THE SEVENTH OF
JOYCE

THE SEVENTH OF
JOYCE

Edited by

Bernard Benstock

INDIANA UNIVERSITY PRESS
BLOOMINGTON
•
THE HARVESTER PRESS
SUSSEX

This edition first published in the United States in 1982 by
INDIANA UNIVERSITY PRESS
Tenth and Morton Streets, Bloomington, Indiana
and in Great Britain by
THE HARVESTER PRESS LIMITED
Publisher: John Spiers
16 Ship Street, Brighton, Sussex

Manufactured in the United States of America

Excerpts from *Ulysses* by James Joyce, copyright © renewed 1961
by Lucia and George Joyce; reprinted by permission of Random
House, Inc., and The Bodley Head. Excerpts from *The Sound and
the Fury* by William Faulkner, reprinted by permission of Random
House, Inc., and Curtis Brown Ltd., London. Excerpt from *Finnegans Wake*, copyright © 1939 by James Joyce; copyright © renewed
1967 by George Joyce and Lucia Joyce; reprinted by permission of
Viking Penguin Inc. and The Society of Authors as the literary
representative of the Estate of James Joyce.

Library of Congress Cataloging in Publication Data
Main entry under title:

The Seventh of Joyce.

Selected papers from the seventh International
James Joyce Symposium held in Zurich, June, 1979.
1. Joyce, James, 1882–1941—Criticism and
interpretation—Congresses. I. Benstock, Bernard.
II. International James Joyce Symposium (7th :
1979 : Zurich, Switzerland)
PR6019.09Z7947   823'.912   81-47775
ISBN 0-253-35184-7   AACR2
ISBN 0-253-20282-5 (pbk.)
1 2 3 4 5 86 85 84 83 82

British Library Cataloguing in Publication Data
The Seventh of Joyce.
1. Joyce, James, *1882-1941*—Criticism and
interpretation—Congresses
I. Benstock, Bernard
823'.912   PR6019.09Z/
ISBN 0-7108-0443-1

Contents

Contents   vii

Preface

The Seventh International James Joyce Symposium in Zurich, Switzerland, in June 1979 fulfilled the long-range plans of the organizers to locate a Joyce symposium in each of the four cities in which Joyce lived a major portion of his life: Dublin, Trieste, Paris, and Zurich. With the first symposium in Dublin, where he was born, and this last in Zurich, where he died, the original intention has been fully realized. From the outset it was our expectation to bring together as diverse a group of Joyce enthusiasts as possible into a functional interaction of people and ideas, breaking down barriers that might have existed between national groups and between various types of Joyceans. Scholars, critics, translators, teachers, students, and readers of Joyce were equally welcome and equally accommodated within the format of our proceedings, and we have all profited greatly from each other's expertise and fields of interest. From its inception the conferences have always been open symposia at which anyone who wanted to participate was given an opportunity to be heard.

It soon became apparent that the traditional sort of symposium, at which auditors are relentlessly subjected to the reading of numerous formal papers best reserved for the printed page, was inappropriate for our purposes, especially once we had expanded from a tentative two-day event (the First) to a week-long extravaganza (the Second and all subsequent symposia). Instead we instituted a symposium in which the panel or the workshop was the basic informative unit, and toward that end the Zurich Symposium was constructed. In most cases the panels consisted of exchanges of ideas and the products of individual research, between the panelists themselves and between the panel and the audience. In some, short presentation statements preceded discussion; in others, more fully developed position papers were introduced.

The essays in this volume represent a "last stage" in the development of ideas and research projects: each is the result of a process that began with the preparation for the panel, the presentation on the panel, and the discussion during the panel, and each is the finished state of the panelist's contribution on the subject under consideration. There is no way of ever recapturing in print the élan of the Zurich Joyce Symposium, and cold type is no substitute for heated debate. Instead, *The Seventh of Joyce* is the Zurich

Symposium recollected in tranquility, and it represents more than the sum total of the individual parts. As a collection of Joyce essays it stands independent of the cultural event that gave it its breath of life, and even for those who attended that event it offers more than they could have taken in during Bloomsweek 1979, where two panels took place simultaneously in separate parts of the building. Even the most diligent symposiast has until now been kept from fully participating, and this printed reconstitution will contain something new for everyone.

To the sessions of sweet silent thought we summon up remembrance of the Symposium past. Some of the excesses may have been honed away, some of the repetitions eliminated, some of the inspirations of the moment reconsidered and given new breath, and some of the static of oral delivery edited out. The multiple approaches, however, remain as varied and differentiated as they naturally would be when several hundred Joyceans gather for a collective effort of communication—as diverse certainly as the topics themselves. Even the definition of a committed Joycean undergoes an overseas change: James Joyce has never existed in a literary or cultural vacuum of his own, as readers of Beckett and Mann, Faulkner and Pynchon, Freud and Jung have long been aware. Several of the "Joyceans" included here may be appearing under that rubric for the first time in their lives, and they are all the more welcome for the range and enlargement of possibilities that they introduce into Joyce studies.

Each author has been allowed his or her own method of annotation, but the pagination for the Joyce texts has been standardized to conform with the volumes most used and most easily available: *Dubliners* (Viking, 1967), *A Portrait* (Viking, 1964), *Ulysses* (Random House, 1961), and *Finnegans Wake* (standard Viking and Faber and Faber).

The complete program of the Zurich Symposium consisted of an embarrassment of riches that no single volume of proceedings could contain. A reading of the printed program reveals three major addresses, twenty-seven short papers, and thirty individual panels, plus two workshops of two sessions each, and seven sessions of a panel of rotating participants spread out over the entire week. Allowing for last-minute cancellations and substitutions (no text is totally reliable, as many a Joycean knows), the program is not an indisputable record of what transpired, nor could one exist on paper or in any single consciousness. *The Seventh of Joyce* is offered to readers both as partial documentation and as a spur to nostalgic recollections. Nor could this volume reproduce the Joyce Exhibit mounted in the Zentralbibliothek, the visit to the Thomas-Mann-Archiv, the receptions hosted by the Canton and City of Zurich and the Suhrkamp Verlag, the Bloomsday banquet, or the performances staged by Ars Nova of London and by the Comedy Club Zürich—nor is it likely that the Guinness and Jameson will ever flow as freely or for free again at the James Joyce Pub on the Pelican-strasse. And over it all hovered the watchful eye of Zurich's most Joycean citizen, Dr. Fritz Senn, and that of the chairman of the English Department of Universität Zürich, Dr. Henri Petter.

Diversity has always been the hallmark of the Joyce Symposia, as they changed locale and formats, experimented with new ways of presentation, and introduced new concepts for consideration. The published proceedings of the various symposia have also been exceedingly different from one another, and *The Seventh of Joyce* is unique in various ways. It is certainly the most extensive coverage of any one symposium, and it concentrates on the basic unit, the integrated panel, which dominated the Zurich event as the most prevalent technique. Included are representatives of more nations, more universities, more disciplines, more schools of thought and walks of life than were initially dreamed of in our philosophy, and consequently this volume mirrors the surprising cross-sections of attitudes and materials on Joyce emerging from the symposium that was the cumulative result of all its predecessors. I am grateful for the cooperation over the past fourteen years of two colleagues who have been co-organizers of almost all the symposia to date, Thomas F. Staley and Fritz Senn (who between them conceived the initial concept), and two colleagues involved in the organizing of several others as well, Morris Beja and Phillip F. Herring.

Bernard Benstock

THE SEVENTH OF
JOYCE

PART I

Joyce and Recent Theory of Narrative

From Narrative Theory to Joyce; From Joyce to Narrative Theory

J. Hillis Miller

My remarks go first from narrative theory to Joyce, then from Joyce to narrative theory.

First a word about the notion in current criticism of fiction about the formal undecidability of any narrative, both on the small scale of word and trope, and on the larger scale of beginning, middle, and end. This undecidability arises from an intrinsic character both of words taken individually and of any narrative line taken as a whole. All words tend to be in one way or another double antithetical words, neither this nor that, but both/and, though one cannot logically have both/and. No narrative line has a clearly identifiable beginning or end, and the line in between wavers, vibrates, and pulverizes itself when the reader tries to pin it down and make it stay still so it can be followed through as a definite trajectory with a definite meaning. One consequence of current narrative theory, at least of the so-called deconstructive sort, has been in various ways to put in question the concept of organic unity or wholeness which has been the central assumption guiding much interpretation of fiction. In place of wholeness has been put the hypothesis of heterogeneity, indeterminacy, or open-endedness.

If these notions in current narrative theory have any validity, then it may not be an accident that critics have tended to disagree about the meaning of Joyce's works, both about the minuscule parts and about the overall patterns. The small-scale parts may have multiple incompatible meanings, and those meanings may not be controllable by reference to other similar words or phrases in other parts of the same work by Joyce, or in other works by him, or in his sources. Such links are broken or may be broken. The model of influence or echo in current theory is not linear, but antithetical. It is organized around one or another twist or trope, so that to say Joyce was in this passage or that influenced by Vico or by Nietzsche or by Swift does not solve problems for interpretation, but rather makes new ones, including the necessity of reading Vico, Nietzsche, or Swift. A critic of Joyce may not take it for granted that the sources may be reduced to a single meaning or a formula, nor may he assume that Joyce necessarily read the sources as we do or even as our most authoritative secondary works do.

In the same way, even the most important large-scale questions about the meaning of Joyce's works may be impossible to answer unequivocally. When, for example, Joyce in *Stephen Hero* says the artist takes the world into himself and flings it abroad again in planetary splendor, or when in *A Portrait of the Artist as a Young Man*, he has Stephen say that art is to "speak of these things and to try to understand their nature and, having understood it, to try slowly and humbly and constantly to express, to press out again, from the gross earth or what it brings forth, from sound and shape and colour which are the prison gates of our soul, an image of the beauty we have come to understand," or when Stephen walks into eternity along Sandymount strand, "Crush, crack, crick, crick," hearing his boots "crush crackling wrack and shells," reading the signatures of all things, one would like to know whether that meaning and that beauty are first made by the artist. One would like to know whether they are created or revealed, and one would like to know whether, for Joyce, those shells, the traces of history, are the remaining signs of some heaven of archetypes or whether the reading makes them signs and they are in themselves mere gross earth and "heaps of dead language." Nothing could be more important than to decide about this, but it may, after all, be undecidable.

Critics of Joyce have by the activity of attempting to interpret his works often been driven to give up the models for the reading of narrative developed for those apparently simpler earlier fictions, though those models were not in fact appropriate even for Dickens or for George Eliot. Nevertheless, it is hard to abandon the motivating ground of a powerful method of criticism. The concept of organic unity has been this for many of us, and I believe that some criticism of Joyce has been inhibited or limited by a lingering hope or expectation that certainty ought to be attainable when it cannot. Current narrative theory may help to liberate critics of Joyce for a fuller recognition of the joyous heterogeneity of his work.

My second point comes from the other direction and can be made briefly. Modern theory of narrative, even in those who are in no narrow sense of the word Joyce specialists, has been strongly motivated in those questionings I have named by Joyce himself. There is little that deconstructive theory of narrative knows about the undecidability of words or of story lines which Joyce did not already know. To conclude with one example, the work of Jacques Derrida has been much influenced, though rather covertly, by his reading of *Finnegans Wake* during a crucial formative year he spent at Harvard during the mid 1950s. What may be Derrida's masterwork so far, *Glas*, would not have taken the form it has without, among other "influences," the example of *Finnegans Wake*.

Formal Re-creation: Re-reading and Re-joycing the Re-rightings of *Ulysses*

Brook Thomas

Perhaps one of the most interesting results of the current fascination with "reader-response" criticism will turn out paradoxically to be an explanation of what for lack of a better term we call the "creativity" of writers such as James Joyce. Of course, normally (another term that requires closer scrutiny) reader-oriented criticism is applied to the role of the reader in literature. Rejecting the textual model, which emphasizes the active role of the writer in producing a text and the passive role of the reader in reproducing it, the advocates of reader-response criticism remind those who need reminding that reading is not merely a passive process. The reader's activity varies from theory to theory, from a reader "adducing" meaning to a reader "producing" meaning, but in almost all cases the reader is seen more and more as an accomplice in the creation of the meaning of a text, a necessary partner who re-creates or, for some, "re-writes" the text.

For me, however, the converse of the argument is just as interesting. If reading is shown to be a form of writing, writing is also shown to be a form of reading. Just as reading is no longer considered merely a passive process, so writing is no longer considered a totally active process. Instead writing itself is shown to involve an act of passivity. As we often tell students of composition, writing is a continued process of revision, and as that master of the craft, Henry James, puts it: "To revise is to see, or to look over, again—which means in the case of a written thing neither more nor less than to re-read it."[1]

This merger of the roles of reader and writer is perhaps no better in evidence than in the case of James Joyce and *Ulysses*. With the widespread availability of Joyce's notesheets and revisions for *Ulysses*, plus Michael Groden's detailed study of Joyce's process of writing the book, we have a privileged opportunity to watch closely how one of the twentieth century's most "creative" users of language wrote his masterpiece.[2] What we find is that Joyce's "passive" act of reading and re-reading what he has already written is one of the reasons why *Ulysses*, which started as a short story for *Dubliners*, kept expanding until Joyce finally had to stop adding to it to meet the publication deadline on his fortieth birthday. As one of those late revisions reminds us, *"It grew bigger and bigger and bigger"* (*U* 172.36).

Groden tries to isolate three major stages in the composition of *Ulysses*:

> In the first stage ("Telemachus"—"Scylla and Charybdis") he developed an interior monologue technique to tell his story. In the middle stage ("Wandering Rocks"—"Oxen of the Sun") he experimented with the monologue and then abandoned it for a series of parody styles that act as "translations" of the story. He balanced his growing attraction to stylistic surface with a continuing interest in the human story. Finally, in the last stage ("Circe"—"Penelope") he created several new styles and revised the earlier episodes.[3]

What Groden does not point out, however, is that the changes from stage to stage correspond closely to Joyce's own re-reading of his text in preliminary form. A major departure from his initial technique occurred soon after Joyce re-read drafts of the early chapters for publication in the *Little Review*. Similarly, Joyce's final revisions, many reflexive in nature, are prompted by his reading of the book in proof before final publication.

That the re-reading of the earlier chapters leads to experiments with the "initial style" and parodies of it only makes sense. Someone as sensitive as Joyce to narrative possibilities would soon see the limitations of any one technique, including the famous "interior monologue," which was once considered a major deviation from narrative norms but is now grasped at by critics seeking to define *Ulysses'* stylistic norm. It is important to remember, however, that not only do the later stages of the book grow out of and depend on the first stage, but by the time *Ulysses* reaches print the first stage has been revised in light of the later strategies and intentions and, thus, depends on them as well as the other way around. As Groden argues, Joyce's strategies and intentions changed and developed as he wrote and read his book, until he created a final draft that would be "a record of all of the stages he passed through and not merely a product of the last one."[4] Joyce's process of writing makes possible a perpetual interaction between all of the book's chapters, styles, and words.

Thus, complaints about Joyce's overly mechanical structure might be reconsidered. Joyce did not simply impose a mechanical structure on the work, since the various structures that he himself discovered grew out of the act of composition. For instance, the famous schema did not appear until late in Joyce's work on the book, indicating that he may not have seen the possibility for many of his elaborate, encyclopedic parallels until after the book amassed more and more words. In fact, as Groden points out, a comparison of the Linati schema with the Stuart Gilbert schema indicates that the schema itself was revised to fit new work on the book. Furthermore, it is typical of Joyce that what Joseph Frank calls the book's spatial structure grows out of the artist's writing process. It is Joyce's continual revisions that give the book the appearance of having a preconceived structure in which all the details fit neatly together. And it is, of course, the book's "spatial" character that allows the reader to participate in a reading *process* with no end, jumping from page to page, reading backwards to forwards as well as forwards to backwards. As Bloom says of the proof-reader in "Aeolus": "Reads it backwards first. Quickly he does it. Must require some practice that" (*U* 122.18).

Joyce, the writer, was such a sensitive reader of his own work that he continually detected new verbal connections and possibilities to be developed in re-writing. In his study Groden lists a number of the most obvious examples, and the interested reader can compare early drafts and final text to find examples of his own. Most readers, however, are more interested in the effect of these revisions in their reading of the final text. For them some of the most interesting additions may be those which, while fitting into the naturalistic tale, also suggest different ways of reading the words of the text. Readers who are apt to take the book too seriously are reminded by a revision in "Hades" that "You must laugh sometimes so better do it that way. Gravediggers in *Hamlet*. Shows the profound knowledge of the human heart" (*U* 109.13). Readers who even before the book was published complained about its randomness might well consider that *Ulysses* consists of "A few well-chosen words" (*U* 140.1). Readers are also invited to enjoy the book's extravagance, as when Joyce adds the comment he made in a letter to Budgen on "Oxen of the Sun" to part of Ned Lambert's response to Dan Dawson's inflated rhetoric: "How's that for high?" (*U* 123.31). Furthermore, many late revisions help steer the reader toward the *Odyssey*, such as when Joyce adds to Mulligan's comment "Ah, Dedalus, the Greeks": "I must teach you. You must read them in the original" (*U* 5.7). Finally, for readers who may forget the metaphoric nature of language, we have late reminders such as: "metaphorically speaking" (*U* 143.38).

Joyce also wants us to read quite literally, for as Fritz Senn remarks, "Part of the dynamism of Joyce's prose arises from the contrast of figurative to literal meaning, or the ironic unfittingness of a metaphor or a cliché fixed in some no longer congruous roles."⁵ Joyce, of course, does not invent either language's figurativeness or its literalness; he merely makes us aware of qualities already contained in language. In fact, as his revisions of "Eumaeus" show, his literal reading of old metaphors is one way in which he breathed new life into what is too often considered that chapter's tired language.

Thus, when we read the following passage, in which Bloom considers the possibility that the stories W. B. Murphy spins might after all have a bit of truth in them, it might be wise to consider what Murphy has quite literally on his chest, although to do so will involve us in a series of not so literal connections with other parts of the text: "Yet still, though his eyes were thick with sleep and sea air, life was full of a host of things and coincidences of a terrible nature and it was quite within the bounds of possibility that it was not an entire fabrication though at first blush there was not much inherent probability in all the spoof he got off his chest being strictly accurate gospel" (*U* 635.36). What we find is that when Murphy unbuttons his shirt, he reveals, "on top of the timehonoured symbol of the mariner's hope and rest . . . the figure 16 and a young man's sideface looking frowningly rather" (*U* 631.21). The young man's face turns out to be none other than a portrait of the tattoo artist himself ("Fellow the name of Antonio done that. There he is himself, a Greek" [*U* 631.27]). In other words, this not entire fabrication which our storyteller is trying to get off his chest is a portrait of the artist as a young man, a connection between Joyce and his fictional character that is reinforced later in the chapter, when we are explicitly warned not to confuse Antonio with "the dramatic person-age of identical name who sprung from the pen of our national poet" (*U* 636.11). Literally, of course, this phrase refers to the character in Shakespeare's *Merchant of Venice*, but it also suggests Ireland's new national poet.

Furthermore, we should not be surprised to find that the key phrase in this connection, "all the spoof he got off his chest being strictly accurate gospel," is a late revision. In the manuscript version that we have, Joyce ends the sentence with the rather bland "though at first blush there was not much inherent probability about it" with "inherent" a marginal addition. In the typescript he revised this to "though at first blush there was not much inherent probability in all he said being strictly accurate," a change that emphasizes the act of narration and makes possible a further revision that will include the reference to Murphy's tattoo, as well as allowing the addition of "gospel" to reinforce the effect of "host" earlier in the sentence. Host and gospel in turn connect the passage to Stephen's and Bloom's comments on the previous page about those "passages in Holy Writ" which Stephen calls proof of "the existence of a supernatural God" and Bloom considers "genuine forgeries" (another late revision) "put in by the monks most probably." Reference to the monks recalls Old Monks, the dayfather in "Aeolus," who, as James H. Maddox remarks, "might well serve as a model of Joyce, dayfather of June 16, 1904."[6] To be sure, Bloom's thoughts about the dayfather could apply as easily to Joyce as to Old Monks. "Queer lot of stuff he must have put through his hands in his time: obituary notices, pubs' ads, speeches, divorce suits, found drowned" (*U* 122.8).

What my example, which is by no means unusual, should make clear is that Joyce's process of writing, re-reading, and re-writing is potentially an endless one. Having once revised a passage, Joyce would re-read his revisions, causing him to discover even more potential verbal connections, causing more re-writing, and so on. Thus, it is easy to see how *Ulysses* came to be more and more about its own creation.[7] The book becomes reflexive because Joyce re-read every sentence he wrote in so many different ways that each one required expansion and qualification. Or, put another way, the material that the book has amassed is not only character, plot, or details of a Dublin setting, but its own language. That language, as part of a language system without beginning or end, allows Joyce continually to create new meanings and formal possibilities for his book. But, in one sense, it is not really Joyce who is "creating" these meanings or potential forms. They are meanings and forms already available in a language that exists prior to any one reader or writer of that language. It is Joyce's awareness of this potentiality of language that allows us to talk about the book writing itself and that makes *Ulysses* the perfect example of Valéry's statement that "a work of art is never finished, but only abandoned." My point is, however, that *Ulysses* has been abandoned only by Joyce, not by its readers. *Ulysses* will never be finished until it is abandoned by its readers, for each time that a reader reads and re-reads *Ulysses*, he repeats with a difference the process by which Joyce created the book, thereby helping once more to bring into existence that "world without end" (*U* 37.31).

Notes

Parenthetical references *U* within the text refer to James Joyce, *Ulysses* (New York: Random House, 1934 ed., reset and corrected 1961).

1. Henry James, *The Art of the Novel* (New York: Scribners, 1934), pp. 338–39. See Walter Benn Michaels, "Writers Reading: James and Eliot," *MLN* 91 (October 1976): 827–49, for a valuable discussion of James's theory of reading.

2. Michael Groden, *"Ulysses" in Progress* (Princeton: Princeton University Press, 1977); James Joyce, *"Ulysses"*: *The Manuscript and First Printings Compared*, annotated by Clive Driver (New York: Octagon Books, 1975); James Joyce, *Ulysses*, general editor Michael Groden (New York: Garland Press, 1978).

3. Groden, p. 4.

4. Groden, p. 203.

5. Fritz Senn, "Book of Many Turns," *JJQ* 10 (Fall 1972): 42.

6. James H. Maddox, *Joyce's "Ulysses" and the Assault upon Character* (New Brunswick: Rutgers University Press, 1978), p. 95.

7. Groden suggest that the "Done" (*U* 291.13) at the end of "Sirens" announces the end of Joyce's experimentation with the "initial style" (p. 42). He also remarks that "It is probably not coincidental that, just as Joyce was about to expand *Ulysses* through innumerable revisions, he wrote a scene extending Bloom's dreams to apocalyptic dimensions" (p. 188). I also like to think that the trial scene in "Circe" owes something to the fact that portions of *Ulysses* published in the *Little Review* were on trial for obscenity at the time Joyce was writing the episode. Similarly, it may not be accidental that Joyce added "Print anything now" (*U* 69.10) to the passage in "Calypso" that Pound had censored because it described Bloom defecating.

The Benstock Principle

Shari Benstock and Bernard Benstock

At its most basic, narative is assumed to comprise two essential elements: a story and a storyteller. In its oral traditions, narrative rested with the bard, who, by his voice and gestures, his nuances of tone and inflection, was inseparable from the story he told: he was recognizably apparent and perfectly audible in his narratives, a status that he frequently exploited for narrative effect. Our critical terminology derives from this oral tradition, despite the conventions of its current sophistication; the terms we use to define and describe narrative ("style," "tone," "point of view," "gesture," "plot," even such weighted terms as *"discours," "recit,"* "signifier," "signified") draw our attention to the role of the teller in the tale. The most common metaphor to characterize that which we read upon a page is "narrative voice": in narrative a speaker speaks to us, hidden though he may be by the person and tense of the narration; he speaks harshly or humorously, in a particular tone, from a particular point of view, in a certain style. He is present in his person ("Let us go then, you and I") or hidden behind a certain impersonality ("Hale knew they meant to murder him before he had been in Brighton three hours"), assumes a limited vision ("On an evening in the latter part of May a middle-aged man was walking homeward from Shaston to the village of Marlott") or a more expansive one ("In the beginning God created the heaven and the earth"). Indeed, the teller can fix himself in the corner of a character's mind ("Sitting beside the road, watching the wagon mount the hill toward her, Lena thinks, 'I have come from Alabama: a fur piece' ") or disappear into the local atmosphere ("London. Michaelmas Term late over, and the Lord Chancellor sitting in Lincoln's Inn Hall"). Whatever its scope and style, the process of narration establishes the notion of an ever-present someone (the narrator) whose voice guides our reading just as it once guided our listening in the "Once upon a time and a very good time it was."

Earlier notions of narrative grounded in a present storyteller whose intervention in his tale was assumed, even demanded, by his listeners are apparent still in the reserve of critical terms used to describe what narrative is and how it works. The illusions presented by narrative (of a voice "heard" in the silent writing on a page) are confirmed and carried on by the critical

10

terminology applied to this narration. These metaphors are actively present in our critical vocabulary, reinforcing the notion that even the most impersonal texts are not generated *ex nihilo* but are the work of a human, work that rests on the conventions of communication between like beings: between a teller and a listener, between a writer and a reader. And regardless of how sophisticated or complicated our terminology becomes, whether we speak of author and reader or whether we acknowledge an implied author and an implied reader, whether we focus on the act of writing or the act of reading, we still invest narrative with a human dimension apparent in the voice of the text: "Lily, the caretaker's daughter, was literally run off her feet."[1]

So long as we are aware of the metaphoric basis of our descriptive terms, perhaps we can escape the trap open to all listeners present at a storytelling—mishearing. Who said Lily was literally run off her feet? Hugh Kenner has told us that Lily herself, were she to describe how she felt, would say—confusing her metaphors—that she was literally run off her feet. And how do we know that this particular expression might belong to Lily and not her maker (or his stand-in, the narrator)? Because we extrapolate what Lily *might* have said, what turn of phrase *might* be hers in this instance, from what she does say. Her voice is inserted in impersonal, third-person narration. This discovery is, of course, of longer standing than Hugh Kenner's reading of *Dubliners*, belonging to a tradition of narrative analysis defined at the turn of the century in Europe.[2] While the French term *le style indirect libre* and the German *erlebte Rede* have significant differences between them, in essence they acknowledge the possibility of a narration inflected from directions other than that of the narrator (even an omniscient one), that the narration can assume its own directions, seemingly separate from—even in contradistinction to—that imposed by the teller, that the subjects of the narration itself (characters) can insert themselves into the fabric of the telling, warping the fictional woof. Once this happens (and it happened very early, with clear signs of its appearance in the eighteenth-century novel),[3] the metaphoric distinctions of "narrator" and "narrative" blurred: at every turn it is possible that a third-rank character (like Lily the caretaker's daughter, who does housework) may shape the narrative in ways that the most vigilant narrator or sharp-eared reader may find perplexing.

Thus the inseparable story and teller undergo a division of labor that allows us to speak distinctly of "narrator" and "narrative," to divide the speaker from his subject, to separate process from product, to effect a cleavage of church and state. That space which separated third-person narration (the mask behind which the voice of the narrator presented itself) and character speech has become blurred, purposely mingling *recit* and *discours*, and at this point the metaphoric overtones of our critical vocabulary can no longer be ignored. The mingling of voices is difficult for the astute listener to dissolve; the blurred perspective produces optical illusions. And while it may sometimes be apparent that the "voice" that intrudes upon a line of narrative prose belongs to a Lily or to Uncle Charles, frequently the source of disruption is not so evident. In some texts, like *Ulysses*, the disruption occurs before the listener has a chance to identify the "initial" narrator; often the disruptions play upon the style in ways that are not just attributable to characters, but belong to physical or abstract processes: peristaltic action, the senses, birth, death, music, rocks, epic poetry, or catechism. The possibility that one voice subsumes all voices, all stylistic and linguistic permutations, becomes conceptually difficult to manage: after all, narrators (even unreliable ones) are known by their consistencies—and here is a narrative that seems to rest on inconsistency. And so we arrive at the 1960s in Joyce criticism, at the birth of a developing school of narrative thought that fixes *Ulysses* at the center of debate over narrative method, the search for new descriptive terms keeping pace with the development—in Europe—of the new stylistics. And the metaphors begin to change: not just one narrator but many, with a supporting cast of an "arranger" (to add musical/dramatic dimensions), and the notion that the text is divided against itself. The textual capacity for anticipation, repetition, inflation, deflation, mockery, sympathy, irony, and comedy is part of a bag of tricks perpetrated to harness subjects that always threaten to wrench the story away from its teller and proceed *tout-seul*, directionless and aberrant.[4] And so we arrive at the 1970s in Joyce criticism: subject is separated from style (indeed, it is pitted against stylistic innovation), teller is divorced from tale, and the widening narrative gap is filled by narrative beings with pernicious motives.[5]

And by 1980 the dualistic concept on which narrative theory rests (*parole* vs. *langue*, signifier vs. signified, deep structure vs. surface manifestation) is a given; the old terms of subject and style, method and matter, story and substance have been replaced by the terms of *la nouvelle critique: histoire* and *discours*. The thrust for generating new terms (and French terms) owes much to recent developments in linguistic theory and the structuralist poetics: whereas it was once *au courant* to speak of "theme," "metaphor," and "symbol," nothing could be more *passé* now. Those interested in the thematic elements of *Ulysses*—whether Bloom and Stephen celebrate some kind of communion over cocoa, whether Molly is a patient Griselda or a lusty Wife of Bath figure, whether or not Bloom is "really" a Jew, couldn't be more "fifties." All the bright young people—many of them European and trained in the rhetoric of Lacan, Derrida, Foucault and readers of *Tel Quel* or *Change*—are persistently pointing out to us where it's at: in the narrative theory that supports so seminal a modernist text as *Ulysses*.

To refresh our memories, we must recall that for the overwhelming number of readers of *Ulysses* the first six chapters are of a piece, consistent in their narrative method, variations on a traditional third-person mode of storytelling, and—by comparison with later chapters—only marginally difficult. These chapters comprise the "initial" style Joyce spoke about in his letter to Budgen. It is with the seventh chapter, "Aeolus," that the text divides against itself, Joyce's notes on the novel telling us that the insertion of the intrusive headlines occurred very late in the game, after the stylistic excesses of the later chapters had carried away the narrative subject with which the novel began. Karen Lawrence's article in the *James Joyce Quarterly* (" 'Aeolus': Interruption and Inventory") focuses on these distinctions, and since it so conveniently arrived in the mail as we write this article, it shall serve to exemplify some recent thoughts about the Ulyssean narrative. She writes:

> In confronting these seemingly arbitrary interruptions in the text [the head-lines], the reader has a number of choices. Because the narration of the story continues beneath the headings, he can try to ignore the intrusions, and proceed, however limpingly, through the chapter to "Lestrygonians." For as bizarre as the headings may be, the texture of the narrative beneath them is largely that of the first six chapters; a combination of dialogue, interior monologue and third-person narration.[6]

The theoretical underpinnings of this analysis are evident in these opening sentences: the headlines introduce a new—and bizarre—element into the smooth progression of narration; they create a "dual text" (upper-case headlines versus lower-case narration); the headlines are significantly different from the narration of the previous six chapters, which is continued in the narrative beneath them. What is the reader to do?

> However, in order to read the seventh chapter in a way similar to the first six, the reader must perform a different operation on the text, an act in this case, of suppression. He must pretend that stitching together the micro-narrative is the same as reading an uninterrupted version of the story. (390)

Here another component of the new poetics is introduced: the text becomes something upon which the reader performs an act, an operation. And the change of text in "Aeolus" constitutes the necessity for a concomitant change in the reading process; we don't read "Aeolus" like we read "Nestor." So how do we define what has happened in "Aeolus"?

> In "Aeolus" the book begins to advertise its own artifice, and in doing so it calls attention to the processes of reading and writing. For the headings not only provide a puzzle to the reader, but also are a sign of a new kind of writing in the book, which undermines the norms established in the first six chapters. (391)

In this assessment of events in "Aeolus" is perhaps the crux of the new narratology: the emphasis is upon the visual elements of the text, what it looks like on the page. And in "Aeolus" the text announces—by its type-face—something new: it disrupts the temporal design it has established; it creates a "visual disturbance"; it emphasizes the printed quality of the text, thus playing "with the distance between written language and oral narra-tive" (393). Most significant, these intrusions seem to come unbidden from any narrative persona; they suggest a process of estrangement from the consciousness to which they are aligned; they emphasize a disturbing notion—that the process of writing (as opposed to narrating) may actually separate the creation from its creator in some undeniable way. As Karen Lawrence writes, "the book now seems cut off from the notion of human origin" (394).

To note briefly one important shift that our text has made in delineating the narrative argument: the metaphors have changed. What began as a concept of "hearing" words on a page, imagining a speaker speaking in that third-person of the first six chapters of *Ulysses*, of supposing a storyteller who by the force of his words and the inflection of his voice bids our attention and participation, we have arrived at "Aeolus," which emphasizes its "printedness," which bids us pay attention to the words as they appear on the page (in caps, abbreviated, punctuated), and which makes us feel that this narrative and its imbedded story have been cut off from human sources, springing from unaccountable regions, that the narrative of this chapter belongs to "a language of common denominator, the received and receivable ideas of society, so different from the language of the initial style" (396), that—in fact—this language is totally divorced from the speech acts of an individual person. Wordplay now exists in visible terms ("K.M.R.I.A."). And the rhetorical devices of the chapter only further this emphasis upon the visible, since our attention shifts to the shape and placement of words on a page rather than to their content. But whether the metaphor is hearing or seeing, all things have conspired to our recognition of the division of things; we seem to have rearrived at the old chestnut of form-versus-content.

At the risk of appearing too *demodé* and shopworn, we should like to return to that question of sources, of narrative impetus, and to pause at the assertion that "Aeolus" represents a schism in the text, a separation of the initial style from the later styles, shifting our attention from a personalized, idiosyncratic (but nonetheless recognizable) narration lodged in the person of its narrator. We shall begin with the narrator.

1. In order for a "narrator" to exist in the text, he must be present in his person. In reality, this leaves only the choice of first-person narration ("I"), since second-person narration is almost unknown and third-person narra-

tion suggests in both its person and syntactical structure the absence of a present, personalized someone who tells us the story. The usual manner of past-tense narration furthers this anonymity, displacing the subject in time ("Stately, plump Buck Mulligan came from the stairhead"), but third-person present-tense narration—although highly unusual—achieves the same effect ("On the veranda, Franck drops into one of the low armchairs and utters his usual exclamation as to how comfortable they are").

2. The constraints upon third-person narration, which achieves in its effect a range extending from "omniscience" to the confines present in Robbe-Grillet, depend in no way upon a conception that resides in the anthropomorphic—even though such terms as "camera eye," "central intelligence," "omniscient narrator" belie the impersonality of narration they try to describe by associating aspects of humanness to the realm of the impersonal. Indeed, the term "omniscient narrator" is in itself a contradiction in terms, since no "narrator" (if we assume the metaphoric elements of humanness, a "he" who "tells" a story) is capable of "omniscience." One must always set aside credulity in using such a term, which strains its metaphoric limits.

3. And it is precisely credulity and our striving for it that has produced the critical notion of "reliability," most often in the services of the narrator: he is either reliable or unreliable. Reliability is something we place great value on, since it guarantees our safe journey through the fictional world: we want to know when we're getting the "straight scoop" (and how) and when we're being led astray. Like Little Red Riding Hood, we need to know when the wolf is hiding in the narrative woods. It is often assumed that reliability is a function of the kind of narration that has been chosen for a given fiction: that it is, perhaps, easier to identify the unreliability in *The Turn of the Screw* because there are two first-person narrators whose motives we are able to assess rather than a vague, slippery, third-person narrator able to evade our efforts at assessing his motives, as in *Ulysses*. Indeed, criticism of both of these works should quickly tell us that no one is quite certain of the whereabouts of unreliability in *The Turn of the Screw*, and many feel perfect confidence in the verbal trickster who manipulates *Ulysses*.

But any method of narration holds the possibility for unreliability because *all* narration is unreliable. We never get the whole story, from every possible angle, and we are never allowed to see (or hear) the choices that were discarded in order that this particular storytelling could advance itself. We can talk about degrees of unreliability, but we cannot distinguish between a fiction that is reliable and one that is not. It is noteworthy that criticism of modernist fiction has tended to emphasize the unreliability of its narration, or its characters' accounts, in large part because modernism is

characterized by the turning of the narrative controls over to the thoughts
and reactions of its characters. How do we assess the trustworthiness of a
Stephen Dedalus or a Clarissa Dalloway? Many would say that we measure
the distance between characters' consciousness and external reality by
assuming a narrator who presents the external reality reliably. This is an act
of faith, rather like turning over the reins of one's conscious decision-
making to an invisible God whose reliability (that is, good will) we trust.
This may make for exemplary religious practice, but it makes for poor
literary criticism.

   And if not God, then who? The author? Joyce himself made the claim
that if Dublin were to be destroyed it could be resurrected from his text.
But which Dublin, exactly, could be resurrected? Certainly not the Dublin
of 1904, since our awareness of certain anachronistic discrepancies in the
text—based on evidence *outside* the text—tells us that between 1904 and
1915, when Joyce began *Ulysses*, history intervened in remarkable ways.
Perhaps, then, one must assume that the work itself presents a certain
"reality," consistent in its effort to render the city in as many forms and
from as many perspectives as possible, and it is to that reality the reader
must attend in an effort to distinguish the personal subjectivity of characters' impressions from the models of physical phenomena present elsewhere
in the text. But most readers feel shy about taking this sort of responsibility
with a text as playful as *Ulysses*, and would rather insert into its workings a
narrator upon whom the reader's subjective responses to the text may be
affixed.

   4. Narrative point-of-view and tone, both terms that associate themselves with a present, on-scene narrator, recognizable as a someone in the
story, are applicable to the impersonal method of narration only if they are
dissociated from the human context. The importance of narrational viewpoint is splendidly demonstrated in "Cyclops" where the prejudice of the
"eye" rests in the "I" of the telling. That a similar prejudice exists in such a
chapter as "Sirens," where the musical forms *seem* to mock Bloom, or in
"Aeolus," where the headlines appear to parody the narration that follows,
risks serious implications for a reading of the text if we say that such
mockery/parody resides in the viewpoint of a narrator.[7] We suggest that
such measures of tone and perspective as irony, parody, sympathy, and so
forth, establish themselves in ways totally separate from the notion of a
personalized narrator who hides himself behind the mask of impersonality
in *Ulysses* (or any other third-person narration).

   5. Another significant area of confusion surrounding critical terminology that invests the impersonal text with a measure of personality resides in
the term "narrative voice," often used as a substitute for "narrator" when
the narrational terrain seems ambiguous. Although there is not room here
for a full explication of the problems of this term or its misleading implica-

tions for a text such as *Ulysses*, we should note that the components of "voice" offer the central false impression. Here we return to the implied notion of a speaker telling a story, a speaker present and identifiable through the story, who cannot be separated from that story, in whom and through whom that story exists and without whom there would be no story.

"Voice" as it resides in a fictional text exists at different levels and serves a variety of metaphorical functions: the most obvious is dialogue (characters' speech acts); the second is narrative voice (when there is a first-person present narrator); authorial voice (in instances—such as in *Tom Jones*—when the author's presence is manifestly apparent in the text). Another whole set of possible voices exists in another narrative context—perhaps best termed "textual" representation—and includes such textual markers as quotation marks, the *tirez*, italics, or run-on sentences to denote thought process (as in "Penelope"), and a whole panoply of other techniques designed to produce the *visual* effect on the page of speech or thought processes which are then internally voiced by the speaker.[8]

These textual effects and their mimetic counterparts work together to produce the illusion that speech acts occur in written narrative: they do not. The notion of present speech in a novel is a supposition, and one that we have lived comfortably with for a long period of time. But it is also one that has led to critical misunderstandings about the nature and role of critical language. To argue, as one critic of *Ulysses* does, that the narrator of "Aeolus" "thumbs his nose at" the reader or, in another critical vision, "with a certain eye for the malapropos, pastes captions across the page through the text of this episode,"[9] is to suggest that this third-person narrator is somehow palpably present, with a nose to thumb and a paste-pot to wield. Our critical language is not innocent; it has the capacity to mislead by its verbal resonances and visual effects. And whereas it might seem possible to adopt such terms as "narrator" or "narrative voice" with the stipulation that we all keep firmly in mind that these terms, like "implied author" or "plot line," rest on metaphoric assumptions, that they are always used in quotation marks, that we can delineate for our various purposes the precise meaning that the term "narrator" shall hold in the numerous cases where we apply, none of this is really possible. Because there is always someone who will take that metaphor out of the realm of the poetic and into the realm of everyday reality, who will give the narrator a nose and a thumb and an eye for the malapropos, who will insist on the literalness of that conception, like Lily the caretaker's daughter.

How is it possible, then, to sort out the complexities of fictional language and critical language, to describe the multiplexities of a text like *Ulysses*? Typically the answer to this plight has been to redefine critical terms that have been in use over hundreds of years,[10] to make them fit present needs by qualifying and categorizing, so that one gets conglomerate terminology like: third-person limited narration, selective omniscience, self-narrated monologue. The alternative is to create new critical terms ("dissonant self-narration" or "subject of enunciation").[11] Behind both of these efforts is a nagging doubt about the language that attempts to describe the fictional representation. Thus if the term narrator can't suffice to describe all of what narrationally occurs in *Ulysses*, then perhaps the addition of "arranger," "stage manager," "interpolator" will.

We suggest that such methods won't solve the problem, since the problem is a conceptual one: no matter by what name we call the narrator, he is still always functioning according to terms delineated by the term "narrator" itself. Adding to his duties, duplicating his job description, giving him a larger staff of helpers and manipulators hardly solves the problem. Moreover, the more power the narrator gains in the creation of the text, the more authority he assumes, the less unity is perceivable between the subject of the text and style: they commence in concurrence in the first six chapters, begin to divide in the seventh, and by the seventeenth are totally divided against each other. Only "Penelope," it seems, is capable of weaving subject with style in a totally convincing production.

We propose, therefore, "The Benstock Principle." *Fictional texts that exploit free indirect speech* (the narrational mode most common to *Ulysses*) *establish the contextual supremacy of subject matter, which influences the direction, tone, pace, point of view, and method of narration.* Examples of this technique at work will follow below, but it is important to understand that what is at stake here is not a kind of "which came first, the chicken or the egg?" riddle, a notion that can be documented by slavish attention to notesheets and early drafts, but a method for establishing, *within the confines of the textual narration*, the sources of its telling.

The "Uncle Charles Principle" is adequate, within its limits. Certainly characters influence the direction of narration in Joyce's works, as they do (and have done) in dozens of novels far less experimental in their narrative devices than *Ulysses*. What the "Uncle Charles Principle" lacks is the capacity for extending narrative influences to include inanimate, mechanical, spontaneous, even organic processes. Such items as cakes of soap, newspapers, clouds, gulls, Elizabethan dance steps, not to mention Homeric correspondences, have the power to structure narrative form, provide images and echoes, and determine the progress of plot at any given moment. The narrative develops in relation to its various subjects, not merely the dramatis personae, but the whole gestalt that we know as the Dublin of *Ulysses*. The later styles of the text may be more palpably evident and more obviously dominant than the styles of the early chapters; they may even bear different relationships to the subjects from which they derive. For instance, the catechism of "Ithaca" provides a metaphysic *category* in which subject and style are wedded at various levels: catechism is obviously the method of narration; it is also its subject, in all the various forms in which "catechism" can exist (method of colloquy, ritualization of concepts, educational process, mnemonic device, a structuring of facts, and so forth); but more importantly, the "subjects" of the catechism cannot be extrapolated from the catechism because they exist only in that context at this moment. We can guess the dialogue of Bloom and Stephen, but we cannot rewrite it separate from its existence in "Ithaca." "Roc's auk's egg" may be Bloom's request for breakfast fare, but we'll never know that based on anything that can be derived from an analysis of "roc's auk's egg."

Still, there exists a major problem in assuming that the styles of the first chapters are either "initial" or "basic," that they somehow form a consistent monolith against which later diversions and digressions can be measured. No narrator guides our entrance to the Martello tower; no narrator introduces us to Stephen and Mulligan; no narrator provides a sustained viewpoint or a recognizable voice on which our responses to the telling can rest. Indeed, we are led to expect guidance where there is none, and we pick our way carefully across the landscape of Sandycove. Whereas we are told that it is Mulligan who gives "the long low whistle of call," we are never told the source of "two strong shrill whistles" (*U* 3) of response. This narration, which is deceptively matter-of-fact, provides the facts without directions; the context is obviously assumed without being stated. And when the reader attempts to state the assumption, either by making a realistic supposition (that the mailboat coincidentally issues two whistles) or by supplying the metaphor appropriate to the circumstance (that the whistles correspond to the bells of the Eucharist), he confronts the various subjects of the text without recourse to an intervening source. He intuits the principles that govern this context even as he supplies the "missing" bases on which the facts of the text rest.

It is obvious, then, that the reader must supply for himself the principles that govern the contextual setting of action in the text, must divine for himself the relationship that exists between the subject as narrated and the process by which it is narrated. Often several readers divine several contexts, which may variously support or undermine each other, depending on the critical viewpoint. To say that the narrative of *Ulysses* is contextually governed, that subject determines both the type of narration as well as its direction, is not to say that only one context is necessarily operative at a given juncture. More likely, several contexts present themselves, each vying with the other for the reader's attention (that narratives present themselves temporally rather than spatially makes the co-temporality of contexts a difficult one to construct, although *Ulysses* offers a multitude of examples—the whole of "Wandering Rocks," for instance—and *Finnegans Wake* is a compendium of such possibilities). The hapless reader is never left totally adrift in the linguistic sea, however; a governing principle always determines the relationships of facts within the fiction, of style to subject, an ordering of contexts and influences available to the attentive reader. Although the principle may change from chapter to chapter, even from sentence to sentence, its evidence can always be remarked; the Joycean method may be ingenious, but it is not haphazard. In the context of Mulligan's pose as officiating priest on the opening page of the text, it is Mulligan who adapts physical phenomena to his preconceived posturing (mirror, shaving-bowl, dressing-gown). Thus the whistles, whatever their source, exist as corollaries to the ritual bell-ringing of the Mass. These bells summon God's presence in His historical narrative; under His presence, the physical properties of bread and wine become the body and blood of Christ. This role has been often noted as an appropriate one for the author of a text (Flaubert was followed in this notion by James Joyce), and one may well wonder about the identity of the "old chap" to whom Mulligan gives a nod of thanks in aid of his ritual comedy. But the author of *Ulysses* is not present in the text under the auspices of Wayne Boothian "implication" or available as an invisible narrator mimicking his characters' voices while quietly guiding our reading. He is apparent under the accidents of the text itself, himself guided by the properties of his multiple subjects. Thus it is no accident of timing that the hour of the morning is just right for the passing of the mailboat to lend two whistles of response to Mulligan's call.

Notes

1. James Joyce, "The Dead," in *Dubliners* (New York: Viking Press, 1967), p. 175.

2. Hugh Kenner, "The Uncle Charles Principle," *Joyce's Voices* (Berkeley: University of California Press, 1978), pp. 15–38. The history of this literary phenomenon is well reviewed in Paul Hernadi, *Beyond Genre* (Ithaca: Cornell University Press, 1972) and Dorrit Cohn, *Transparent Minds* (Princeton: Princeton University Press, 1978).

3. See Roy Pascal, *The Dual Voice: Free Indirect Speech and Its Functions in the Nineteenth-Century European Novel* (Manchester: Manchester University Press, 1977), for the roots of this technique in the eighteenth-century novel.

4. The division of labor between subject and style in *Ulysses* has recently become a popular one in Joyce criticism. Its almost forgotten origins are in Arnold Goldman's *The Joyce Paradox: Form and Freedom in His Fiction* (London: Routledge and Kegan Paul, 1966).

5. The breakthrough was David Hayman's *"Ulysses": The Mechanics of Meaning* (Englewood Cliffs, N.J.: Prentice-Hall, 1970), whose closest followers have been

Marilyn French, *The Book as World* (Cambridge: Harvard University Press, 1977) and Michael Groden, *Ulysses in Progress* (Princeton: Princeton University Press, 1977).

6. *James Joyce Quarterly* 17 (Summer 1980): 389. Hereafter cited in the text.

7. Marilyn French, "The Voices of the Sirens in Joyce's *Ulysses,*" *The Journal of Narrative Technique* 8 (Winter 1979): 1–10.

8. Stephen M. Ross, " 'Voice' in Narrative Texts: The Example of *As I Lay Dying,*" *PMLA* 94 (March 1979): 300–10.

9. French, *The Book as World*, p. 101; Kenner, p. 75.

10. There are dozens of examples of this kind of exercise available in current work on narrative, but Dorrit Cohn exemplifies the effort to redefine critical terms in *Transparent Minds*, as does Wayne Booth in his *Rhetoric of Fiction* (Chicago: University of Chicago Press, 1961) and, more recently, Franz K. Stanzel in "Second Thoughts on Narrative Situations in the Novel: Towards a 'Grammar of Fiction,' " *Novel* (Spring 1978): 253–63.

11. See Nomi Tamir-Ghez, "The Art of Persuasion in Nabokov's *Lolita,*" *Poetics Today* 1 (1979): 68.

Enjoying Invisibility:
The Myth of Joyce's Impersonal Narrator

J. P. Riquelme

       Critics of Joyce's fiction have been living with a myth, the myth of the teller's impersonality. That impersonality is an illusion; it fools us, yet we know it is not real. Impersonality is simply one among many possible disguises, or personae, in storytelling. As a persona, it can be neither wholly personal nor wholly impersonal, and never absolutely invisible. Part of the difficulty in discussing Joyce's narrator is inherent in the notion of a narrator as persona, for that notion is potentially self-contradictory. We can easily, and perhaps do necessarily, oversimplify the complications of narration in our assertions about a teller's presence or absence. We can mean at least two things when we speak of a narrator. We can mean the teller as the writer's consciousness inscribed in the tale's language, whatever specific forms that language may take. And we can mean the teller as the effect of the tale's language on the reader, an effect that may seem to exclude the writer's presence as a personal consciousness. The two possibilities create the potential for an oscillating perspective, one that sees double by perceiving both the author as the teller and the author's double, the teller, as a fiction. We can sense both a seemingly real consciousness as creating or reporting presence and a fictive presence, of a different order from the author, that is the language of fiction. In all fiction, the language indicates at once the author's previous, ineluctable presence during the writing and his necessary absence during the reading. We designate that presence and that absence by the single term, the narrator.

We have strong grounds for probing the odd aspects of Joyce's fiction, grounds for asking whether there is a narrator at all in any traditional sense. Does the narrator disappear? Can the narrator become invisible, be refined out of existence, like the artist as Stephen describes him in *A Portrait*? While I would not ascribe to Joyce's narrator a full, fictive personality of the sort we might claim for Stephen Dedalus or Leopold Bloom, I am just as sceptical about a disappearing narrator. The teller disappears only when the page becomes blank, once the book is complete. During the course of the narration, although the teller does not appear in the conventional ways.

that is, as a commentator in the manner of the nineteenth-century English novel, he *does* appear in other forms. In the case of Joyce's fiction, the narrator's supposed disappearance is also his presence everywhere. Like Poe's purloined letter, he is hidden out in the open, where anyone who cares to look can find him.

In his aesthetic theory in *A Portrait*, Stephen's comments on the artist's impersonality echo the similar ones of Flaubert. But Flaubert claims that the artist resembles God in *two* ways, not just as invisible but also as all-powerful ("tout-puissant"). For Joyce's all-powerful narrator, the choice of invisibility and the acts of withdrawing mark his presence. The narrating situation is especially complicated, arrestingly so, in the final episode of *Ulysses*. Does no one besides Molly Bloom narrate "Penelope"? Even the stream of consciousness needs banks, in this case provided implicitly by the chameleonic narrator of the preceding seventeen episodes. His change of state reveals him. The paradox here may make us uncomfortable, but it seems to me unavoidable and indisputable: the author's persona makes itself felt through its apparent invisibility. Like the boy from the pantomime "Turko the Terrible" alluded to several times in *Ulysses*, the narrator announces that he *enjoys* invisibility. He enjoys it in two senses of that verb: he enjoys, that is, he possesses, the power to efface himself, and he enjoys, that is, he relishes, the role of invisibility, at least sufficiently to choose it as his ultimate narrating stance. Insofar as we perceive the teller's enjoyment of the role, the act of effacing becomes an indication of presence.

Besides invisibility, Joyce gives us other metaphors *in* and *of* the narration that reflect the odd nature of his persona in *Ulysses*. Like Macintosh, he earns a name, attains a status as present because of the apparently anonymous garment he wears. But anonymous becomes, as in *Finnegans Wake*, "Anonymoses" (*FW* 47), a mythic figure. As in Yeats's poem "A Coat," style is the coat the author has made for his work as song or tale, and that tale is the coat he wears. Through his choice of styles, Joyce emphasizes attitudes similar to Yeats's. We can never see the writer actually walking naked, never know the dancer solely on the evidence of the dance, or the author as teller on the evidence of the tale alone. On the other hand, we can only know the dancer from the evidence of the dance, and the author on the evidence of the tale. We may not be able to see the figure of the writer, but we have figures for the writer: his figurative language, the figures who speak for him as personae, and the figure woven and unwoven, Penelope-like, by styles.

Joyce's narrator in *Ulysses* is a bit like gravity. We don't see gravity but we do perceive its manifestations. It would be as silly to deny a narrator's presence as to deny gravity. Though neither is directly visible to us, both clearly exist. We couldn't get along without them. The narrator's presence is of a structural sort, and that is an odd kind of presence indeed. It reveals itself through difference: through the difference between the character's interior voice and the surrounding narration and through the differences between styles as the narration proceeds from episode to episode. Through these differences, these shifts of language, in the interstices between the different styles, the narrator's structural presence emerges as the rationale for the book's arrangement, as the pattern in the carpet, the spectrum of a coat of many colors, with its teller and wearer, like the Shakespeare of "Scylla and Charybdis," a "man all hues," "myriadminded." That rationale is polytropic and Odyssean. Like the hero of the *Odyssey* in Homer's opening invocation to the muse, the teller is not named. We know him only by his actions and by the figure left behind as the linguistic trace of his acts of telling. In this regard, the book's title becomes the structural metaphor for the narration as well as for the narrative. Through wanderings of style, Joyce as teller attains a mythic status different in kind from the critical myth of invisibility. He earns his title as mythic artificer, an agnomen that happens also to be the title of his mythic artifice. The styles *of Ulysses* are the styles of its teller *as* Ulysses, *as polytropos*. For Joyce, the heroic teller, *-tropos* can only mean trope.

PART II

Joyce and Beckett

Prefatory Note

Melvin J. Friedman

Samuel Beckett was the subject of two sessions at the Seventh International James Joyce Symposium. The essays that follow offer a representative sampling of the papers presented.

From the early days of Beckett criticism commentators have wondered about the exact nature of the personal and literary rapports between the two self-displaced Dubliners, Joyce and Beckett, who found life on the Continent more congenial than anything offered by their native Ireland. Richard Ellmann's *James Joyce* (1959), that most elegant of literary biographies, began to set the record straight. In two artfully turned sentences Ellmann managed this tableau: "Beckett was addicted to silences, and so was Joyce; they engaged in conversations which consisted often of silences directed towards each other, both suffused with sadness, Beckett mostly for the world, Joyce mostly for himself. Joyce sat in his habitual posture, legs crossed, toe of the upper leg under the instep of the lower; Beckett, also tall and slender, fell into the same gesture." Hugh Kenner offered a compelling though different kind of juxtaposition in his *Flaubert, Joyce and Beckett: The Stoic Comedians* (1962). A Beckett issue of *James Joyce Quarterly* (Summer 1971), edited by David Hayman, enlarged further the critical apparatus. In his "A Prefatory Note," Hayman set down these knowing judgments: "Across the chasm which separates his [Beckett's] career and writing (and personality) from Joyce's we begin to see the qualities which make him Joyce's most distinguished successor, the only living writer who can compete for his laurels. This is evident in his very refusal to compete with Joyce, to accept such competition as vaguely significant, or in his enormous success in the area of Joyce's most depressing failure, the theatre. The narrative tradition which Joyce so brilliantly projected into outer space, Beckett has pulled back to the pole of negative capability by a parallel process of attenuation and mockery."

Deirdre Bair's *Samuel Beckett: A Biography* (1978) adds some useful details to the ups and downs of the friendship, but does little to engage the literary relationships. Barbara Reich Gluck's *Beckett and Joyce: Friendship and Fiction* (1979), while it gently but firmly leads us by the hand in mapping out the circuitous route Beckett took while cutting the Joycean umbilical cord, sadly fails to live up to expectations: it never quite manages to rid itself of its musty origins as a Columbia University Ph.D. dissertation. (For a judicious assessment of Gluck's book, see S. E. Gcntarski's review in the Spring 1980 *James Joyce Quarterly*.)

All of this emphatically proves that the case is not closed. We are now aware, of course, that Beckett started his career in the shadow of Joyce and in the "wake" of the *Wake*: he contributed an essay on Joyce to *Our Exagmination Round His Factification for Incamination of Work in Progress* (1929); he was involved in the translation of the "Anna Livia Plurabelle" into French, which was published in the May 1931 *Nouvelle Revue Française*; he wrote the acrostic "Home Olga" in 1932, with James Joyce's name spelled out by the first letters of the ten lines of the poem. Reverberations of *Finnegans Wake* are certainly heard in the background of Beckett's early verse, just as echoes of *Dubliners* resound through the pages of *More Pricks Than Kicks*. The "Cyclops" chapter of *Ulysses* surely comes to mind when one reads these sentences from *Murphy*: "He was a low-sized, clean-shaven, grey-faced, one-eyed man, triorchous and a non-smoker. He had a curious hunted walk, like that of a destitute diabetic in a strange city."

These essays, in quite different ways, expand upon the material mentioned above. Their counterpointing of the two Irish writers works extremely well. We understand better now, I think, the kinds of debts the younger owed the older.

Samuel Beckett, James Joyce's "Illstarred Punster"

S. E. Gontarski

Sam knows miles bettern me how
to work the miracle. . . .
Illstarred punster, lipstering
cowknucks. 'Twas the quadra
sent him and Trinity too. And
he can cantab as chipper as any
oxon ever I mood with, a tiptoe
singer! He'll prisckly soon hand
tune your Erin's ear for you.

(*Finnegans Wake*, p. 467)

      Samuel Beckett's early years in Paris, especially that two-year tenure at the École Normale, from 1928 to 1930, were critical to the developing artist, and although James Joyce was only one of the forces at work on the young Beckett, he may certainly have been both the most formidable and finally the most burdensome, for Joyce was for Beckett a messiah who finally had to be denied if the younger Dubliner was to develop as an independent prophet. In fact, it may not have been until Beckett abandoned, albeit temporarily, his native tongue, that he could shed the Joycean influence enough to develop his most distinct, personal, original voice.

      Beckett apparently met Joyce through Thomas McGreevy soon after the former's appointment to the École Normale in the fall of 1928. McGreevy was Beckett's predecessor at the École from 1926 to 1928, was the friend of many artists of the time, and became Beckett's primary link to the Joyce circle. McGreevy received his appointment to the staff of the arts magazine *Formes* with the help of James and Nora Joyce and was to become Beckett's confidant until his death in 1967.

      The relationship with Joyce had far-reaching consequences for Beckett. On a superficial level, as biographers of both men report, Beckett began to imitate, if not mock, Joyce's mannerisms: assuming the Joycean posture while sitting, dangling his cigarettes in the Joycean fashion, reading books

and papers closer to his glasses than necessary, ordering the same brand of
wine as Joyce. According to some reports Beckett even wore pointed-toe,
patent leather shoes in Joyce's size, which were much too small for the
lanky Beckett and evidently caused him considerable pain. It is, of course,
possible to take such posing too seriously, since the early Beckett is as much
slashing satirist holding little sacred as he is idolator—witness his Trinity
satire, *Le Kid* (1931).

Beckett was one of the coterie around Joyce willing to donate the time to
the relationship that Joyce demanded, so much so that the popular (but
erroneous) notion was that Beckett was Joyce's private secretary, an attribu-
tion that Beckett denies in his interview (or rather noninterview) with Israel
Shenker: "I was never Joyce's secretary, but like all his friends, I helped
him. He was greatly handicapped because of his eyes. I did odd jobs for
him, marking passages for him or reading to him. But I never wrote any of
his letters." But so much of Beckett's life was taken up with Joyce's errands
that Richard Aldington referred to Beckett as "James Joyce's white boy."[1]

The relationship was further complicated by psychological and emotional factors: Beckett's need for a father figure, Lucia's demands on Beckett's affections, which, if nothing else, caused a two-year hiatus in the
Beckett/Joyce friendship, from about May of 1930 to Bloomsday of 1932.
The breach was at least in part closed by Beckett's gift for that Bloomsday
celebration, his poem "Home Olga," an ironic gift for the resumption of a
friendship since, while it is homage in imitation of the master, it is also the
poem in which Beckett announces his attempt to break with Joyce, artistically at any rate.

The intellectual and artistic grip that Joyce had on Beckett in these early
years was profound. Becket was only too pleased to be chosen by Joyce,
even as a last-minute replacement, to be one of the essayists for Joyce's
planned defense of *Work in Progress*, published as *Our Exagmination Round
His Factification for Incamination of Work in Progress*. And Beckett was willing
to let Joyce suggest the subject matter of the essay and even its thesis. But
such hegemony was characteristic of Joyce. Richard Ellmann reports,
"Joyce admitted to [Valery] Larbaud [that] he had stood behind 'those
twelve Marshals more or less directing them what lines of research to
follow.' "[2] Beckett's task was to outline Joyce's debt not only to Dante, a
writer for whom both had a passion, but to two other Italians: Giordano
Bruno and Giambattista Vico, neither of whom Becket had previously
read. As Deirdre Bair suggests, "Joyce was at pains to instruct Beckett not
only to show his indebtedness to them [i.e., Dante, Bruno, and Vico] but
also to make it plain that he moved beyond them to create his own particular
work of art."[3] The result of Beckett's effort, however, was an essay that
served both writers: it is a highly original, perceptive work by the twenty-

three-year-old scholar, one that still serves as a useful entrée to both Joyce and Beckett and anticipates the critical acumen Beckett brings to his 1931 study of Proust.

Beckett's poetry of the time also shows strong Joycean traces. Three of the four poems he published in Samuel Putnam's *The European Caravan* (1931) are based to one degree or another on mythic structures from Dante: "Hell Crane to Starling," "Text," and "Yoke of Liberty." Beckett's own blurb for the book notes that he "has adapted the Joyce method to his poetry with original results."[4] (So much for our image of a shy, modest Beckett.) The fourth poem, an account of a disastrous New Year's Eve party, "Casket of Pralinen for a Daughter of a Dissipated Mandarin," was used the following year in Beckett's first (and still-unpublished) novel, *Dream of Fair to Middling Women*, begun in May of 1932, about the same time that Beckett was writing "Home Olga." Another poem, "Enueg II," which Beckett wrote during the crisis winter of 1931 while back in Dublin struggling with thoughts of his future and his academic career at Trinity College, not only uses a mythic structure, in this case a Christian myth (partly Veronica and the *via dolorosa*, and partly Judas's betrayal), but concerns a subject near to Joyce's heart: exile, a theme that in later years Beckett was to extend to make his own. As he suggests in *Murphy*, "asylum (after a point) is better than exile" (33). In "Enueg II," the narrator compares himself to Judas, the betrayer. The poem develops a Dublin setting and uses the private imagery characteristic of Beckett's poetry: "lying on O'Connell Bridge / goggling at the tulips of the evening / the green tulips / shining round the corner like an anthrax / shining on Guinness's barges." Shortly after writing the poem, Beckett chose: he too became an exile. He resigned his position at Trinity, essentially abandoning his academic career, in December of 1931, and by mid-March was back in Paris. The following year when Beckett sat down to write *Dream*, he reused the "Enueg II" material, altered only slightly: "A man, a burly man . . . paused on O'Connell Bridge and raised his face to the tulips of the evening, the green tulips, shining round the corner like an anthrax, shining on Guinness's barges" (*Dream*, p. 25). Beckett, in these years, seems to have picked up many of Joyce's pack rat or encyclopediast tendencies, an artistic direction that in later years he would revise and make his own.

One of the few comprehensive statements that Beckett has (apparently) made about his relationship with Joyce appears in an account, actually a sham interview, by Israel Shenker. Although the account appears as an interview, evidently no direct interview ever took place. Beckett has said, at least, that the material that Shenker presents is misleading. And yet the observations seem so accurate, so Beckettian, that it is difficult to believe that Shenker's information has no merit. The position Beckett (or Shenker, or someone) puts forth in the account is corroborated by the sort of artistic struggle that Beckett was having in those early years and that manifests itself in "Home Olga" and *Dream of Fair to Middling Women*:

> the difference is that Joyce was a superb manipulator of material, perhaps the greatest. He was making words do the absolute maximum of work. There isn't a syllable that's superfluous. The kind of work I do is one in which I am not master of my material. The more Joyce knew the more he could. His tendency is toward omniscience and omnipotence as an artist. I'm working with impotence, ignorance. I don't think that impotence has been exploited in the past. There seems to be a kind of esthetic axiom that expression is an achievement—must be an achievement. My little exploration is that whole zone of being that has always been set aside by artists as something unusable—as something by definition incompatible with art.[5]

Beckett echoed these sentiments to John Gruen in 1969: "If my work has any meaning at all, it is due more to ignorance, inability and intuitive despair than to any individual strength. I think that I have perhaps freed myself from certain formal concepts." Beckett then goes on to compare himself to Schönberg and Kandinsky.[6] The inability, ignorance, and impotence Beckett speaks of here are more than matters of his creating helpless characters. They also suggest the fundamental inability of the author to control his art, i.e., the lives of his characters and the forms of his expression. Beckett's aesthetic here is more phenomenological or existential, closer to Sartre's argument that one measure of the quality of literature is the amount of freedom characters have independent of their authors; this is far from Joycean control.

But earlier in his career Beckett himself evidently strove for a sort of literary omniscience and formal control. The above analysis may describe Beckett's relationship to Joyce after Beckett had been able to make his break, after he began to write in French; during the late twenties and early thirties, however, Beckett was still trying to be the word man, still trying to model himself after Shem the Penman. The 1932 homage to Joyce, "Home Olga," is a revealing statement about the relationship in these early years. The poem is called "Home Olga," or *Home* Olga! since the title is based partly on a private joke, a comment made at a party in Ireland by a bored husband, who, after getting his wife's hat and coat, said to her, "*Home, Olga!*" and left without a word to the hostess. According to Lawrence Harvey, "At subsequent parties the phrase signaled ennui and became a covert call for relief and regroupment at a pre-selected cafe."[7] But the title also, or especially, plays on *Homo Logos*, word man, a direct reference to Joyce, and further outlines something of the poem's pattern of development, since it also suggests the Greek-derived *homologous* and even might call to mind the word *homage*. The poem builds to an epiphany, where we see Joyce and Christ as homologous or, to borrow one of Joyce's titles from *Dubliners*, counterparts. Moreover, by virtue of the fact that the poem is so Joycean, an acrostic filled with arcane allusions and word play, and is structured around emblematic patterns, Beckett himself becomes one of the counterparts. In the poem's linguistic virtuosity Beckett seems to be trying to out-Joyce Joyce, as in his later works he seems almost to be trying to out-suffer Christ.

In addition to each of the poem's ten lines beginning with a letter of Joyce's name, the poem is structured around Christian and Joycean symbols: the three theological virtues, hope, charity (or its equivalent, love), and faith, each developed with its corresponding color, green ("Jade of hope"), red ("erythrite of love"), and white ("opal of faith"). To strengthen the ties with Joyce, the poem develops Stephen Dedalus's three defenses to the world (see *Portrait*, pp. 246–47), "silence, exile, and cunning," a position that itself may be heavily indebted to Balzac, who has his character Lucien de Rubempré say in *Splendeurs et misères des courtisanes*: "J'ai mis en pratique un axiome avec lequel on est sûr de vivre tranquille: Fuge . . . Late . . . Tace."[8] Moreover, the poem is filled with Joycean word play: "In stomacho," plays on *in petto*; Dante's *dolce stil nuovo* is written "sweet noo style." How much of this poem is playful satire and how much reverential imitation is difficult to tell, but one suspects at least a large smattering of the former. The poem's epiphany in the last line is most revealing of how Beckett saw the relationship. The line begins with an example: "*Exempli gratia: ecce* himself and the pickthank agnus." Here Joyce is the Man himself, *Ecce homo*, the Christ rejected by his people; Beckett the "pickthank agnus," the peccable (i.e., sinful), thankless lamb. "Home Olga" is finally so compact a poem that it indeed seems to be an example of a poet trying to make words do the absolute maximum. The one touch of modesty can be found in the closing, symmetrical cryptogram, "—e. o. o. e.," i.e., errors or omissions excepted. The relationship depicted in the poem is as complex as the analysis of friendship Joyce offers through Richard Rowan in *Exiles*: "There is a faith still stranger than the faith of a disciple in his master. . . . The faith of a master in the disciple who will betray him."

Beckett begins his first extended piece of prose fiction in May of 1932, and the novel includes the same sort of conflict evident in "Home Olga." While less tightly structured and considerably more fragmented than the poem, *Dream of Fair to Middling Women* reflects the same flirt with linguistic virtuosity as "Home Olga." Part of the disorganization may be the result of its incomplete state, but part is surely Beckett's design. And with *Dream* Beckett begins to plot an artistic course away from Joyce. As his narrator suggests in the text: "The only unity in this story is, please God, an involuntary unity" (118).[9] In fact, in *Dream* Beckett begins his examination of how to contain the chaos of life, of reality, within the forms of art, and much of what is rejected here is a Joycean control. Speaking to the Mandarin, Belacqua, Beckett's protagonist in *Dream*, expostulates: "The reality of the individual . . . is an incoherent reality and must be expressed incoherently. . . . I was speaking of the incoherent continuum as expressed by, say, Rimbaud and Beethoven. Their names occur to me. The terms of whose statements serve merely to delimit the reality of insane areas of silence, whose audibilities are no more than punctuation in a statement of silences. How do they get from point to point. That is what I meant by the incoherent reality and its authentic extrinsecation" (91). *This* is the impotence, the ignorance that Beckett will spend his life trying to express. Even Beckett's technically omniscient narrator has his lapses into impotence: "What she meant by that," he admits, "and what pleasure she hoped to get out of that, cannot be made clear" (97). In *Dream* Beckett clearly rejects the sort of artistic omniscience that he associates with Balzac (and, in later years, with Joyce):

> The *procédé* that seems all falsity, that of Balzac, for example, and the divine Jane [Jane Austen] and many others, consists in dealing with the vicissitudes, or absence of vicissitudes, of character in this backwash, as though they were the whole story. Whereas, in reality, this is so little the story, this nervous recoil into composure, this has so little to do with the story that one must be excessively concerned with a total precision to allude to it at all. . . . So all the novelist has to do is to bind his material in a spell, item after item, and juggle politely with irrefragable values, values that can assimilate other values like in kind and be assimilated by them, that can increase and decrease in virtue of an unreal permanence of quality. To read Balzac is to receive the impression of a chloroformed world. *He is absolute master of his material*, he can do what he likes with it, he can foresee and calculate its least vicissitude, he can write the end of his book before he has finished the first paragraph, because he has turned all his creatures into clockwork cabbages and can rely on their *staying put wherever needed or staying going at whatever speed in whatever direction he chooses*. The whole thing, from beginning to end, takes place in a spellbound backwash. We all love and lick up Balzac, we lap it up and say it is wonderful, but why call this distillation of Euclid and Perrault *Scenes from Life*? (P. 106)

If Belacqua is a sad specimen, there is nothing the narrator is free to do for him. Of him the narrator can say: "He remembers the pleasant gracious bountiful tunnel [i.e. womb], and cannot get back" (110). "And we cannot do anything for him," announces the narrator; "how can you help people, unless it be on with their corsets or to a second or third helping" (110). The aesthetic that Beckett is developing in these early years is diametrically opposed to the one Joyce expresses through Stephen Dedalus, where the artist is "like the God of creation" (481), and develops in the structure of both *Ulysses* and *Finnegans Wake*. As Joyce has said to Beckett, "I can justify every line of my book." And at a later time, "I have discovered I can do anything with language I want."[10]

Further, the aesthetic that is gestating in *Dream* is not one in which art is viewed as a lasting monument, as an achievement, as the author's defense against Time, but the opposite. Of Belacqua's character the narrator notes, "Then the gestures, the horrid gestures, of the little fat hands and the splendid words and the seaweed smile, all coiling and uncoiling and unfolding and flowering into nothingness, his whole person a stew of disruption and flux" (104). And very early in the novel: "Without going as far as Stendhal,—who said—or repeated after somebody—that the best music (what did he know about music anyway?) was the music that became inaudible after a few bars, we do declare and maintain stiffly (at least for the purposes of this paragraph) that the object that becomes invisible before our eyes is, so to speak, the brightest and best" (9–10). The technique of effacing, of cancelling what has just been said, the technique that suggests the impossibility of communication because "there is nothing to express, nothing with which to express, nothing from which to express, no power to express, no desire to express, together with the obligation to express"[11] is already taking shape in *Dream*. The aesthetic developing here seems very close to that stated by Jean-Paul Sartre in his essay "The Unprivileged Painter: Lapoujade": "On his canvas the artist paints the rudiments of intuition only to blot them out immediately thereafter."[12]

If "Home Olga" is Beckett's announcement of his intention to pursue his own independent artistic course, *Dream of Fair to Middling Women* may be Beckett's first faltering steps along that path. He may not have written the novel he wanted to in *Dream*. He may not have written it until *Molloy*, but once it was written he could not stop, has not stopped.

Notes

1. Deirdre Bair, *Samuel Beckett: A Biography* (New York: Harcourt, Brace, Jovanovich, 1978), p. 71.
2. Richard Ellmann, *James Joyce* (New York: Oxford University Press, 1959), p. 626.
3. Bair, p. 76.
4. Raymond Federman and John Fletcher, *Samuel Beckett: His Works and His Critics* (Berkeley: Unversity of California Press, 1970), p. 10.
5. Israel Shenker, "A Portrait of Samuel Beckett, the Author of the Puzzling *Waiting for Godot*," *New York Times*, May 6, 1956, Section 2, pp. 1, 3.
6. *Vogue* (December 1969), p. 210.

7. Lawrence E. Harvey, *Samuel Beckett: Poet and Critic* (Princeton: Princeton University Press, 1970), p. 296.

8. Ellmann, p. 365.

9. Quotations with permission of Samuel Beckett.

10. Cited by Ellmann, p. 715.

11. Samuel Beckett and Georges Duthuit, "Three Dialogues," in *Samuel Beckett: A Collection of Critical Essays*, ed. Martin Esslin (Englewood Cliffs, N.J.: Prentice-Hall, Inc., 1965), p. 17.

12. Jean-Paul Sartre, *Essays in Aesthetics*, trans. Wade Baskin (New York: Washington Square Press, 1966), p. 109.

Joyce → Beckett/Joyce

David Hayman

The question of Beckett in relation to Joyce could be a fine test case for Harold Bloom's theory about the anxiety of influence and creative misreading. In terms of that theory the later Beckett will occult and sublimate the Joycean roots, disclose himself by distorting his former model.

It is already recognized that the early Beckett was influenced, reacting to, reflecting upon Joyce, and that he was capable by the time he wrote *Watt* of beginning the writing-off process, a process of rejection followed more or less consciously by Joyce himself in relation to his own early influences. Recently, Barbara Gluck has written a whole book on the topic, confirming earlier findings but uncovering relatively little that is new or revealing about either Joyce or Beckett.[1] I propose only to rediscover the topic in a general way, pointing up Joyce's place in a panoply of influential writers, indicating similarities, and examining briefly two unexplored shared traits: the use of a complex voice and of self-generating texts.

Apart from the obvious use of puns, the tendency to call upon an encyclopedic range of associations, the more or less obvious allusions to moments in Joyce's work, the occasional use of opposite equivalence (as in the obvious case of Molloy and Moran)—apart from these, what are the marks of Joyce's impact on the later Beckett? Gluck points to his use of cyclical development, a trait too common to have specifically Joycean roots. I have spoken of his tendency toward inclusiveness, his archetypal thrust, and, rightly or not, I have connected this with the *Wake*.[2]

We might say that along with Céline, Kafka, and Proust, though in a radically different way, Joyce gave Beckett a precedent for the sort of intercraneal discourse that characterizes the later prose. The locus of *Finnegans Wake*, like Beckett's trilogy, is the psyche of a stylized individual and, by extension, that of the reader. The Joycean theater is clearly the human brain, in which civilization sleeps. Though his vision of that situation is perhaps more positive than Beckett's, it is noteworthy that neither of them sees it as an heroic arena, that both find in it the detritus of life and of the living process, the picnic litter of past times' pastimes. In both cases the reader is obliged to create his/her own space in the inner universe, to

37

participate in a sort of intransitive discourse, one that bears no fixed meaning in relation to external reality, which tends in fact to destroy referentiality and with it the reader's sense of balance.

Along these lines, Joyce also provided a model for a major attribute of Beckett's work, the suspension of the suspension of disbelief or, better, the unwilling suspension of *b*elief. This is a deliberate play upon the reader's *urge* or *impulse* to accept as valid that which is presented as a controlled fiction. Beginning with the arranged passages in *Ulysses*, that is with the headlines in "Aeolus," Joyce, like Sterne and few other writers since the eighteenth century, has refused to play the reader's game, has insisted on violating the apparent decorum of his own work by introducing noncon- forming literary techniques into the fabric of his discourse. Beckett has always found ways to undermine credibility, to underscore artifice. We may point to the Sternean narrators of *More Pricks*, *Murphy*, and *Watt*, with their interpolations, as well as to the underlying narrative strategies of the trilogy and the later fictions. But in neither Joyce nor Beckett is suspension of the suspension of disbelief dependent only on narrative hijinks. The Beckettian circumstance itself undermines credulity. If Molloy seems to some a viable character, what do we make of Moran taking up in his wake, a palpable music-hall straight man, an absurd private eye whose discourse turns him gradually into a clown? It is the attainment of belief on another, deeper level of awareness that characterizes both Beckett and Joyce, the affirmation of flux as an essential component of our experience. While affirming this, we must not overlook the obvious differences: the amplitude of Joyce's vision, the minimal-art quality in Beckett's, the fact that the postwar Beckett chooses to write pellucid prose while Joyce deliberately squid-screens his very language, that Beckett develops a starkly human situation while Joyce, in the later work, lets experience shine darkly through his text. Still, both seem to achieve by means that are not unrelated a double reversal: the suspension of the suspension of disbelief imposes yet another suspension of disbelief.

To my mind, two other shared traits are even more striking than those listed above: self-generation/auto-destruction and the voice as medley. Joyce did not invent self-generation as a procedure, since almost any aesthetically viable text can be seen on inspection to grow out of its own inner needs, but his later texts do seem to foreground their processes, to evolve not so much out of the necessity of plot, situation, or character as out of the rhythmic and associative flux. "One world burrowing on another," as Joyce puts it.[3] Beckett must have been aware of this when he collaborated in the translation of "Anna Livia Plurabelle" or when he participated in the composition and revision of *Finnegans Wake*. But in applying it to *Molloy*, for example, he had different ends in view. Joyce was building a world; Beckett was dismantling one, proving the verbal nature of the known, shaping the void. His prime tool was and is the evolving text, which by its very progress denies its own existence and validity. By means of such denials it affirms its own existence in the presence of absence. The method in both cases is farcical. That is, in both cases language reinforces or subverts action by taking pratfalls. Life and language are held up to ridicule, which the reader experiences and in which he/she participates. Our laughter destroys not only the world we inhabit but also the language of the text that projects an image of that world. Take the following passage from *Finnegans Wake*, in which the thunderclap of parental applause/authority disperses the children at play in the chapter Joyce called "The Mime of Mick, Nick and the Maggies":

> Uploudermainagain!
> For the Clearer of the Air from on high has spoken in tumbuldum tambaldam to his tembledim tombaldoom worrild and, moguphonoised by that phonemanon, the unhappitents of the earth have terrerumbled from fimament unto fundament and from tweedledeedumms down to twid-dledeedees.
> Loud, here us!
> Loud, graciously hear us! (258)

Among the generating principles operating here, beyond the situation of parental applause/command, is a cluster of oppositions: those between the elevated and the debased, the serious and the comic, the divine and the mundane, the sad or even catastrophic and the hilarious. Thus we have references to the Egyptian Book of the Dead ("For the Clearer of the Air from on high"), to Carroll's *Through the Looking Glass* ("tweedledeedumms" etc.), to the fall ("tumbuldum" etc.), to a prayer to the Christian God, to the rumbling of bowels ("terrerumbled from fimament unto fundament"), to human misery ("unhappitents of the earth"), etc., etc. These references tend to interlock and perpetuate themselves in such a way that the Twee-dledee allusion calls forth its echo syllables and relates to the fall, which is also that of Humpty Dumpty/HCE, another Carrollian figure. The expression "the unhappitents of the earth," which itself conceals self-generated details like "tent" and "inhabitants," leads quite openly to the pun on earth/*terre* in "terrerumbled," a word that contains both the fear of the terrestrials and the rumble of the thunder-god while preparing for the rumble of the bowels mentioned earlier. Not only are joy and terror united, but practically every element in the passage conceals its own negation, or finds a precise negative echo. Statement in Joyce is always ready to give way to antistatement, though no true synthesis is elicited and the dynamic of the word persists. This is of course only the sketchiest possible treatment of Joycean auto-generation/destruction, but it will enable us to compare and contrast it with Beckett's use of a similiar device for very different ends, noting that both writers draw much of their material from a text that perceptibly folds in on itself.

Self-generation/auto-destruction in Beckett is perhaps best illustrated by the unnamable's telling and untelling of its self. But, even earlier, the voice of Molloy provides us with many examples of telling *ex-nihilo*, of words generating words that are later erased. The following passage shows him in the process of generating the details of a landscape out of the concept of the men A & C, and finally out of the language itself. The conventions of naturalist discourse are under fire as their text responds to its own givens, as each phrase calls forth amplification:

> Each went on his way, A back towards the town, C on by ways he seemed hardly to know, or not at all, for he went with uncertain step and often stopped to look about him, like someone trying to fix landmarks in his mind, for one day perhaps he may have to retrace his steps, you never know. The treacherous hills where fearfully he ventured were no doubt only known to him from afar, seen perhaps from his bedroom window or from the summit of a monument which, one black day, having nothing in particular to do and turning to height for solace, he had paid his few coppers to climb, slower and slower, up the winding stones. From there he must have seen it all, the plain, the sea, and then these selfsame hills that some call mountains, indigo in places in the evening light, their serried ranges crowding to the skyline, cloven with hidden valleys that the eye divines from sudden shifts of colour and then from other signs for which there are no words, nor even thoughts.[4]

Molloy continues, calling forth other tropes, words for sights, but this quotation may be enough to make the point, especially if we see that the passage, which generates the experience of a third party, is, in many respects, similar to the *locus classicus* of Joycean composition of place, the "Parable of the Plums," another self-generating narrative. It is to Stephen's method that reference is covertly being made here. But Molloy goes further (much as Stephen does in "Scylla and Charybdis"), making the accidents of this passage the essentials of what follows. We note that A is dismissed from the narrative, brushed off by the pursuit of a history and motivation for C, who quickly takes on the density of a novelistic persona. The sea in this citation eventually generates the seashore at which Molloy spends time later in the narrative, but the sea reference itself seems to derive from the liquid component in his description of the rolling landscape.

In this same passage we have inklings of what I meant by the voice as medley, a technique introduced early in *Finnegans Wake* and especially evident in passages seemingly delivered in a single voice. In such monologues, though the register seems stable, we find fragments in various voices run together with borrowings from literature and even popular discourse. The procedure is a modification of formulaic composition, and as such it is not rare in fiction. More immediately it is a continuation of *style indirect libre*, which inserts the persona's voice into the texture of the narrator's discourse. The difference here is that the alien voice penetrates the discourse of a seemingly stable persona. Both Beckett and Joyce fore-ground the disjunctions, undercutting the seamless discourse of the unified persona. Coherence persists, but only within a random field as a quality among others and largely through the tenacious efforts of the reader, who must at all costs make sense of the verbal experience. There are of course many instances to cite, the prime example being the inquisition chapter of Book III, where all voices emanate from the recumbent Shaun. But perhaps the following passage from Book I, chapter 6, is appropriate, in which the young Issy lectures her ambiguous (androgynous?) lover:

> I know, pepette, of course, dear, but listen, precious! Thanks, pette, those are lovely, pitounette, delicious! But mind the wind, sweet! What exquisite hands you have, you angiol, if you didn't gnaw your nails, isn't it a wonder you're not achamed of me, you pig, you perfect little pigaleen! I'll nudge you in a minute! I bet you use her best Perisian smear off her vanity table to make them look so rosetop glowstop nostop. I know her. Slight me, would she? For every got I care! Three creamings a day, the first during her shower and wipe off with tissue. Then after cleanup and of course before retiring. Beme shawl, when I think of that espos of a Clancarbry, the foodbrawler, of the sociationist party with hiss blackleaded chest, hello, Prendregast! that you, Innkipper, and all his fourteen other fullback maulers or hurling stars or whatever the dagos they are, baiting at my Lord Ornery's, just becups they won the egg and spoon there so ovally provencial at Balldole. (143–44)

At first glance this seems a fairly unified, if outrageously flirtatious and coy, voice. But closer study shows it to be an amalgam—or perhaps it is better to say that it tends to alternate between the childish Issy voice and the mature voice of ALP, between Issy's sweet voice and her dark and sadistic one. In short, it contains elements from several if not all aspects of the female persona, plus a variety of literary and popular voices. Our example quickly shifts from a pleasant to an angry mood, from sweet to perverse, and includes a fully developed commercial for a skin cream. But the principal shift is from the childish voice to an echo of the mature one, of ALP as letter writer. The final sentence is a clear reference to the style of her famous missive, the apologetic "Letter" that the reader will first encounter only at the end of the book, some 470 pages later. We note among other things the direct address to the absent one, whose "hiss" links him to the serpent in

ALP's garden: "Wriggling reptiles, take notice," she says, after describing her beloved and benighted husband as "hairy of chest." But it is the general tonality with its direct address that points up the relationship between our passages, though Issy is at this point less emphatic than ALP, being, after all, one of the "two Peris" (see the "best Perisian smear") or temptresses who caused the fall in the Phoenix Park encounter of which ALP speaks in the following extract:

> How delitious for the three Sulvans of Dulkey and what a sellpriceget the two Peris of Monacheena! Sugars of lead for the chloras ashpots! Peace! He possessing from a child of highest valency for our privileged beholdings ever complete hairy of chest, hamps and eyebags in pursuance to salesladies' affectionate company. His real devotes. Wriggling reptiles, take notice! Whereas we exgust all such sprinkling snigs. They are pestituting the whole time never with standing. (616)

Both discourses contain all sorts of foreign matter, of course. Song tags, citations, clichés, bits of formal discourse mingle with commercials, echoes from within the text itself, etc. But note particularly the expressions of anger and outrage. The reference to "sellpriceget" is a citation from Issy, whose presence infiltrates this passage as the seductress of the fall. The full range of tonalities cannot be studied here, but we may suggest that as sentence follows sentence we dip into a variety of shifting masks as well as moods.

In the Beckett passage cited earlier, there is an inkling of the medley effect, though one would need a much longer sample to make its nature transparent. Here again the register seems stable even though, on a second reading, we may recognize amongst the tonalities of Molloy the intonations of Moran. Beckett has challenged himself to undermine and maintain the oldest and most solid pillar of narrative discourse, the first-person speaker (reliable and unreliable). He has done this without recourse to an obviously heterogeneous overarching style (like Joyce's in the *Wake*). In this passage the matter-of-fact voice of the narrator is interspersed with a variety of elevated and clichéd utterances. Typically there is the heavily qualified aside: "for one day *perhaps* he *may* have to retrace his steps, *you never know*." This uncertainty is generated by the imagined uncertainty of C, who "*seemed* hardly to know." In a radically different and comically more assured voice, Molloy falls into the lyrical clichés of the composition of place generated by the "treacherous hills." A bit further down on the same page we find a remarkable sentence alliterating in *s*, *n*, and *r* and broken by random ejaculations:

He looks old and it is a sorry sight to see him solitary after so many years, so many days and nights unthinkingly given to that rumour rising at birth and even earlier, What shall I do? What shall I do? now low, a murmur, now precise as a headwaiter's And to follow? and often rising to a scream. (*Molloy*, p. 11)

We note that the sentence melts at one point into the utterance of the imaginary persona. It is to such internally motivated modifications of voice that the text owes much of its interest. Ultimately, by virtue of Molloy's intransigence, they define the speaker so well that we tend to overlook the heterogeneous texture and to assume a nonexistent coherence. This is one of the miracles and joys of the Beckettian, like the Joycean, text, the stillness composed of motion.

Notes

1. *Beckett and Joyce: Friendship and Fiction* (Lewisburg, Pa.: Bucknell University Press, 1979).

2. "Some Writers in the Wake of the *Wake*" in *In the Wake of the "Wake"* (Madison: University of Wisconsin Press, 1978), pp. 12–18.

3. *Finnegans Wake* (New York: Viking Press, 1958), p. 275. Future references in the text are to this edition.

4. *Molloy* (New York: Grove Press, 1955), pp. 10–11.

From Joyce to Beckett:
The Tale That Wags the Telling

Richard Pearce

Molloy is in his mother's room. He is filling up empty pages
with what he knows. Which is his story. What he knows, then—indeed
what he is—is what he writes. And he knows nothing beyond his present
situation. His present situation includes the words he has just written into
the empty space. Whether they are in the past or present tense, they are
presences. And it is through his engagement—through his toying, struggling, and intercourse—with these physical presences that his story comes
to life.

He doesn't know how he got to his mother's room. He doesn't know
whether his mother was dead when he arrived or only died later, that is,
enough to bury. He tells us, though, that he has taken her place: "I must
resemble her more and more. All I need now is a son." And then Molloy
gives birth to a son. Watch how: "Perhaps I have one somewhere. But I
think not. He *would be* old now, nearly as old as myself. It *was* a little
chambermaid. It *wasn't* true love" (my emphases).[1]

Molloy speculates upon the possibility, reflects upon the improbabil-
ity—and then creates a son by shifting from the conditional present to the
indicative (or actual) past: "He *would be* old now. . . . It *was* a little
chambermaid." This grammaculate conception is also generated by a shift
from "he" to "it." And while "it" has no antecedent in the text, we easily
apprehend its referent, for such ellipses are common in everyday speech.[2]
In this case "it" refers to the dalliance that led to his son's conception—
which is itself conceived by Molloy's pencil dallying with the grammar and
filling in the empty space after a sentence defining his son as no more than
what Stephen Dedalus called a "Godpossibled soul."[3]

We know that Beckett was attracted by the fecundity and procreative
power of Joyce's language, especially in *Finnegans Wake*. But if we turn to
Ulysses we will see where Joyce's language liberated itself from the consciousness of his characters and even from the narrator—and became the
autonomous physical presence and the self-generating element that Beckett
would exploit.

As we enter the world of *Ulysses*, we look through Stephen's eyes across his "threadbare cuffedge" to see a "ring of bay and skyline" that holds "a dull green mass of liquid" which becomes the "bowl of white china . . . holding the green sluggish bile" torn up from his mother's liver (5). We see something of Mr. Deasy's school but very little of the Sandymount strand through the waves of Stephen's recollections, obsessions, and musings. We see a great deal of Dublin through the eyes of Leopold Bloom, but these scenes are continually fragmented by the singular associations that emerge from his consciousness. Then suddenly we encounter neither a scene nor a stream of consciousness but a *page*—where what Bloom sees and thinks is continually interrupted by boldface headings. Indeed, Bloom's stream of consciousness is only part of a pattern that includes—is in fact dominated by—the typography.

It is only at the bottom of the page that we discover we are in a newspaper world, and that the boldface headings are like newspaper headlines. Still, we cannot locate their source. They are not part of what any character sees or thinks, nor are they part of what the narrator sees or says. The headlines are just *there*: gratuitous, obdurate, physical presences that intrude into the narrative, interrupt, fragment, and sometimes comment upon the scene. The printed words, the very material that composes the novel, come out into the open in a form that calls attention to itself—and becomes a dramatic element in its own right. It becomes what David Hayman defines as a "counterforce,"[4] and what I have described as an antagonist against which the narrator, the characters, and the readers will have to contend.[5] As a pattern of arbitrary sounds and a series of literary parodies, this counterforce will obscure our view of Bloom when he becomes a cuckold and when he finally meets Stephen as a father. As an arbitrary point of view, it lifts us high above the streets of Dublin, reducing all the characters to the same level, while, from time to time, zooming down to fragment them into parts. As language issuing from no source within the narrative world, feeding upon itself and gathering momentum, it generates an intensity of danger far out of proportion to the hurtling biscuit tin. As a set of stage directions, it transforms characters into the shapes of their deepest anxieties. As a series of impersonal questions and answers, it transforms the quality of the novel's most significant encounter into a set of quantitative results, and threatens to reduce Bloom to one of the many inanimate objects in 7 Eccles Street.

Joyce's language in *Ulysses*, then, has more than the power to call up Dublin on June 16, 1904, and embody the streams of its characters' consciousnesses. It becomes a fully autonomous element, issuing from no source within the narrative world—a counterforce that is self-generating, arbitrary, intrusive, comic, and dramatically threatening. In Beckett, it is not a counterforce but the only force; it does not intrude into a narrative world, it is all the world.

On the opening page of *Watt*, Mr. Hackett turns a corner and sees, in the failing light, at some little distance, his seat. But what is the corner he turns? It is not like the stairhead from which Buck Mulligan emerges; we never see enough of the scene to place or define it. We do not even know—cannot even see—what it is the corner of. It has only a single dimension. It is no more than a point, an intersection, between what never was and what will become, as one word after another fills up the page. It is the point from which Mr. Hackett emerges, first as a name—an abstraction, a virtual character like a line drawing—and from which he and his world will develop as the line of the story burgeons into further dimensions. The virtual becomes actual, the world begins to solidify, as one event follows another. Mr. Hackett stretches out his left hand and fastens it around a rail. And now that the rail is *there* to support his hand, he can strike his stick against the pavement and feel the thudding rubber in his palm. When he gets closer to the seat, the occupants appear part by part: "the lady held the gentleman by the ears, and the gentleman's hand was on the lady's thigh, and the lady's tongue was in the gentleman's mouth."[6] Even though the clauses of the sentence are joined by coordinating conjunctions, signifying the simultaneous presence of all the parts, we discover them one by one, incrementally. Each new element is a surprise. Mr. Hackett has called a policeman, although we don't discover this until the policeman arrives. The policeman sees no indecency. After the lovers leave, Mr. Hackett can take his seat. And in his seat he emerges, part by part, until he is fully three-dimensional: "Mr. Hackett's nape rested against the solitary backboard, beneath it unimpeded his hunch protruded, his feet just touched the ground, the stick hooked around his neck hung between his knees" (9).

In *Watt* we are engaged in the extension of a story line—in its most concrete and elemental form. The opening section (which has been passed over or only treated thematically) begins the process that extends through the whole length of the novel, and through the trilogy as well. For the story line—an autonomous, self-generating element—develops incrementally in two ways: first, as one word succeeds another; and, second, as one story succeeds another. A gentleman and lady pass Mr. Hackett. They become husband and wife when the gentleman introduces Mr. Hackett to his wife. Then they become parents, Goff and Tetty Nixon, when they tell the story of Larry's birth. Larry is literally born and the husband and wife literally become parents in the telling of the story. Or, to put it another way, Larry exists as a character and they exist as his parents only in their story. And this is just what happens in the body of the novel. Beckett's narrative strategy has been described in terms of combinations and permutations.

But it is important to realize that each new combination and permutation is a new increment—extending the story line as it extends the world of Watt. Which is just what we experience as the Lynch family grows.

So far as I know, every critic has accepted Sam as the ultimate storyteller, for Sam has taken careful notes from the time Watt began to "spin his yarn." Sam's mind is like Watt's, and he is seeking to know Watt just as Watt was seeking to know Knott. He is obsessed by the same kinds of questions and generates the same incredible multiplicity of possibilities. And he brings into focus the nature of Watt's language—as well as the language he is constrained to compose in. "How hideous is the semi-colon" (158), he complains; and he is often forced to resort to question marks to make an ultimately enigmatic point. But what are we to make of those distinctly editorial interpolations: "Hiatus in ms" (238) and "ms illegible" (241)? Shouldn't they lead us back to see the question marks and semi-colon complaint as interpolations as well? If so, can the ultimate narrator really be Sam, at least the Sam who appears in the first person in the manuscript? And, if not, can we find any other voice in the novel to assure us of a narrative presence? No! What we have, from the first to the last page of *Watt*, is a story line extending itself, a yarn spinning itself out of empty space—bringing characters, objects, and events into existence through the addition of new words, which continue to develop every conceivable combination and permutation through the addition of new stories. The story line issues out of the empty space in the opening page, disappears in the empty space after the Hackett section, turns Watt from "a roll of tarpaulin, wrapped up in dark paper and tied about the middle with a cord" (16) into a singular individual, burgeons out of the generative capacity of words as they succeed one another, comes nearly full circle—past where Sam sees Watt disappearing into the undergrowth for the last time—to where the train first took Watt to Mr. Knott's house. Watt is created out of the story line and is ultimately cancelled by it. For we are finally left with the station attendants watching his train leave, looking from one to the other until Mr. Nolan looks "at nothing in particular, though the sky falling to the hills, and the hills falling to the plain made as pretty a picture, in the early morning light, as a man could hope to meet with, in a day's march" (246). And then continuing through an appendix.

Watt is the process of words, as autonomous physical presences, extending themselves into a story line, creating and finally cancelling a world by the addition of new increments. *Molloy*, as I began to show at the beginning of my paper, is also the product of an autonomous, procreative language, but not of a burgeoning story line. Rather, it is a process we can understand more graphically by comparing it to Beckett's plays. Krapp listens to what he recorded in the past, but the words exist only in the present; their autonomous presence is made dramatically evident by their issuing from a tape recorder. And Krapp creates himself from moment to moment by reacting to the sounds he hears. In *Act Without Words I*, Beckett's mime creates himself silently through his intercourse not with words but with objects: a carafe, a tree, a rope, and a pair of scissors. And Winnie creates perhaps the most memorable character on the modern stage through her verbal intercourse with the objects in her purse. So Molloy is challenged by, challenges, teases, laments over, and engenders new life out of the words he has just written—that are *there* on the page just as Krapp's sounds, the mime's objects, and Winnie's purse are *there* on the stage. He questions them, is disturbed by them, undermines or contradicts them, shifts their tense or mood, creates ellipses. He also engenders alternative characters by mitosis (Was it A or C? Lousse or Mrs. Loy? Edith or Ruth?), evinces surprise at what he creates ("Well, well, I didn't know I knew this story so well" [58]), and completely abandons many of his offspring.

Molloy creates his own elusive self by filling up the empty pages with words and interacting with them, continuously creating new presences and a new present. But he is also aware that the language he toys with has its own autonomous power: "Saying is inventing. Wrong, very rightly wrong. You invent nothing, you think you are inventing, you think you are escaping, and all you do is stammer out your lesson" (32). Molloy, after all, may be the creation of Moran. And even if he is not, even if Moran is his creation, the final lines of the novel undermine the entire creative process: "It is midnight. The rain is beating on the windows. It was not midnight. It was not raining" (176).

As we read through the trilogy, one storyteller yields to another. On the one hand, the story line generates continually new possibilities. But on the other hand, it continually reduces one storyteller to the figment of another storyteller's imagination—or to the product of another storyteller's words. In the end, there is nothing but the words, still generating possibilities, but also undermining and denying them. The Unnamable tries to tell the story of Mahood but finds that it was Mahood "who told me stories about me . . . his voice continues to testify for me, as though woven into mine, preventing me from saying who I was" (309). Once again we encounter the power of grammar. Molloy could create a son by shifting from the conditional present to the indicative (or actual) past. Now the Unnamable is denied existence by a past tense belonging to a third person. He cannot say I am because he cannot say I was. The language of the trilogy, issuing from no source within the narrative, denies the very existence of what it has brought into being.

In *Ulysses* Joyce discovered the potential of language as an autonomous, self-generating force. And while he realizes its threatening potential, his medium attaining the level of a dramatic antagonist or counterforce, he ultimately affirms its creative power. In the final chapter we have more than Molly's monologue. It is the language that transforms her into an earth goddess; language gives rise to an experience of fullness and affirmation, which continues to develop in *Finnegans Wake*. Beckett begins by realizing the creative power of language—and this is his debt to Joyce. But he ends by discovering its full autonomy as a capricious, threatening—and literally self-denying—force.

Notes

1. *Molloy*, in *Three Novels by Samuel Beckett* (New York: Grove Press, 1965), p. 7. Subsequent citations will be made in the text.
2. I am indebted to Carlotta Smith and Jeanne Whitaker, who are preparing an article on ellipses in Flaubert's *Un coeur simple*. Molloy's "it" would be called "unanchored pronoun."
3. James Joyce, *Ulysses* (New York: Random House, 1961), p. 389. Subsequent citations will be made in the text.
4. *"Ulysses": The Mechanics of Meaning* (Englewood Cliffs, N.J.: Prentice-Hall, 1970), Ch. V.
5. "Experimentation with the Grotesque: Comic Collisions in the Grotesque World of *Ulysses*," *Modern Fiction Studies* 20 (Autumn 1974):378–84. What follows is a summary of my argument.
6. Samuel Beckett, *Watt* (New York: Grove Press, 1959), p. 8. Subsequent citations will be made in the text.

PART III

Joyce and Freud

Introduction

Chester G. Anderson

The three essays presented here are substantially the talks given during the Zurich Symposium. They form part of the new wave of scholarly appraisal of the relationship of Joyce to Freud that swelled during the decade of 1970s, cresting with the news, published as an appendix to Richard Ellmann's *The Consciousness of James Joyce* (1977), that Joyce had purchased in Trieste several works by Freud, Jung, and Ernest Jones, perhaps as early as 1909–11.

Joyce himself, as is well know, constantly disparaged both "the Swiss Tweedledum" and "the Viennese Tweedledee" in his letters, his reported conversations, and his fictions. In *Ulysses* he has Stephen mention "the new Viennese school" only to fight against it by implying that St. Thomas's definition of incest is more interesting (205). Stephen's fight against Mulligan and the "lancet" of the art of medicine begins at the opening of the "Telemachus" episode and continues throughout the book. That is, it begins at 8:00 A.M. on June 16, 1904. In the "Scylla and Charybdis" episode Stephen tells us why he as poet fears that lancet—"Will they wrest from us, from me the palm of beauty?" (204). Joyce seems to have shared that fear of the usurpation of the poet's power by the medicinemen.

Nevertheless, it became clear in the 1970s that Joyce knew Freud's work, knew it well, and knew it early. *How* early remains a question. Although Professor Ellmann's listing of the books in Joyce's possession in Trieste has made certain some of the texts he surely knew by 1911 or thereabout, I think it would be misleading to consider that date as the beginning of his knowledge of Freud.

In 1972 I convinced myself that Joyce used Freud's *The Psychopathology of Everyday Life*, *Jokes in Relation to the Unconscious*, and *The Interpretation of Dreams* in presenting Bloom in the "Lestrygonians" episode, and I wrote this conviction out in excruciating detail in "Leopold Bloom as Dr. Sigmund Freud" as I was on my way to spend six weeks in Dublin.

While there, I visited the libraries where Joyce might have read Freud before he left for Paris in 1902 and 1904. I found that even if he had used these libraries during his visits to Dublin in 1909 and 1912, his opportunity for reading Freud would have been all but nil. None of the four major medical libraries in Dublin had, save for a single book, anything by Freud until the National Library acquired his *Selected Papers on Hysteria and Other Psychoneuroses*, 2nd edition, translated by A. A. Brill, Nervous and Mental Disease Monograph Series, No. 4 (New York: Journal of Nervous and Mental Disease Publishing Co., 1912). The following year the National Library acquired *The Interpretation of Dreams*, 3rd edition, translated by A. A. Brill (London: G. Allen, 1913). This same work was received in 1913 by the Trinity College Library as its first book by Freud, and in 1914 Trinity received *On Dreams*, translated by M. D. Eder (London: International Psychoanalytic Library, 1914).

Even in the 1970s, then, it would have been a mistake to have gone to Dublin to study Freud's works. The library of the Royal College of Surgeons had *no* works by Freud in August 1972. The Royal College of Physicians had two—*The Psychopathology of Everyday Life*, translated by A. A. Brill (London: Fisher Unwin, 1920), and another, discussed below. The National Library had Freud's collected works in German only. Altogether, the National Library had fifteen volumes by Freud, aside from the *Gasammelte Werke*, and twelve about him, tending toward "reevaluations" (apparently preceding evaluations): Rudolph Alters's *The Successful Error: A Critical Study of Freudian Psychoanalysis* (London: Sheed and Ward, 1941), Jonathan Hanaghan's *Freud and Jesus* (Monkstown, Dublin: Runa Press, 1966), and so on. Trinity College was somewhat better off, with the standard works in English (but not in German)—altogether about forty volumes, most of them published in the 1950s and 1960s.

The single exception to all this is an interesting one. The only volume in the four medical libraries that antedates 1913 is the second of the two in the library of the Royal College of Physicians. It is Freud's first book, *Zur Auffassung der Aphasien* (Leipzig und Wien: Franz Deuticke, 1891). The volume was "Presented to the Library of the Royal College of Physicians of Ireland by Mrs. C. Norman," according to a card within it. There is no date. The librarian, however, says that the book is from the library of Dr. Conolly Norman, who died suddenly in February 1908, aged fifty-five.

Readers of *Ulysses* will recognize that "Conolly Norman" is mentioned early in the first episode by Buck Mulligan, the medicineman. Between Mulligan's offhand accusation that Stephen "kills his mother" and his admonition that Stephen "Look at yourself," he says: "That fellow I was with in the Ship last night . . . says you have g.p.i. He's up in Dottyville with Conolly Norman. General paralysis of the insane" (6). Conolly Norman was a Dublin psychiatrist who for twenty-two years was Medical Superintendent of the Richmond District Asylum ("Dottyville"). He was one of the leading psychiatrists of the United Kingdom, a member of psychiatric associations in Dublin, London, New York, Brussels, and

Paris. He wrote many professional articles and edited the *Journal of Mental Science*, which became *The British Journal of Psychiatry*. In his office as editor he probably received *Zur Auffassung der Aphasien* as a review copy.

Norman's main achievement in his own estimation (as he implied in his inaugural speech as president, 1894–95, of the Medico-Psychological Association of Great Britain and Ireland) was that he helped see that "clinical instruction in mental disease is a necessary portion of the medical curriculum throughout the United Kingdom." Similarly, the writer of his obituary for the *Dublin Journal of Medical Science* (April 1908) says: "In addition to his many scientific and literary studies in psychiatry, he was one of the most successful and practical exponents of clinical instruction in lunacy. It was during his term of office as Resident Superintendent of the Richmond Lunatic Asylum that certificates in clinical lunacy became a necessity for candidates for the Degree in Medicine in the University of Dublin."

It seems likely, then, that Joyce first heard of Freud in conversations with Dublin medical students, possibly from Conolly Norman's extern in the Ship, possibly from Oliver St. John Gogarty himself. He may, too, have read reviews, such as the one of Freud's *Ueber den Traum* by Havelock Ellis in the *Journal of Mental Science* for April 1901. He heard enough, perhaps, so that when he went to Paris in the fall of 1902 as a student of "Paysayenn. P.C.N., you know: *physiques, chimiques et naturelles*" (*U*, 41), he could hear more—Freud had been a student there himself twenty years before—and read Freud for the first time.

This kind of research increased my regard for Leonard Albert's "Joyce and the New Psychology," his unpublished doctoral dissertation accepted at Columbia University in 1957, though his argument was then not well received. Albert makes a case entirely from internal evidence taken from *Ulysses* and from Joyce's notes for the "Cyclops" episode that Joyce read *Die Traumdeutung* in the *Bibliothèque Nationale* during the winter of 1902–1903.

Leaving Dublin for Trieste at the end of September 1972, I had the great pleasure of being introduced there to Italo Svevo's daughter, Signora Fonda-Savio. She told me charmingly that when she and her husband-to-be were first keeping company in 1910, as young teenagers, they discussed whether or not they should "be Freudians." It is a proper question, well put: for *being* a Freudian is a lot like being a Christian or an existentialist or a structuralist or a Joycean. Freudian psychoanalysis is very hard to *use* a bit of, mixing it with this and that. Freudian thought is, rather, a complete world view—complete and deterministic, with its own god (anatomy), theology (id, ego, superego), style (aggressive high seriousness), and so on. Joyce considered Signora Fonda-Savio's question and decided not to.

He decided, rather, to continue writing "the book of himself," tracing the "features of infancy" in the adolescent portrait and, later, in the portrait of

the middle-aged everyman-self. His project from the beginning had similarities to Freud's, concerning as it did dreams and the life of the unconscious, the psychopathology of everyday life, the dynamic interaction of
body and soul, and the determining power of infancy and childhood—as
well as of family, nation, and church—on adult character and behavior.
Furthermore, Joyce proved to have a remarkably clear eye for the obsessions, compulsions, fetishisms, etc. of neurotic behavior.

But his whole procedure was that of the artist rather than the scientist.
He believed that he *chose* this procedure (or at the very least accepted the call
of his destiny) and saw himself in opposition to the Viennese school. We
should not forget his choice. Joyce came to understand more about the self
than any other person of his time: more about the oedipus ("eatupus")
conflict, the castration threat ("pull out his eyes"), the infantile stages of
development ("the features of infancy"), coprophilia, the "vagina dentata"
("scrotumtightening sea"), and the rest than any other man or woman
before or since. His choice was not to become a Freudian about it, but
rather to create fictions about it. If he was driven, he was driven differently
from the rest of us—in a way that Freud, in the works on Leonardo and
Dostoevski, repeatedly categorizes as being "inaccessible along psychoanalytic lines."

Even so, Joyce's last word on the subject may be embedded in his choice
of the passive voice in the astonishing sentence uttered by ALP on her way
out to sea at the end of *Finnegans Wake*—"All me life I have been lived
among them. . ." (627). For this summarizes, surely, Joyce's understanding
of Jacques Lacan's "Insistence of the Letter in the Unconscious" (and the
conscious by way of language)—beyond Freud's understanding, and
Jung's.

Freud, Leonardo, and Joyce:
The Dimensions of a Childhood Memory

Jean Kimball

"The features of infancy," Joyce's earliest portrait of the artist begins, "are not commonly reproduced in the adolescent portrait," and his own 1904 essay is no exception, for the reader first glimpses its subject praying in the wood as a boy of fifteen.[1] By 1914, however, when the manuscript of *A Portrait of the Artist as a Young Man* was ready to be set in type,[2] the "features of infancy" had been expanded into a dramatic overture, opening with the meeting of "baby tuckoo" and "the moocow," and throwing its symbolic shadow not only over the whole of *A Portrait* but, as Hugh Kenner claims, over "the entire lifework of James Joyce."[3]

Between 1904 and 1914, of course, infancy had assumed a more powerful significance and a much more explicit identity—not only for Joyce but for a growing portion of the intellectual world of the twentieth century—with the publication in 1905 of Freud's *Three Essays on the Theory of Sexuality*, which focused on the crucial effect of infant sexuality on the psychological destiny of the adult.[4] And in 1910 Freud published a biographical study of Leonardo da Vinci,[5] explaining peculiarities of his character on the basis of his childhood, centering on Leonardo's memory of being visited in his cradle by a vulture. We now know that this monograph was in Joyce's personal library, purchased in Trieste, in all probability not long after its publication.[6]

The certainty that Joyce was acquainted with psychoanalytic theory well before the publication of *Ulysses* and probably even before the completion of *A Portrait* clears the way for a new perspective on Freudian motifs in both novels, motifs that have indeed been identified and discussed almost from the beginnings of Joyce criticism,[7] but with almost no attempt to trace these motifs to a specific source in the body of Freud's writings.[8] With the discovery, however, that as early as 1911 or 1912 Joyce owned Freud's essay on Leonardo, which highlights the artist's relationship with his mother (a relationship that is central also in *Ulysses*), an examination of the

Reprinted from the *James Joyce Quarterly* 17 (Winter 1980):165–82, by permission of the Editor.

links between Joyce's text and Freud's promises something different from another "Freudian" reading. For Joyce's great and unique gift is his uncanny ability to recognize and appropriate insights and ambiences not his own and to transform them into an integral part of his own symbolic statement without sacrificing their original integrity. He has so transformed the work of still uncounted thinkers and artists, and he has so transformed Sigmund Freud and his Leonardo da Vinci. For the congruences between Freud's picture of this supreme artist and Joyce's fictional portrait of the artist in his own time bear witness to Joyce's unapologetically conscious use of what he finds in Freud. To be sure, since Joyce's portrait is always subject to the constraints of his autobiography, he has adapted these insights to conform to his own artistic needs, but there are distinctive features of Freud's portrait of both the adult Leonardo of history and the reconstructed Leonardo as a child that appear to be integrated into Joyce's portrait, as his artist develops from infancy to adulthood.[9]

Thus the picture of the historical Leonardo presented by Freud exhibits curious affinities with the fictional surrogate of Joyce's middle years, Leopold Bloom, which can hardly be accidental, especially as they relate to Freud's emphasis on "Leonardo's double nature as an artist and as a scientific investigator" (*L* 73). For in *Ulysses* Bloom embodies the scientific half of this double nature, which is explicitly assigned by the catechizer of "Ithaca" to Stephen and Bloom: "What two temperaments did they individually represent? The scientific. The artistic" (*U* 683). And the "proofs" then offered by Bloom of his aptitude for science read like a parody of Leonardo's notebooks, which, as Freud comments, "not only deal with the greatest scientific problems but also contain trivialities that strike us as scarcely worthy of so great a mind" (*L* 69–70).

The affinities between Leonardo and Bloom, however, extend beyond shared scientific propensities to certain "unusual traits and apparent contradictions." In a society characterized, Freud says, by "energetic aggressiveness towards other people," and in that respect no different from the Dublin milieu in *Ulysses*, Leonardo, like the "prudent member" in Dublin, "was notable for his quiet peaceableness and his avoidance of all antagonism and controversy" (*L* 68). Seemingly "indifferent to good and evil," he nevertheless had such feeling for birds that he was said to have made a habit of buying them in the market in order to set them free (*L* 69). Bloom cites his own feeding of the gulls (*U* 153) as evidence of "doing good to others" (*U* 453) and having a "good heart" (*U* 471). Leonardo, Freud relates, "condemned war and bloodshed," though "this feminine delicacy of feeling did not deter him from accompanying condemned criminals on their way to execution in order to study their features distorted by fear" and sketch them (*L* 69). And Bloom, who rises to eloquence in his rejection of "force, hatred, history, all that" in "Cyclops" (*U* 333), has earlier in the episode expanded at length, as "Herr Professor Luitpold Blumenduft," on the "codology" of the anomalous effect on a hanged man of having his neck broken (*U* 304–05).

Beyond these contradictions, however, what points most clearly to the kinship between Leonardo da Vinci and Leopold Bloom is the "peculiarity of [their] emotional and sexual life." For "in an age which saw a struggle between sensuality without restraint and gloomy asceticism, Leonardo represented the cool repudiation of sexuality" (*L* 69).[10] In Leonardo, in fact, "love and hate threw off their positive or negative signs and were both alike transformed into intellectual interest"; as he "converted his passion into a thirst for knowledge," investigating took the place of "acting and creating as well," and research became "a substitute for sexual activity" (*L* 74, 75, 80). Bloom's day is filled with this kind of substitution, but two obviously paired examples will serve as a kind of synecdoche. At two o'clock, when Bloom sees Blazes Boylan, who is scheduled to cuckold him in a couple of hours, he seizes in his panic on the memory of his project of examining the anatomy of the statues of the goddesses in the National Museum: "Cold statues: quiet there. Safe in a minute" (*U* 183). Again, at the end of Bloomsday, as he enters the bed Boylan has shared with Molly, he systematically nullifies all passion through a succession of "scientific" reveries (*U* 731–34).

The resemblance, then, between Joyce's mature creation of Bloom, who is, after all, "a bit of an artist in his spare time" (*U* 653), and the Leonardo re-created by Freud is inescapable, and though we can be sure that the Bloom in Joyce was alive when Joyce read Freud, we cannot be sure to what extent his shape was revealed to Joyce or even determined for him by the factual details and interpretations offered by Freud. In any case, this kinship is extended to the Stephen who was before Bloom, and the childhood memory crafted for him by Joyce in the opening section of his *Portrait* reveals remarkable parallels with Freud's interpretation of the childhood memory that he makes the focus of his study of Leonardo. At the same time, however, Joyce has adapted features of the memory to conform to autobiographical fact without losing touch with the Freudian context, and the resulting symbolic construct prefigures themes that deepen and darken from the *Portrait* to *Ulysses*, where the central importance of the artist's resolution of his radical ambivalence toward the simultaneously supportive and menacing tie with his mother—drawn from Leonardo's memory by Freud—is complicated by his need to accept his relationship with his father, a figure who is significant in Freud's interpretation only through his absence. This characteristic combination of appropriation and transformation operates in both novels, but in *A Portrait* implications of the Freudian portrait of Leonardo are more or less superimposed on a form already substantially complete, whereas in *Ulysses* this portrait fuses with Joyce's own perspective and becomes an integral part of the symbolic pattern of the novel.

It is in the second chapter of *Leonardo da Vinci and a Memory of His Childhood* that Freud quotes the very brief memory with which Leonardo interrupts his discussion of the flight of vultures:[11] "I recall as one of my very earliest memories that while I was in my cradle a vulture came down to me, and opened my mouth with its tail, and struck me many times with its tail against my lips" (*L* 82). Recognizing that this almost certainly describes not an actual memory, but a later fantasy transposed back to earliest childhood, Freud identifies it as a reminiscence of being suckled at his mother's breast (*L* 84, 87), but finds it odd that the fantasy, in contrast to the active nature of a baby's nursing, is "so completely passive in character" (*L* 86) and that the mother has been "replaced by—a vulture" (*L* 87–88). In fact, what Leonardo describes, with the vulture "opening the child's mouth and beating about inside vigorously with its tail, corresponds to the idea of *fellatio*," a fantasy, Freud points out, which resembles dreams and fantasies produced by passive homosexuals, but also by women who have no awareness of the sexual practice itself (*L* 86–87). And Freud hypothesizes that the universally pleasurable "organic impression" of sucking on a nipple merges with the "repellant sexual phantasy" through the homely intermediary figure of the cow. For every cow has a visible udder, "whose function is that of a nipple, but whose shape and position under the belly make it resemble a penis" (*L* 87).

Joyce's *Portrait* opens with the story told to Stephen by his father about the "moocow coming down along the road" that "met a nicens little boy named baby tuckoo" (*P* 7), a childhood memory authenticated by John Joyce's birthday greeting to his son in 1931 (*Letters* III, 212). Chester Anderson sets the stage for his Freudian reading of this memory with a series of autobiographical assumptions about the connections between the story and the arrival of more Joyce babies,[12] which may well be true but which are not necessary to establish the textual fact that the memory, like Leonardo's, arises out of the suckling period. We have, after all, the cow, and we also have the lemon platt, a "tit-bit" made of lemon-flavored barley-sugar,[13] which also requires sucking. But from the beginning Stephen's memory departs significantly from Leonardo's because it starts from the father, whereas a significant factor in Freud's analysis of Leonardo is that Leonardo, an illegitimate son, was separated from his father in his earliest years (*L* 81, 91–92).[14] Stephen's father "looked at him through a glass: he had a hairy face," an image that Kenner sees as "a traditional infantile analogue of God the Father," linking at the same time the phrase "through a glass" with Paul's "through a glass darkly" ("Perspective," pp. 137–38), and the link may well be intended. But the hairy face and the glass are also found in Freud's 1909 "Analysis of a Phobia of a Five-Year-Old Boy," to which he refers in his discussion of Leonardo's early "sexual researches" (*L* 79).[15] And in Freud's study of "Little Hans," the hairy face and the glass are found together in a context that brings both mother and father into the picture.

The five-year-old Hans had developed a phobic fear of horses, and his father, an early adherent of psychoanalysis, had been working with his son—and Freud—along the lines of Freud's hypothesis that intellectual enlightenment was the avenue to freedom from neurotic fear. They had already established that somehow the horses Hans was afraid of were connected with "affectionate feelings towards his mother" and that "he was particularly bothered by what horses wear in front of their eyes and by the black round their mouths" (*SE* X, 41). Then Freud relates:

> As I saw the two of them sitting in front of me and at the same time heard Hans's description of his anxiety-horses, a further piece of the solution shot through my mind. . . . I asked Hans jokingly whether his horses wore eyeglasses, to which he replied that they did not. I then asked him whether his father wore eyeglasses, to which, against all evidence, he once more said no. Finally I asked him whether by "the black round the mouth" he meant a moustache; and I then disclosed to him that he was afraid of his father, precisely because he was so fond of his mother. (*SE* X, 42)

Freud then reassured Hans that he had known long before Hans was born that "he would be so fond of his mother that he would be bound to feel afraid of his father because of it," but that his father was fond of him in spite of his great affection for his mother. The happy ending is signaled by the father's recognition of Hans's phobia about horses as "an expression of the little boy's hostile disposition towards him, and perhaps also as a manifestation of a need for getting punished for it" (*SE* X, 42).

The case study of Little Hans could thus provide Joyce with a bridge between the exclusive maternal relationship that Freud posits for the child Leonardo and his own more normal family constellation, which in turn defines Stephen's memory. His father, who, like Hans's father, has a "hairy face,"[16] looks at Stephen "through a glass," because, unlike Hans's father, Simon Dedalus wears a monocle, which he is shown using at the Christmas dinner and later at the Whitsuntide play (*P* 29, 77). And Stephen's memory, through association with Freud's explanation of Hans's phobia, becomes colored with a repressed hostility and fear toward the father, which is connected with excessive affection for the mother, who appears in her proper person (assuming the cow to be a symbol for the boy's earliest relationship with her) only after the father's place in his babyhood has been acknowledged.

When Stephen's mother does appear, she is putting on the oilsheet after Stephen has wet the bed, and Joyce is quite certainly aware of the sexual connotations of this typical happening. In Jung's essay on the significance of the father, which he purchased in Trieste, for example, he could read the casual comment that "from the Freudian standpoint . . . bed-wetting must be regarded as an infantile sexual substitute,"[17] and when Stephen's memory moves from the "queer smell" of the oilsheet to the observation that "his mother had a nicer smell than his father," Joyce is carefully setting up an associational progression that is also sexually tinged. When he rounds this off by producing the memory of Stephen's mother as she played "the sailor's hornpipe for him to dance," the chain of sexual associations is subtly continued, for "horn" is one of the battery of phallic synonyms that Joyce uses in the notorious pornographic letters written to Nora in 1909 (e.g., December 3, *Selected Letters*, 181–83), and the "hornpipe" is not, I think, used neutrally here but rather points to the image of the "phallic mother," which is also the source for the vulture-mother of Leonardo's fantasy.

Freud links the appearance of the mother figure as a vulture in Leonardo's fantasy to an association between the vulture and motherhood, originating in ancient Egypt, but familiar to Leonardo through the writings of the Church Fathers, a familiarity that Freud carefully documents. The vulture, that is, is found in Egyptian hieroglyphics as the symbol for motherhood, an association explained in certain classical sources cited by Freud by the fact that "only female vultures were believed to exist," a belief that was in turn useful to the Church Fathers because of the correlative belief, "mentioned by almost all of them," that vultures were impregnated by the wind with no assistance from a male, a natural-history fable of obvious relevance to the dogma of the Virgin Birth (*L* 88–90). Furthermore, Freud points out, the association of the mother with the vulture is also found in the ancient Egyptian mother goddess Mut, a woman with a vulture's head (*L* 88), who "was usually represented with a phallus; her body was female, as the breasts indicated, but it also had a male organ in a state of erection." Thus in this figure "we find the same combination of maternal and masculine characteristics as in Leonardo's phantasy of the vulture" (*L* 94) and may identify the "common source" of both images as the infantile theory of the mother with a penis (*L* 97). The prominence of the vulture's tail in Leonardo's fantasy may then be translated: "That was a time when my fond curiosity was directed to my mother, and when I still believed she had a genital organ like my own" (*L* 98). Just so, Stephen's association of his mother with the "hornpipe" veils the repressed memory of this theoretical construct which is common to most boys.[18]

For it is the mother who is the central figure motivating the small boy toward his earliest investigations into the two great sexual problems: the problem of birth, including the obscure part played by the father, and the problem of the difference between the sexes.[19] Though a boy may or may not have a sister, he almost necessarily is close to a mother or mother-surrogate. "Most children," Freud explains in his discussion of Leonardo's overdeveloped instinct for research, "or at least the most gifted ones, pass through a period of infantile sexual researches" (L 78), and it is to be expected that Joyce would have Stephen participate in this process, though Joyce's sensitivity to the reality of the psychoanalytic concept of repression is such that he veils the most significant of Stephen's researches and discoveries behind screen memories. Thus, what Stephen does remember of his sexual research is only the episode with Eileen, whose nature is indicated by the parallel in *Finnegans Wake* (FW 327), "playing house of ivary dower of gould and gift you soil me peepat my prize," and whose general outlines could be supplied by most adults from their own childhood memories. The terrible threat that the episode brings down on Stephen's childish head of the eagles' pulling out his eyes seems monstrously dispro-portionate, but this "childish naughtiness" almost certainly screens, as Ruth von Phul asserts, "a greater guilt," the spying on the parents.[20] Though the memory has been repressed below the level of consciousness, Stephen's mother has surely been the object of the same kind of investiga-tion—a prototype of the episode with Eileen—and the punishment of blindness suggests the oedipal nature of the offense. Stephen's researches are brought to an end in the typical way, according to Freud: by "a wave of energetic sexual repression" (L 79).

Though it is Mrs. Dedalus herself who promises that Stephen will apologize, a promise that prefigures her cry of "Repent!" in "Circe" (U 581), it is Dante, "the terrible mother" of Anderson's reading ("Baby Tuckoo," p. 149), who threatens that "the eagles will come and pull out his eyes," a punishment of extraordinary resonance. The designation of the eagle as the instrument of punishment may point obliquely to Prometheus, as Kenner has suggested ("Perspective," p. 141), but Dante's threat calls on eagles much closer to Stephen's actual world, the imperial eagles of Rome, sym-bols of her church and the sexual repression it represents for Stephen's future. And if the threat of blindness recalls the legendary figure of Oedi-pus, it also represents an acutely personal threat to Stephen and to Joyce himself. The link between blindness and punishment is, of course, involved in Stephen's first questioning of the authority of the church, after his unjust punishment at Clongowes, and the punishment of the pandybat echoes throughout *Ulysses* until, in "Circe," it attaches again to Oedipus. For Stephen's reference to breaking his glasses "sixteen years ago" is juxtaposed with the final term of a complicated allusion to Oedipus, as Stephen adds to the riddle of the Sphinx, solved by Oedipus, a sexual component of his own: "the beast that has two backs at midnight" (*U* 560), through which he links Oedipus to Hamlet and to Stephen.[21]

The self-inflicted blindness of Oedipus as punishment for his transgression against the parental bond relates in turn to Freud's version of blindness as self-inflicted punishment in his 1910 essay "The Psycho-Analytic View of Psychogenic Disturbances of Vision" (*SE* XI, 314–21). Though this essay is not cited in the Leonardo study, to which it has no relevance, it is extremely relevant to Stephen's memory, since in it Freud introduces the idea of "talion punishment" by the ego when the sexual instinct makes excessive demands on the eyes.[22] In the "obscure psychical processes concerned in the repression of sexual scopophilia and in the development of the psychogenic disturbance of vision," Freud writes, it is "as though a punishing voice was speaking from within the subject, and saying: 'Because you sought to misuse your organ of sight for evil sensual pleasures, it is fitting that you should not see anything at all any more' " (*SE* XI, 216–17). And it is significant that, though Dante defines the punishment, it is Stephen himself, hiding under the table, who makes a litany of it. Literally, as the small boy repeats the rhyme to himself, the "punishing voice" of Freud's reconstruction is "speaking from within the subject," and the lifelong punishment of the fear of blindness is indeed, in true oedipal fashion, self-inflicted.

Thus, Joyce keeps intact the lines to Leonardo's fantasy, which includes no hint of blindness or punishment, even as he adapts its implications to the facts of his historical and spiritual autobiography. The vulture is replaced by another bird of prey, the eagle, which pulls the church into the orbit of the multifaceted allusion, while the menace of the phallic mother remains strong through her association with the fear of blindness. But there is another fear, present as a hidden threat in *A Portrait* but not made thematically explicit until *Ulysses*, where it dominates Stephen's Bloomsday choices and is identified with his mother: the fear of homosexuality as a life pattern. And the "causal connection between Leonardo's relationship with his mother in childhood and his later manifest, if ideal, homosexuality" (*L* 98) is the most significant implication that Freud draws from Leonardo's fantasy of the vulture-mother: "It was through this erotic relation with my mother that I became a homosexual" (*L* 106).

Any erotic relationship with the mother in Stephen's childhood memory must be deduced from sexual connotations attaching to the chain of associations presented, and Stephen's repressed memory is a far cry from Freud's reconstruction of Leonardo's infancy, for the mother as a menacing seductress does not really appear directly in either *A Portrait* or *Ulysses*. True, Freud's comments on "a mother's love for the infant she suckles and cares for" as "a completely satisfying love-relation, which not only fulfills every mental wish but also every physical need" (*L* 117), are echoed in Cranly's paean to motherhood in *A Portrait* (*P* 241–42), which in turn prefigures Stephen's thematically significant musings in *Ulysses* about "*amor matris*" as "the only true thing in life" (*U* 27–28, 207). Freud's further reminder that some of the satisfactions may be considered perverse,[23] however, finds no echo, but his picture of the "fateful" consequences for Leonardo of his mother's tenderness (manifest in the "double meaning" of Mona Lisa's smile—"the promise of unbounded tenderness and at the same time sinister menace" [*L* 115]) resonates in Stephen's Shakespeare discussion in *Ulysses*.

"Like all unsatisfied mothers," Freud hypothesizes of Leonardo's mother, "she took her little son in place of her husband, and by the too early maturing of his erotism robbed him of a part of his masculinity" (*L* 117). This cause-and-effect situation is paralleled by what Stephen proposes for Shakespeare. The mother, to be sure, is replaced by the wife, Ann Hathaway, "who tumbles in a cornfield a lover younger than herself" (*U* 191), but Freud's tracing of a causal relationship between the too-early arousal of erotic feelings and the later sexual disability is echoed by Stephen's assertion that through Shakespeare's seduction by an older woman, "Belief in himself had been untimely killed. He was overborne . . . and he will never . . . play victoriously the game of laugh and lie down. . . . No later undoing will undo the first undoing" (*U* 196). If we then reread the microcosmic description in *A Portrait*—"She played on the piano the sailor's hornpipe for him to dance. He danced"—in the light of this attack on Ann Hathaway, which Mark Shechner sees as "significantly related" to Stephen's "maternal obsession,"[24] there are darker shadows in the innocent picture of the mother encouraging her son.

And the darker shadows, specifically the connection between mother love and the problem of homosexuality, which Freud highlights in his reconstruction of Leonardo's childhood, are suggested even in the early pages of *A Portrait*. The "erotic attraction" of his mother for the very young boy "soon culminates," Freud says, "in a longing for her genital organ, which he takes to be a penis"; his later discovery that women are not so equipped often turns this longing to disgust, which may lead to permanent homosexuality. "The fixation on the object that was once so strongly desired," however, may well persist in "fetishistic reverence for a woman's foot and shoe" as a "substitutive symbol" (*L* 96). And the picture of himself before the fire at home, which the homesick boy at Clongowes conjures up to ward off the memory of the "cold slimy water" of the ditch into which Wells has pushed him, focuses on his mother's feet on the fender—"and her jewelly slippers were so hot and they had such a lovely warm smell" (*P* 10).

This picture, then, is followed almost immediately by the introduction of Simon Moonan as "McGlade's suck," the homosexual connotations of which are reinforced by the association with the "cocks" of the lavatory at the Wicklow Hotel (*P* 11). And the combination of the dirty water in the white lavatory and his own feelings of being "cold and then a little hot" repeat the antithesis of the cold, slimy water and the hearth fire in the earlier picture, an antithesis that is first set up in Stephen's earliest memory of his mother as she changes his bed, which first "is warm then it gets cold" (*P* 7).[25] The juxtaposition of the memory of the comforting mother with the dimly grasped implications of the relationship between Simon Moonan and McGlade points to the same contradictory mixture in the "queer word" *suck* (*P* 11) as is found in Leonardo's memory of being suckled at his mother's breast and its association with the homosexual fantasy of fellatio.

In *A Portrait*, as the scene shifts from playground to classroom to refectory, the boy's longing "to be at home and lay his head on his mother's lap" (*P* 13) is set off against his relationship to other males, again in the context of Simon Moonan and the prefect of studies, for as Wells teases him about kissing his mother goodnight, Simon is knotting the prefect's false sleeves (*P* 14), an act that in the earlier scene has been identified with his being "McGlade's suck." Once again Stephen experiences heat and cold— the heat of embarrassment alternating with the memory of the cold slime of the ditch water—as he tries to determine whether it is right or wrong to kiss his mother, examining the idea of *kiss* as he has earlier examined the idea of *suck*; and again there is a sound, but only "a tiny little noise" (*P* 14–15), and we might remember that a nursing baby also makes a tiny little noise. The comforting mother fades out of the early pages with that kiss, but the inner conflict that her image sets off is picked up again much later, in Stephen's response to "the unspoken speech behind the words" of Cranly's outburst about mother love: "Pascal, if I remember rightly, would not suffer his mother to kiss him as he feared the contact of her sex" (*P* 242), and we have returned to Freud's question of the "causal connection" between Leonardo's relationship with his mother and his homosexuality.

And this is the question that broods over the opening pages of *Ulysses* and is picked up again in distorted form in "Scylla and Charybdis," where the question attaches itself to Stephen's Shakespeare discussion. For in both these episodes Stephen's obsession with his dead mother is played against his relationship with Buck Mulligan, a relationship that is shadowed by the ghost of Oscar Wilde's "love that dare not speak its name." Mulligan's assurance as the novel opens that Stephen has "the real Oxford manner"

(*U* 5) surfaces in "Scylla and Charybdis" as "Manner of Oxenford" (*U* 217), in a context that identifies it explicitly with homosexuality; Mulligan's laughing taunt, "If Wilde were only alive to see you" (*U* 6), is sandwiched between allusions to Wilde's *Dorian Gray* and "The Decay of Lying,"[26] one of the "Platonic dialogues Wilde wrote" (*U* 214), to which Best refers in the Library scene. Mulligan's response to Stephen's question about Haines— "Yes, my love?" (*U* 4)—is echoed in Stephen's reference to Shakespeare's "dearmylove," followed by his inner association: "Love that dare not speak its name" (*U* 202), the phrase that comes into his mind in "Proteus" as he contemplates "his broadtoed boots, a buck's castoffs" (*U* 49)—Mulligan's discarded boots, which he wears on Bloomsday, and which replace the fetishistic symbol of the mother's slippers in *A Portrait*.

The mother appears in death, both in "Telemachus" and in "Scylla and Charybdis," but in the later episode her living influence is projected onto Ann Hathaway, whom Stephen charges with responsibility for Shakespeare's sexual malaise, a charge that includes an allusion to a passage in Wilde's *De Profundis* about his mother's death while he was in Reading Gaol (Thornton, p. 181). And the terms of Stephen's charge suggest the submerged, unconscious character of the early maternal influence: "The soul has been before stricken mortally, a poison poured in the porch of a sleeping ear" (*U* 196). Buck Mulligan appears as Stephen winds up this charge, and the ensuing discussion of the Sonnets throws the shadow of the homosexual threat over the remainder of the episode, a threat regularly associated with Mulligan, most explicitly in Stephen's unspoken "Catamite" (*U* 204). But as they leave the library together, they separate to make way for Bloom, who embodies the alternative to Mulligan,[27] and Stephen sees the beginnings of a solution to the threat—so far as *Ulysses* provides solutions, which is never through straightforward narrative, but rather through multiple associations of words. The word *becomes* the event, a peculiarity also of dreams, and it is his dream that points the way for Stephen. Remembering that before his departure from Ireland the year before, he had "watched the birds for augury" from these same steps, he recognizes a development from that time to his dream of the night before: "Last night I flew" (*U* 217), a flight whose significance *as* a solution is clarified by reference to Freud's analysis of Leonardo.

Leonardo links his memory of the vulture with his being destined to study the flight of birds, and "in admitting to us that ever since his childhood he felt bound up in a special and personal way with the problem of flight," Freud says, "Leonardo gives us confirmation that his childhood researches were directed to sexual matters" (*L* 126). For in dreams "to fly or to be a bird" regularly disguises "a longing to be capable of sexual performance" (*L* 126.) The symbolic importance of bird imagery in Joyce's

Portrait has received considerable attention, and Stephen's own reiterated determination to fly complements this imagery, reaching an impassioned climax in his vision of "the winged form of . . . a hawklike man" as "a prophecy of the end he had been born to serve," a climax that is sustained through the companion vision of the wading girl (*P* 169–72)—all of it highly charged sexually. In contrast, however, and suggesting the diversion of sexual energy into research that Freud claims for Leonardo, when Stephen later watches the birds outside the library, it is to escape the raw emotion of his struggle with his mother, her "sobs and reproaches," in the cool contemplation of the flight of birds, which, he reminds himself, Swedenborg links to "things of the intellect." And he turns finally from this soothing contemplation back to the "calmly lit" library (*P* 224, 226).

But in *Ulysses*, the matching scene on the library steps ends with Stephen's departure from the library, the home of "coffined thoughts" with "an itch of death in them" (*U* 193–94). On Bloomsday there are "no birds,"[28] and Stephen's vision is dominated by his own flight in the context of his sensual dream of the gift of Haroun al Raschid, a dream that confronts and competes with his dream of the dead mother throughout Bloomsday: "Last night I flew. Easily flew" (*U* 217). And, unlike his unuttered "cry of triumph" in *A Portrait*, which exults in "the freedom and power of his soul" (*P* 169), Stephen's cry of "Free!" at the renewed memory of this dream in "Circe" (*U* 572) is a response to the physical, sensual solution the dream contains to that morning's inner cry to his dead mother: "Let me be and let me live" (*U* 10), a cry that Leonardo da Vinci, as Freud reconstructs his development, never knew how to make.

But then Stephen's cry is addressed to his father, who represents a feature of infancy missing from Leonardo's early childhood, and the vulture, which doubles as the mother in Leonardo's fantasy and which, according to legend, has no male counterpart, is absent from *A Portrait* and appears in *Ulysses* as an exclusively male symbol, associated with the father-son relationship. In "Circe" Rudolph Virag feels Bloom's face "*With feeble vulture talons*" (*U* 437), and Stephen, as he declares his freedom, cries to his father, "*his vulture talons sharpened*," while Simon, answering him, "*swoops uncertainly through the air . . . on strong ponderous buzzard wings*" (*U* 572). The fable of the vulture's impregnation by the wind is, to be sure, included in Stephen's list of primitive beliefs about conception in "Oxen of the Sun" as "bigness wrought by wind," followed closely by "potency of vampires mouth to mouth" (*U* 390), a figure that is explicitly, if obscurely, associated with Stephen's obsession with his mother.[29] But this is in turn followed by his assertion that the female power of creation in the flesh is superseded by the preeminent creative power of the male artist to build "eternity's mansions" from "time's ruins": "In woman's womb word is made flesh but in the spirit of the maker all flesh that passes becomes the word that shall not pass away. This is the postcreation" (*U* 391).

And in "Circe" this bridge to eternity is—verbally at least—guaranteed by the father. For, confronted by the apparition of his dead mother, who reaches for his heart with the crab's claws (*U* 582), Stephen, denying the power of her memory to paralyze him, smashes the chandelier with his ashplant, which for this purpose he transforms verbally into "*Nothung*" (*U* 583), Siegfried's mystical sword handed down from father to son. In the ensuing darkness—"ruin of all space" and time's ruin as well—the way is cleared for the building of eternity's mansions, the postcreation, and Joyce, through a dreamlike word magic, has affirmed his artist's release from the dominance of the maternal fixation that Freud pictures as Leonardo's fate.

This release of the son from the power of the mother is further signaled by the replacement of Mut, the vulture-headed mother goddess of Freud's analysis of Leonardo, by the bird-headed Egyptian god Thoth, who, with his "narrow ibis head" is "the god of writers" in *A Portrait* (*P* 225) and in *Ulysses*, "god of libraries, a birdgod, moony crowned" (*U* 193). And in E. A. Wallis Budge's *Gods of the Egyptians*, which Joyce almost certainly used,[30] Thoth is credited with powers not inferior to those of the Word in St. John's Prologue. For it is Thoth who in the beginning "spoke the words which resulted in the creation of the heavens and the earth" and, "as the personification of the mind of God," is "the all-pervading, and governing, and directing power of heaven and of earth" (Budge, I, 407, 415). Like Mut, "who giveth birth, but was herself not born of any" (II, 30), Thoth was "self-begotten and self-produced" (I, 401). Though Mut gives birth, Thoth creates a world, and the Egyptian connection suggested by Freud is thus used by Joyce to affirm the freedom and the power of the artist as self-created creator.

Richard Ellmann, discussing the nature of Joyce's identification with great figures who appealed to his imagination, speculates that what Joyce wanted was "an interplay among their images and his own" (*JJ* 47), and the authors of *The Workshop of Daedalus* have concluded that he deliberately designed his *Portrait* so that material relating to other artists was interwoven with the events of his own life, making it "both a self-portrait of the author and a portrait of the artist in general,"[31] a design that carries over into *Ulysses* and of which Freud's Leonardo is a part. Conditioned by traditional Jesuit assumptions to accept Freud's claims for the overwhelming formative significance of the very early years of childhood, Joyce was undoubtedly also conditioned by the sexual repression of his Irish Catholic upbringing to accept the predominantly sexual emphasis of Freud's analysis of Leonardo, and most of the threads of this analysis have been interwoven with those of his own self-portrait with no discernible break or joint. Leonardo's features fuse with Stephen's and with Bloom's, and beyond the fictional portrait there appears to be an "interplay" with the Joyce of the postwar years as he shifted gears in *Ulysses*[32] and turned to the staggering intricacies of *Finnegans Wake*.

For the question Freud raises about Leonardo remains a significant unanswered question about James Joyce: "Though he left behind him masterpieces . . . the investigator in him never in the course of his development left the artist entirely free, but often made severe encroachments on him and perhaps in the end suppressed him" (*L* 63–64).[33] And the development he describes in Leonardo is clearly relevant to Joyce's final development: "He was no longer able to limit his demands, to see the work of art in isolation and to tear it from the wide context to which he knew it belonged." Freud concludes that "the artist had once taken the investigator into his service to assist him; now the servant had become the stronger and suppressed his master" (*L* 77).

Having said this, however, Freud admits that "the nature of the artistic function is . . . inaccessible along psycho-analytic lines" (*L* 136), an admission that he reaffirmed years later in the opening paragraph of his "Dostoevsky and Parricide": "Before the problem of the creative artist analysis must, alas, lay down its arms" (*SE* XXI, 177). This comprehensive disclaimer should serve as a caution to the rest of us, but we can recognize the interplay between James Joyce, who denied Freud's influence, and Sigmund Freud. For Joyce, through his embodiment in his many-layered portrait of the artist of those psychoanalytic insights he accepted did more to transfuse this new perspective into the mainstream of Western literature than many a declared disciple, while his own deep acceptance of those same insights, as they fused with his vision of his artist self, may well have changed the shape of that self.

Notes

1. Robert E. Scholes and Richard M. Kain, "The First Version of 'A Portrait,' " *Yale Review* 49 (Spring 1960): 360.
2. See Hans Walter Gabler, "The Seven Lost Years of *A Portrait of the Artist as a Young Man*," in *Approaches to Joyce's "Portrait": Ten Essays*, ed. Thomas F. Staley and Bernard Benstock (Pittsburgh: University of Pittsburgh Press, 1976), p. 35, on the probable late date of the completion of the opening section.
3. "The *Portrait* in Perspective," in *James Joyce: Two Decades of Criticism*, ed. Seon Givens (New York: Vanguard, 1948), pp. 137, 142.
4. In *The Standard Edition of the Complete Psychological Works of Sigmund Freud*, trans. and ed. James Strachey in collaboration with Anna Freud, et al. (Hereafter *SE*.) (London: The Hogarth Press and the Institute of Psycho-Analysis, 1953–

1974), VII, 130–243. See also Appendix, VII, 244–45, "List of Writings by Freud Dealing Predominantly or Largely with Sexuality."

5. *Eine Kindheitserinnerung des Leonardo da Vinci* (Leipzig and Vienna, 1910). Eng. trans. by Alan Tyson, *Leonardo da Vinci and a Memory of His Childhood*, *SE* XI, 63–137 (hereafter *L*). For a summary of Freud's argument in this essay, see *Minutes of the Vienna Psychoanalytic Society*, ed. Herman Nunberg and Ernst Federn, trans. M. Nunberg (New York: International Universities Press, 1967), II, 338–46.

6. See Richard Ellmann, *The Consciousness of James Joyce* (New York: Oxford University Press, 1977), pp. 53–59, and see Appendix, pp. 114, 115, for bibliographical information about the other two early psychoanalytic essays purchased in Trieste: the German translation of Ernest Jones's 1910 essay on Hamlet and Oedipus and C. G. Jung's *Die Bedeutung des Vaters dur das Schicksal des Einzelnen*.

7. Most comprehensively by Sheldon Brivic in his "Joyce in Progress: A Freudian View," *JJQ* 13 (Spring 1976): 306–27, and his earlier "James Joyce: From Stephen to Bloom," in *Psychoanalysis and the Literary Process*, ed. Frederick Crews (Cambridge, Mass.: Winthrop Publishers, 1970), pp. 118–62. See the latter, p. 124, n. 14, for a representative list of discussions of Stephen's Oedipus complex, to which should be added William Wasserstrom, "In Gertrude's Closet," *Yale Review* 48 (Winter 1959): 245–65. See also Mark Shechner, "James Joyce and Psychoanalysis: A Selected Checklist" *JJQ* 13 (Spring 1976): 383–84. Jeanne McKnight's "Unlocking the Word Hoard: Madness, Identity and Creativity in James Joyce," *JJQ* 14 (Summer 1977): 420–33, centers, as does Freud's analysis of Leonardo, on the ambiguity of the mother/son relationship, but her expanded conception of this relationship, as Shechner points out in the same issue ("Joyce and Psychoanalysis: Two Additional Perspectives," p. 418), is really post-Freudian in perspective and "beyond Joyce's own myths," or indeed any "conceptual guides" he might have had.

8. An exception is Chester Anderson's detailed evidence for Joyce's use of Freud's *The Psychopathology of Everyday Life* in *Ulysses* ("Leopold Bloom as Dr. Sigmund Freud," *Mosaic* 6 [Fall 1972]: 23–43). See my "James Joyce and Otto Rank: The Incest Motif in *Ulysses*," *JJQ* 13 (Spring 1976): 336, on the reluctance to connect Freudian elements in Joyce with Freud or psychoanalysis.

9. Cf. Shechner's note on Joyce's "deliberate mythmaking" as a response to his "need to tie his own emotional life to larger patterns of experience in order to universalize and aggrandize himself" ("Two Perspectives," pp. 417–18). I should perhaps emphasize that in this essay I am concerned not with identifying Joyce's psychic needs or contributing to what Shechner calls "a composite psychoanalytic picture of Joyce's mind," but with examining Joyce's always highly conscious transformation of Freud's material—an aim that, I think, separates my view sharply from Brivic's, for example, who has seen many of the same "Freudian"motifs in many of the same passages that I cite in this essay, but from a different perspective. I might note that in Freud's discussion of Leonardo's personality, with its characteristically human emphasis, there is no "castration anxiety" or "phallic threat" or even "Oedipus complex" in evidence.

10. Freud includes in this repudiation of sexuality the active homosexuality of which Leonardo was once accused, an accusation that Joyce attaches to Bloom through Mulligan: "He looked upon you to lust after you. . . . Get thee a breechpad" (*U* 217). See also *U* 413, where Bloom, surrounded by the young men in the hospital, reflects, "Now he is himself paternal and these about him might be his sons," paralleling the relationship that Freud sees for Leonardo with his young apprentices, whatever the emotional undertones, except that in Freud's interpretation of Leonardo it was a *maternal* relationship (*L* 102–104).

11. See the editor's discussion of Freud's mistranslation of the Italian *nibio* (*kite*) as *Geier* (*vulture*), *SE* XI, 60–62.

12. See "Baby Tuckoo: Joyce's 'Features of Infancy,' " in Staley and Benstock, *Approaches to Joyce's "Portrait*," pp. 141–42. Anderson's note that "tuckoo" is related to "tuck" as a word for food (142) seems to me reasonable and helpful, though I am not so ready to go along with his connection between the excretory birth theories of children and Simon's story, or indeed a number of features of his Freudian reading.

13. See Don Gifford, with Robert J. Seidman, *Notes for Joyce: "Dubliners" and "A Portrait of the Artist as a Young Man"* (New York: Dutton, 1967), p. 86.

14. It is ironical that in the face of Freud's long insistence on the primary importance of the father, his one complete biographical study should have focused on the mother's influence. See, however, *L* 119–25 on the effect of the absence of Leonardo's father on the artist's freedom of inquiry, especially his freedom from inhibition by orthodox religion.

15. *SE* X, 5–149. Other works by Freud that he cites in the Leonardo Study are the following: "Fragment of an Analysis of a Case of Hysteria [The Case of 'Dora']" (1905), *SE* VII, 7–122; "Character and Anal Erotism" (1908), *SE* IX, 169–75; "On the Sexual Theories of Children" (1908), *SE* IX, 209–26; *Three Essays on the Theory of Sexuality* (1905), *SE* VII, 130–243.

16. Cf. Stephen's recognition of the Jesuits as a separate species, outside male categories: "It was hard to think what [they would have become if they had not become Jesuits] because you would have to think of them in a different way with . . . beards and moustaches" (*P* 48).

17. "The Significance of the Father in the Destiny of the Individual," in *Freud and Psycho-Analysis*, Vol. 4 of *The Collected Works*, Bollingen Series XX (New York: Pantheon, 1969), p. 319. Note the similarities between the child Stephen and the enuretic eight-year-old subject of Case 4, pp. 317–19. See also Anderson's discussion in "Baby Tuckoo," pp. 145–47.

18. There is no suggestion in the Leonardo essay that this image is connected with any castration anxiety (cf. Brivic, "Stephen to Bloom," p. 127); the implication is that the problem is more nearly narcissistic (*L* 95–99).

19. See *L* 78, ff. See also Hans's father's comment that "it is not clear to him in what way he belongs to me" (*SE* X, 100), and "On the Sexual Theories of Children" (*SE* IX, 211–14). See also *SE* X, 133n, on Freud's emendation to his first assumption that the primary riddle was that of birth.

20. "Joyce and the Strabismal Apologia," in *A James Joyce Miscellany*, ed. Marvin Magalaner, Second Series (Carbondale, Ill.: Univ. of Southern Illinois Press, 1959), pp. 121, 126. See also Little Hans's dialogue with his father (*SE* X, 61–63), in which his account of "looking-on" episodes with Berta runs into related episodes with his mother, and note Freud's observation that "the pleasure taken in looking on while some one one loves performs the natural functions" represents a "confluence of instincts" (*SE* X, 127).

21. For details of this compound allusion, see my "Incest Motif," p. 368, and note Freud's comment on "the great riddle of where babies come from . . . of which the riddle of the Theban Sphinx is probably no more than a distorted version" (*SE* X, 133).

22. Freud's essay does not extend the literal self-punishment through the eyes to symbolic castration, which Brivic sees as a probable interpretation of the punishment in *A Portrait* ("Stephen to Bloom," p. 125). Though this essay is not cited in the Leonardo study, it seems reasonable to assume that Joyce, with his continuing eye problems, would have read it. See Stanislaus Joyce's comment that if Joyce read a

book that appealed to him "he tried to read as many by the same author as he could lay his hands on" (*My Brother's Keeper*, ed. Richard Ellmann [New York: Viking, 1958], p. 79).

23. Freud's comment that if motherhood "represents one of the forms of attainable human happiness, that is in no little measure due to the possibility it offers of satisfying, without reproach, wishful impulses which have long been repressed and which must be called perverse" (*L* 117) is followed by a reference to *Three Essays* (*SE* VII, 223), where he spells out the sexual nature of mother love. Note also that he introduces the idea of rivalry and antagonism between father and son (*L* 117), which crops up in Stephen's discussion of fatherhood (*U* 207–208).

24. *Joyce in Nighttown: A Psychoanalytic Inquiry into "Ulysses"* (Berkeley: University of California Press, 1974), pp. 27–28. See also my "Incest Motif," pp. 375–77, on the connection between the mother and homosexuality, and cf. Brivic, "Stephen to Bloom," 129–30.

25. Cf. Freud's elucidation (*SE* VII, 71–74) of the antithesis between fire and water as specifically related to bed-wetting and its sexual connotations in his analysis of one of "Dora's" dreams in "Fragment of an Analysis," to which he refers in the Leonardo study (*L* 87), and note that there is also a reference in his analysis to the question of a kiss. Note also that Brivic sees this antithesis as related to the conflict in Stephen between "phallic threat" and "maternal haven" ("Stephen to Bloom," p. 126, and "Joyce in Progress," p. 308). He identifies as fetishistic not only the mother's slippers but also details of her farewell kiss ("Stephen to Bloom," p. 127).

26. See Weldon Thornton, *Allusions in "Ulysses": An Annotated List* (Chapel Hill: University of North Carolina Press, 1968), p. 14. See also references to Wilde in Thornton's index.

27. Cf. my "Incest Motif," p. 377, and my "The Hypostasis in *Ulysses*," *JJQ* 10 (Summer 1973): 435–36.

28. In *Ulysses* the birds of the scene in *A Portrait* appear to be paralled by the bats that Bloom sleepily contemplates on the Strand (*U* 377–82), and Leonardo also compares the bird and the bat in connection with his efforts to build a flying machine. See Edward McCurdy, ed., *The Notebooks of Leonardo da Vinci* (New York: Braziller, 1958), p. 416.

29. Cf. *U* 48, 132, and see also Anderson's interpretation of the "ugly fantasy—at once homosexual and incestuous" ("Baby Tuckoo," p. 136).

30. *The Gods of the Egyptians or Studies in Egyptian Mythology*, 2 vols. (New York: Dover Publications [1904], 1969). On Joyce's probable use of this work in *Finnegans Wake*, see Mark L. Troy, *Mummeries of Resurrection: The Cycle of Osiris in "Finnegans Wake*," Diss., Uppsala 1976 (Uppsala: Almquist & Wiksell, 1976), pp. 20–21, and James S. Atherton, *The Books at the Wake: A Study of Literary Allusions in James Joyce's "Finnegans Wake"* (New York: Viking, 1960), p. 197.

31. Robert E. Scholes and Richard M. Kain, *The Workshop of Daedalus: James Joyce and the Raw Materials for "A Portrait of the Artist as a Young Man"* (Evanston: Northwestern University Press, 1965), p. xiii.

32. See Michael Groden, *"Ulysses" in Progress* (Princeton: Princeton University Press, 1977) on the three stages in *Ulysses*.

33. Cf. John Livingston Lowes, *The Road to Xanadu: A Study in the Ways of the Imagination* (Boston: Houghton Mifflin Co., [1927] 1955), p. 391: "For some of the greatest poets . . . have had, like Faust, two natures struggling within them. They have possessed at once the instincts of the scholar and the instincts of the artist, and it is precisely with regard to facts that these instincts perilously clash."

The Father in Joyce

Sheldon Brivic

Although the earliest psychoanalytic work Joyce purchased was by Carl Gustav Jung, "The Significance of the Father in the Destiny of the Individual" (*Die Bedeutung des Vaters dur das Schicksal des Einzelnen*, 1909), it was written while Jung was still the *prima Freuderina*. The tone of this piece was set by its first word, which was "Freud." Joyce may have been attracted by its un-Jungian emphases on sexuality and on the oppressive effects of fathers on children. The essay presented powerful support for the revolt of Stephen Dedalus by showing how parental authority can operate unconsciously to blight lives and marriages. Stephen makes one of his psychoanalytic statements when he tells Cranly that what he fears more than damnation is "the chemical action which would be set up in my soul" (*P* 243) by praying to venerable authority, for he perceives an unknown process operating within. And Jung's essay emphasized Freud's finding that religion has a factual basis for the individual in an unconscious, neurotic image of father. Thus it prefigured the Jungian idea that the ultimate conditions of an individual's life are built on a framework of projected parental imagoes.[1]

Hans Walter Gabler indicates that most of *A Portrait of the Artist as a Young Man* was revised or newly written after 1911,[2] so we are now in a position to see *Portrait* rather than *Ulysses* as the first work Joyce informed with an awareness of depth psychology supported by the theories of the man who bore his name in German. The influence on Joyce's *Portrait* of Jung's essay is probably not as great as that of Freud's Leonardo da Vinci study of 1910, but there are points Joyce may have picked up from or seen corroborated in the earlier work. One of Jung's case histories, for example, presents an eight-year-old who wets his bed as an expression of oedipal anxiety. Jung also refers his readers to "Obsessive Acts and Religious Practices" (1907), in which Freud identifies religious rituals with neurotic ones. This linkage could have clarified for Joyce his conception of the rituals of self-control Stephen goes through in his religious phase: "he drove his soul daily through an increasing circle of works of supererogation."

Supererogation, doing more than you have to, is motivated by the superego, an internalized parental voice, usually the father's, which constitutes an intensification of necessity. The protest of the early Joyce against the restriction of freedom is aimed precisely at the force that makes Dubliners revolve in their sterile rituals of superfluous self-control. This force is a measure of fear or need beyond immediate necessity, which will keep the child obeying the father when he is not present—or more than obeying him. And the same constant, unconscious dread is used by such institutional extensions of father as school, society and church.

A malign current, but Jung here agrees with Freud that the image of the father is extremely ambivalent, and within this polarized imago, tyranny is hard to separate from benefit. If Joyce had not done more than he had to, his destiny would never have freed him from the expanding circles through which he was driven, but he managed to make himself at home in those cycles by internalizing his father insofar as he understood or got behind the voice of compulsion within himself.

The qualities of John Joyce that transferred directly to the artist are extensive, and the fiction shows Simon Dedalus's wit, articulateness, energy, egotism, irony, alchoholism, anticlericalism, idealism, and sentiment. Moreover, Simon views facts through a filter of imaginative language, and this pattern transmits through Stephen's tendency to recite magic styles to himself as he walks through squalor (especially in *Portrait*, p. 176), to lead to Joyce's elaborate experiments with the imposition of style on reality in the later works. Crucial roles are played by Simon's decline from glory to debility and his extremely conciliatory attitude toward his eldest son: these tendencies allow Stephen to expand his powers at the same time that they implant in him a deeply rooted guilt over this expansion.

Stephen realizes that he will never be able to confront reality except through rituals (*P* 159), so he concentrates on using these rituals toward that end. To reach toward reality by making ritual conscious is to take the father's weapon and turn it against him, for the initial function of the ritual handed down by the old man is to keep the individuality of the son subordinate. The son takes from the father the strengths he uses to oppose him. In fact, the relation of son to father undergoes a complete reversal: simply put, the boy spends his first ten years trying to get as close to his father as possible and the next ten trying to get as far away as possible.

The essential functions of the two parents may be distinguished by saying that the father's role is to push forward while the mother's is to draw back. The liquid paradise the mother withholds from her son is the source of his dreams, and maternal lineaments are dimly discernible in the unsubstantial images Stephen pursues constantly as fantasy, whore, Virgin, and muse. Opposed to this pursuit are the voices of male authority Stephen strives to escape. The father strengthens the son by thrusting forward hard reality, and the dreams of the boy are pressed into conscious definition when he meets the father's challenge. In *Portrait* the threat of the father Stephen meets in each chapter is creative because it forces him to imagine a new version of mother to aim at.

While a good father must provide some measure of maternal kindness and encouragement, his real job is to present the boy with an obstacle that will force him to draw back and build up his strength. Thus, the father activates rebirth by enacting the harshness of reality without quite playing for keeps, and anyone who has this effect plays a paternal role. As a son, however, Joyce was most concerned with the excess of the father's authority. Jung says in his essay that when we encounter threats, our minds flow back into the old channels of childhood, and Joyce shows such regression to be a tool of the church when Stephen is at retreat and "the figure of his old master" makes "his soul" become "again a child's soul." A dam, however, can lift water to a higher level, and the father who forces innocence on his son may be giving him a source of strength. Joyce's sensual side could generate great art only by working in opposition to the discipline the church instilled in him.

Stephen says in *Ulysses* that fatherhood is a "necessary evil" and that father and son are opposed irrevocably because the growth of the son is the decline of the father. A glint of his keen competition with Simon occurs in *Portrait* in a Cork pub, when Simon offers to beat Stephen in athletics or singing. An old man puts his finger to his forehead and prophesies truly: "But he'll beat you here." The context of the Dedalus fiction shows why this victory has to be mental. In Joyce the relation between men is virtually always one of duelling in what Stephen calls "the joust of life." That this male competition must imply a female prize becomes most obvious in the *Wake*: whenever Shem and Shaun begin to argue, the image of Issy appears in the background. If, as I have maintained, competition with father over mother is a major key to Stephen's attitude toward the world, it becomes clear why he must relinquish any attempt to win at competitive activity:

> Some weeks Jack Lawton got the card for first and some weeks he got the card for first. His white silk badge fluttered . . . as he worked at the next sum and heard Father Arnall's voice. Then all his eagerness passed away and he felt his face quite cool. He thought his face must be white because it felt so cool. He could not get out the answer for the sum but it did not matter. White roses and red roses: those were beautiful colours to think of. And the cards for first place and second place and third place were beautiful colours too: pink and cream and lavender. Lavender and cream and pink roses were beautiful to think of. Perhaps a wild rose might be like those colours and he remembered the song about the wild rose blossoms on the little green place. But you could not have a green rose. But perhaps somewhere in the world you could. (*P* 12)

At the crucial point in the pursuit of the rose, Stephen stops paying attention, loses, and rationalizes his loss. The signal that triggers this loss is "Father Arnall's voice." Arnall is called *Father* because the church understands his role, as outlined above. Stephen has no idea why his eagerness passes away at the voice of the father, but Joyce probably understood. Stephen gives up the real rose for an imaginary one that he analyzes in esthetic and intellectual terms. He can't bear to win because to possess the bloom of life would be incestuous, and so the father deflects the son onto the abstract rose of the spirit. Whenever Stephen establishes himself in a comfortable matrix in pursuit of some goal, whether it is *alma mater*, a prostitute, the Virgin or Emma Clery, a paternal threat will arise that will make this mode of life intolerable and force him to turn to a search for a new goal, a new receptivity. To project this paternal threat is as easy as stirring up a sense of male competition. The opposition Stephen touches at the limit of his ability to extend himself toward his object is congruent with the role of the father, the one who can never be beaten.

In the course of a discussion of how the obsessive serves the unknown "master" in his superego, Jacques Lacan describes what happens to Stephen during the class of elements: "Thus the symbol manifests itself first of all as the murder of the thing, and this death constitutes in the subject the eternalization of his desire."[3] Stephen actually becomes a symbolist in this passage (perhaps a poet of seven years) as he shifts his concentration from the direct goal of reality onto the clear beginnings of a personal system of magic numbers and colors. This imaginary system can be pursued forever with little fear of physical satisfaction. Stephen seeks power in the subjective realm through control over words here, remembering what he made out of words.

In fact, this scene is a repetition of the earlier one, for the pattern of turning from the externalized mother back into the self because of the threatening father first appears when Stephen does. The first paragraph of *Portrait* ends with Stephen meeting a moocow. Then there is an ellipsis, for the fairy tale breaks off as the cow appears and Stephen is confronted with the threatening image of his father reading the story to him, which obliges him to turn inward and make up his own scene of imaginary roses. The mental shuttling back and forth between a maternal attraction and a paternal threat that generate each other continues to operate through the rest of Stephen's life at a rate of about one turn per page, until those two final major gestures of turning from satisfaction to conflict, in which he runs out of an orgy when his mother's ghost appears, only to pick a fight with some soldiers, and then he refuses Bloom's offer of a warm hearth and a soft couch.

Of course, Stephen was only a part of Joyce's mind, and we know the name of the figure who stands for the part that finally was able to accept the bloom of physical life with maternal help. But the opposition represented by Stephen remained part of Joyce, who could only see acceptance of a world one never quite possesses as cuckoldry. And the discontinued runner, failed potential priest, and second-prize tenor could never quite confront the risks or rewards of social reality. This ineluctable trait shows father operating in the role of nemesis that the Jung essay assigns to him. But if the old man who looks at him through a glass finally sets him behind a glass that withholds him from reality, Simon is also germinal, because he forces Stephen to build his mansion in the realm of eternity or potentiality. Because a satisfying relation to the world will always bring the apparition of father, the artist is motivated to devise sophisticated means to compete without physical competition. And because he can never possess in certainty a matrix of reality, the artist is driven continuously to cast off what is perfected and to create new perspectives, new styles, and new languages at such an impressive rate and with such an accession of personality that since Joyce, any writer who uses the same style twice seems just a bit old-fashioned.

The fruitful aspect of confrontation with the father or male competitor is increasingly prominent in the later works. It is the crux of cruxes in *Ulysses* and it is explicit in *Finnegans Wake*, which says of H. C. E.: "we go into him sleepy children, we come out of him strucklers for life" (*FW* 132.8). Confrontation with father is seen here as a regenerative communion that partakes of his substance. Such male communion through conflict is so important in Joyce's view of life that most of the episodes and structural units of his work may be seen as organized around it. At the risk of simplifying (mainly by leaving out lesser paternal confrontations and visions of mother), I want to trace some of the main examples of this process in the Dedalus-Bloom cycle.

In the first chapter of *Portrait*, Father Dolan impels Stephen to define himself in a quest for justice. The trip to Cork on which Simon takes Stephen in the second chapter confronts the son with mutability and impotence, and this disturbance galvanizes his quest for physical satisfaction, while the sermons on hell oblige Stephen to lift his consciousness above such satisfaction and develop his spiritual functions. The Jesuit director's attempt to ensnare Stephen in the fourth chapter forces him to realize his vocation. And in the fifth chapter Cranly makes Stephen realize that he will have to reject social normality. In every case the threatening male imprints his image on Stephen in reverse.

The pattern of negative contact with a father figure that generates vital realization continues to form the core of most of the episodes in *Ulysses*. Stephen has to pass outside the enclosure of his present home by disagreeing with Mulligan, and it is necessary for him to be sundered from the social context of his occupation through his dialogue with Deasy. Both of these differentiations prepare him to meet Bloom and to be receptive to him. The force of change represented by Proteus must be confronted and grasped before Stephen can be reconciled to physical reality, and in "Aeolus" he is propelled beyond the false language of cynics toward truth.

In his struggle with Shakespeare, Stephen gains new understanding by projecting his mind into the role of father. A final stage of young manhood involves defeating the father, a task so difficult it can only be done indirectly. Defeating the father allows the son to relax his defenses enough to understand him. Because it is the only way to feel father's subjective mind, it teaches the son the illusory nature of victory. After Stephen undermines Shakespeare's authority by psychoanalysis, he realizes that he can't quite believe his theory; similarly, his rather cruel rebuff of Bloom must plant in his mind glowing seeds of regenerative *agenbite of inwit*. Stephen is hostile because he is afraid when Bloom presents him with the world, with a long course of acceptance that will be traumatic as any birth. The father's part of every enemy is the part you are unable to defeat insofar as you are still a boy. To defeat such fatherhood is to ingest it, to exchange boyhood for it.

Moreover, youths are not the only ones fathered in this fashion, for every manchild remains part boy. Bloom is impelled by Blazes Boylan toward a spiritual birth into a world of new feelings and possibilities. Simon's singing of *M'appari*, which is obviously presented as a sexual union between Simon and Bloom, is an injection of spiritual energy that makes Bloom more aware of his desires. This and the stirring of his pride by the citizen are stages of his preparation for Stephen. And Stephen leads him to a confrontation with evil and with his own mortality, which, whatever his subsequent development, will leave him with a greater charge of life than he has absorbed in a decade.

The shape of male conflict in Joyce's work tends to metamorphose through his career from emphasis on the destructive aspect to emphasis on the creative. The father figures of *Dubliners*, such as Father James Flynn, the old man of "An Encounter," and Farrington, have little productive effect on the young people they run into, but the male conflicts in the *Wake* stream with generative energy as they cast the archetypal seeds of history. The conflict grows more beneficial as Joyce's focus shifts from the son's point of view in *Dubliners* and *Portrait* to that of the parents in *Ulysses* and the *Wake*. In the long run, the role of the son is to win, while that of the father is to lose. In the early "Hero" phase, Joyce's work is driven by a need to be right at the expense of the world. But the later phase accepts the possibility of being overwhelmed by experience. The inevitable victory of the son tends to be destructive to others, while the defeat of the father is creative.

The son takes life while the father gives it. Yet the victories of sonship are ultimately justified as preparation for fatherhood, and Joyce became his own cause only by accepting the secret, fateful identity of his enemy.

Notes

1. "Significance," *Freud and Psychoanalysis, The Collected Works of C. G. Jung*, 4, trans. R. F. C. Hull, ed. Sir Herbert Read et al. (Princeton: Bollingen, 1961), pp. 301–23. The original text of 1909 is here distinguished from Jung's revisions of 1949.
2. Gabler, "The Seven Lost Years of *A Portrait of the Artist as a Young Man*," in *Approaches to Joyce's "Portrait*," ed. Thomas F. Staley and Bernard Benstock (University of Pittsburgh Press, 1976), pp. 52–53.
3. Lacan, *The Language of the Self: The Function of Language in Psychoanalysis*, trans. Anthony Wilden (Baltimore: Johns Hopkins University Press, 1968), p. 84.

Mollyloquy

Gabriele Schwab

Molly Bloom has been subjected to a great deal of psychological criticism; to be more precise, *male* psychological criticism. As a result, the history of her critical reception has turned out to be more a documentation of male fears and wishes regarding women than an analysis of her character limited strictly to textual considerations.

My objective here is to point out not only some of the different possibilities but also some of the limitations of psychoanalytical criticism. My main interest does not lie in an analysis of Molly's character as it is portrayed in the manifest text. Instead I want to show the way one could speak of the "unconscious" of a literary figure, which is presented in the textual form of an interior monologue. I will attempt to demonstrate how one can approach Molly's "unconscious," even though all that is in the text is her "conscious" utterance.

I would like to examine a short passage in light of the analytical principles of Freud's *Interpretation of Dreams*. One of the most striking aesthetic achievements of the Penelope chapter lies in the fact that the strategies of the manifest text always signal an implicit dimension of "unconscious meaning" comparable to the latent meaning of a dream or of free association.

Taking place at night just before going to sleep, when the need for daily censorship is reduced, Molly's monologue is such a highly suggestive text, so full of condensed intratextual associations and fragmentary allusions to her past, that the reader reacts unconsciously to Molly's implied "unconscious." This reaction is reinforced by strategies that reveal to him, sometimes only at an unconscious level, more about Molly than she knows herself. At times, latent negations or internal contradictions in Molly's web of thought become quite obvious. Thus guided, the reader may learn to "see through" Molly.

A psychoanalytical interpretation based on formal textual signals that provide connections to unconscious material differs greatly from a common reader's conscious experience, but may designate textual motivations for his possible unconscious reactions.

81

ANALYSIS

. . . what was it she told me O yes that sometimes he used to go to bed with
his muddy boots on when the maggot takes him just imagine having to get
into bed with a thing like that that might murder you any moment what a
man well its not the one way everyone goes mad Poldy anyway whatever he
does always wipes his feet on the mat when he comes in wet or shine and
always blacks his own boots too and he always takes off his hat when he
comes up in the street like that and now hes going about in his slippers to look
for £10000 for a postcard up up O Sweetheart May wouldnt a thing like that
simply bore you stiff to extinction actually too stupid even to take his boots
off now what could you make of a man like that Id rather die 20 times over
than marry another of their sex of course hed never find another woman like
me to put up with him the way I do know me come sleep with me yes and he
knows that too at the bottom of his heart take that Mrs Maybrick that
poisoned her husband for what I wonder in love with some other man yet it
was found out on her wasnt she the downright villain to go and do a thing like
that of course some men can be dreadfully aggravating drive you mad and
always the worst word in the world what do they ask us to marry them for if
were so bad as all that comes to yes because they cant get on without us white
Arsenic she put in his tea off flypaper wasnt it I wonder why they call it that
if I asked him hed say its from the Greek leave us as wise as we were before
she must have been madly in love with the other fellow to run the chance of
being hanged O she didnt care if that was her nature what could she do
besides theyre not brutes enough to go and hang a woman surely are they[1]

Molly has slipped into a train of thought revolving around Josie Powell
(Mrs. Breen), which reveals jealousy and a need for self-consolation.
Abruptly, associations of death and murder emerge—at first on a linguistic
level: "a thing like that might *murder* you"; "bore you *stiff to extinction*"; "I'd
rather *die* 20 times over than marry another of their sex." The theme of
death culminates in Molly's recollection: "take that Mrs Maybrick that
poisoned her husband for what I wonder in love with some other
man. . . ." The tone of her following reflections on Mrs. Maybrick[2] clearly
reveals a secret identification behind her open condemnation of the evil
deed. Thus the boat of Molly's consciousness steers clear of the shallows of
a death-wish toward her own husband. The wish itself is so near to
conscious thought that it becomes fairly obvious to the reader.

Much less accessible is a double unconscious overdetermination of the
censored wish. The key to its understanding is Molly's exclamation "O
Sweetheart May," which is interspersed in her associations of death. The
words come from a song, "Sweetheart May,"[3] which Molly has often sung
herself. There are two doubly significant lines in that song, not quoted in

the text, but presumably known by Molly: "Your dear boy has gone and left you, sweetheart May. . . . Don't you fear for him or cry, sweetheart May, for the boys must win or die, sweetheart May."

From the exclamation "O Sweetheart May" the thread of associations leads on to Mrs. Maybrick—on the surface, because of the occurrence of "May" in both expressions; at a deeper level, because the song's content touches upon material that remains unconscious throughout the associations of death. With its two implicit motifs—a dead son and a lover—the song reaches down to Molly's memory of her dead son (Rudy) and to her fantasy of a son-lover (Stephen). This reading is confirmed by another passage thirty pages later, where, thinking about Simon Dedalus, Molly passes from "dearest goodbye *sweet*heart he always sang" to "he was married at the time to *May* Golding" (emphasis mine), then on to Stephen, and from there directly to Rudy: "I was in mourning that's 11 years ago now yes hed be 11. . . ."[4]

From a psychoanalytical perspective, Molly's seemingly arbitrary exclamation "O Sweetheart May" turns out to be the highly condensed vehicle of a whole bundle of unconscious feelings. It reveals the fate of her son Rudy as a hidden motif behind the latent death-wish against Bloom and her fantasies of a young lover.

All this, of course, is not allowed to get through to Molly's conscious. The conflict arising out of all these ideas and wishes is solved in a characteristic manner: she disavows her maternal feelings and her sorrow, which then return in her fantasies of a son-lover. And she disavows her own feeling of guilt concerning Rudy's death, projecting the guilt onto Bloom, and taking her revenge by means of the death-wish and the fantasy of a son-lover.

By analyzing "O Sweetheart May" as a private symbol and bearer of unconscious meaning, I have introduced the two main themes that continually affect Molly's unconscious life. At first glance, the aforementioned critics may feel that their viewpoint has been confirmed. For them Molly is the literary concretization of the archetypal "Great Mother": to some the nourishing and devouring mother, to others the "satanic mistress," if not a "thirty-shilling whore."[5] Indeed, does not Molly's fantasy of a son-lover, together with her latent death-wish toward her husband, correspond to the second interpretation? And do not her mourning, her feeling of guilt, and the tenderness in her thoughts of Stephen express a profound motherly feeling?

Yet the psychoanalytical interpretation demonstrates what is wrong with that controversial split among Molly's critics who conclude that Molly is one *or* the other. She is both. Behind her death wish, there are mother and lover motifs; behind her son-lover fantasy there is the mother's interest of winning back a son. Molly's text does not dissolve her fundamental ambivalence but thematizes it.

A close reading shows that this strategy is constitutive: every feeling expressed in Molly's thoughts and belonging to one side of the ambivalence is counterbalanced by opposite feelings. Even her famous female "yes" is quite often nothing more than a self-disguised "no." All her manifest utterances are made ambiguous by latent negations, and it is neither in the manifest nor on the latent level but in the interaction of both that one may find the "truth" about Molly. Critics who decide in favor of one or the other version in fact reproduce a common activity of consciousness, which is the reduction of ambivalence. Yet the textual strategy of portraying Molly in terms of her irreducibly ambivalent feelings works against that habitual tendency.

As such, the portrayal of Molly also subverts the presentation of consciousness in previous chapters: it puts an end to the vanity fair celebrated by and for consciousness in Joyce's *Ulysses*. The permanent doubling and counterbalancing of Molly's utterances by latent negation show that her conscious thoughts very often distort and disavow the feelings from which they derive. This is as true for her motive of revenge and her desire for a son-lover as it is for her death-wish toward Bloom. Thus consciousness is revealed to be a means of self-deception rather than one of self-knowledge. Molly's conscious is always less or other than her self. This self is often hiding or hidden in the stream of her consciousness but is nonetheless latently present and accessible to the reader.

Until now, one important dimension of the text has been neglected: the archetypal pattern of the whole novel. What is the link between "Penelope" and "Molly," if Molly is now considered as part of the whole system of *Ulysses* as a meta-novel?

The myth of Penelope stresses a reading of "Molly" as a concretization of the archetypal "Great Mother." Yet all the Ulysses references in the Joycean manifestation of the archetypal pattern differ so much from their literary origin that the aesthetic achievement cannot be found in the reference itself. The passage analyzed above shows that archetypal patterns like that of the son-lover or of the nourishing and devouring mother underlie Molly's psychic system. But it becomes quite clear that Molly as a character can never be reduced to or even explained by such a pattern. She is certainly not just a representation of the archetype. It might well designate hidden motives of her behavior or provide a key to the order of her seemingly arbitrary recollections and thoughts. Thus one could work out a whole dynamic system of interacting archetypes that permeates Molly's nocturnal monologue.

But far from giving *the key* to her personality, such a system can only underline the fact that Molly transcends every concrete manifestation of her self. This is quite an unusual way to be confronted with a literary figure. Before Joyce we had been used to getting very specific views of a character. But our view of Molly remains strikingly contingent, for the text abstains from guiding and evaluating the selection of archetypes, which creates a need in the reader to make a selection himself. By doing so he may become aware that the archetypes have undergone a change of function. Their consciousness-forming power, still viable in the mythical foil of *Ulysses*, has been lost in our civilization. The archetypes underlying Molly's psyche no longer shape her consciousness. In the context of everyday life in Dublin, they melt into the clichés of the pulp novels she reads and become vehicles of unconscious meaning, comforting to a subject who is not allowed consciously to experience the precluded significance. Thus, the archetypes have taken on a new function. They are no longer a means to bring ambivalent feelings to a conscious level but still serve to connect our lived experience with parts of ourselves excluded from consciousness.

Just as Penelope, night after night, secretly unweaves her web in order to hold off her suitors, so Molly's nocturnal web of associations secretly unweaves the diurnal social net in which she is caught. She does this, of course, not in order to avoid suitors, but to fill her imaginary life with them. In thus affirming her own self and its desires, she creates an imaginary order of present and past events, fantasies and fears, which allows her to approach her unconscious. Molly's monologue thus demonstrates how consciousness finds means and ways to live out what it nonetheless refuses to recognize.

Notes

1. James Joyce, *Ulysses* (Random House, p. 744; Penguin, p. 665).
2. Mrs. Florence Elisabeth Chandler Maybrick (1862–1941) was tried for the murder of her husband; at the trial it was established that she had a lover or lovers; also that she had tried to obtain arsenic in the way Molly recalls. She was condemned to death, but her sentence was commuted to life and she was released on 25 January 1904 (cf. Don Gifford with R. J. Seidman, *Notes for Joyce: An Annotation of James Joyce's "Ulysses,"* New York: Dutton, 1974, p. 500).
3. A song by Leslie Stuart and Charles K. Harris; cf. *Notes for Joyce*, p. 499.
4. Random House, p. 774; Penguin, p. 695.
5. Cf. Mark Shechner, *Joyce in Nighttown* (Berkeley: University of California Press, 1974), chapter 5, "Das Fleisch das stets bejaht," pp. 195–226.

PART IV

The Narrative Structures of Joyce and Faulkner

Prefatory Note

Bernard Benstock

The subject of influence has been approached at various times in charting the relationship of William Faulkner to James Joyce, despite Faulkner's disclaimer that he had not read *Ulysses* before writing *The Sound and the Fury*. Rather than reopen the same issues for reinvestigation, the panel of Faulkner scholars concerned itself with comparative analyses of narrative structures in the complex development of selected passages from Joyce and Faulkner. Each of the participants chose a passage from a Faulkner text, and the panel coordinator undertook to find comparable portions from Joyce's *Ulysses* for their deployment in relation to those by Faulkner. In each case the two passages precede the comparative treatment presented by members of the panel.

Joyce's and Faulkner's "Twining Stresses": A Textual Comparison

François L. Pitavy

Woodshadows floated silently by through the morning peace from the stairhead seaward where he gazed. Inshore and farther out the mirror of water whitened, spurned by lightshod hurrying feet. White breast of the dim sea. The twining stresses, two by two. A hand plucking the harpstrings merging their twining chords. Wavewhite wedded words shimmering on the dim tide.

A cloud began to cover the sun slowly, shadowing the bay in deeper green. It lay behind him, a bowl of bitter waters. Fergus' song: I sang it alone in the house, holding down the long dark chords. Her door was open: she wanted to hear my music. Silent with awe and pity I went to her bedside. She was crying in her wretched bed. For those words, Stephen: love's bitter mystery.

Where now?

Her secrets: old feather fans, tasselled dancecards, powdered with musk, a gaud of amber beads in her locked drawer. A birdcage hung in the sunny window of her house when she was a girl. She heard old Royce sing in the pantomime of Turko the terrible and laughed with others when he sang:

> *I am the boy*
> *That can enjoy*
> *Invisibility.*

Phantasmal mirth, folded away: muskperfumed.

> *And no more turn aside and brood*

Folded away in the memory of nature with her toys. Memories beset his brooding brain. Her glass of water from the kitchen tap when she had approached the sacrament. A cored apple, filled with brown sugar, roasting for her at the hob on a dark autumn evening. Her shapely fingernails reddened by the blood of squashed lice from the children's shirts.[1]

Then it [noon] was past. I got off [the car] and stood in my shadow and after a while a car came along and I got on and went back to the interurban station. There was a car ready to leave, and I found a seat next the window and it started and I watched it sort of frazzle out into slack tide flats, and then trees. Now and then I saw the river and I thought how nice it would be for them down at New London if the weather and Gerald's shell going solemnly up the glinting forenoon and I wondered what the old woman would be wanting now, sending me a note before ten oclock in the morning. What picture of Gerald I to be one of the *Dalton Ames oh asbestos Quentin has shot* background. Something with girls in it. Women do have *always his voice above the gabble voice that breathed* an affinity for evil, for believing that no woman is to be trusted, but that some men are too innocent to protect themselves. Plain girls. Remote cousins and family friends whom mere acquaintanceship invested with a sort of blood obligation noblesse oblige. And she sitting there telling us before their faces what a shame it was that Gerald should have all the family looks because a man didn't need it, was better off without it but without it a girl was simply lost. Telling us about Gerald's women in a *Quentin has shot Herbert he shot his voice through the floor of Caddy's room* tone of smug approbation. "When he was seventeen I said to him one day 'What a shame that you should have a mouth like that it should be on a girls face' and can you imagine *the curtains leaning in on the twilight upon the odour of the apple tree her head against the twilight her arms behind her head kimono-winged the voice that breathed o'er eden clothes upon the bed by the nose seen above the apple* what he said? just seventeen, mind. 'Mother' he said 'it often is.' " And him sitting there in attitudes regal watching two or three of them through his eyelashes.[2]

The influence of Joyce has long been a moot point in the field of Faulkner criticism, especially in view of the contradictory declarations of Faulkner concerning his acquaintance with *Ulysses*. These statements are too well known to bear repetition at this point, and of little use in the matter of textual criticism. Coming from a writer, claims or denials of influences obviously cannot be taken at their face value, but should rather be considered in the light of the only admissible evidence, the texts—evidence, however, not to be regarded as indisputable, except in the case of obvious quotations or borrowings.

Hence the interest of juxtaposing short texts by Joyce and Faulkner, so as to point out specific similarities or differences, which might eventually justify the word "influence," or simply "convergence."

Surface similarities between Stephen Dedalus on June 16, 1904, and Quentin Compson on June 2, 1910, have been generally recognized, such as the occurrence within one day of their wanderings in or around Dublin or Boston, the assumption of a symbolic or ritualistic significance by seemingly trivial acts, the interaction of past and present, and the intermingling of "interior" monologue with the description of "exterior" setting.[3] Moreover, though these two texts do not hold parallel positions in the *diegesis* of each novel, the situations of the two young men bear comparison. Both are confronted with the death of a woman, Stephen with that of his mother, whose deathbed wish that he kneel down to pray he refused to comply with, Quentin with the spiritual death of his promiscuous sister Caddy, with "her clothes upon the bed": tainted by sex, she no longer conforms to his private image of an ethereal beauty.[4]

In *Ulysses*, just before the text studied here, Mulligan's voice "booms out" the first three lines of the second stanza of Yeats's short lyric "Who Goes with Fergus?" The stanza must be quoted here in its entirety, if the first paragraph of the text is to be properly understood.

> And no more turn aside and brood
> Upon love's bitter mystery;
> For Fergus rules the brazen cars,
> And rules the shadows of the wood,
> And the white breast of the dim sea
> And all dishevelled wandering stars.[5]

Although Fergus's song is here explicitly linked with Stephen's mother, who wanted to hear it on her deathbed, Mulligan's partial quotation suggests a masculine, or a father image, Fergus being here the lord of heaven and earth, ruling the brazen cars—a suggestion borne out in the "Telemachus" episode by the discussion on *Hamlet* and Mulligan's assertion that Stephen "proves by algebra . . . that he [Hamlet, or Stephen?] himself is the ghost of his own father" (18); the chanting by Mulligan of the "Ballad of Joking Jesus," "the queerest young fellow that ever you heard," since a bird, and not "Joseph the joiner," was his father (19); and Stephen's thinking of various heretics—Arius, Valentine, Sabellius—all denying one way or another the sonship of Christ (21).[6]

But such a father image, or more specifically that of a man being his own father, i.e., the dream of the artist, self-engendered (which sends the reader back to the *Portrait*), is precisely the temptation that Stephen the bard—as Mulligan jeeringly calls him—must turn aside from: that he may come to terms with himself, his guilt-ridden conscience must first confront the memory of his mother. He has, so to speak, to go through the body of his mother (hence the blood), so as to acknowledge his subjection to the conditions of life—his submission to Fergus. Here, however, Stephen cannot recall the deathbed scene to its end: veering away from it (with the question "Where now?"), he turns to reminders of his mother's happiness *before* him, and to her own memories of a past in which he has no part. Contrary to Turko the terrible in a never-never land of fairy-tale metamorphoses, it is impossible for him to be "the boy that can enjoy invisibility." Such prelapsarian mirth, as it were, such a vision of a time antedating his feeling of guilt, is just phantasm, to be "folded away" among the muskperfumed memories of his dead mother. So he broods again over his mother's illness, and then reverts to a final memory in which her fingernails are reddened with his own blood. He may feel that he has her blood on his hands—as Mulligan has just told him, "The aunt thinks you killed your mother" (5)—but he also realizes that even dead she is a mortiferous presence: "Ghoul! Chewer of corpses!" his rebellious mind tells her (10).

The ambiguity of his feelings, or the irreconcilability of his views, makes the dramatic climax later on in the day inevitable, when he recalls that deathbed scene completely (580–81): as he eagerly requests that she tell him "the word," she answers asking him to pray and repent. Loving and protecting, but also related to the Logos, "the mother" thus reveals herself as a double-faced God, as mother and father: and Stephen cannot reconcile himself to this duality: *"Non serviam!"* (582). At the end of his traumatic night (the end of the "Circe" episode), beaten unconscious by Private Carr, "doubling himself together" into the position of the fetus, he finally acknowledges the dominion he had so bitterly rejected, and "goes with Fergus": apparently, the whole poem then comes back to his mind. Only by submitting to the point of fainting does his conscience bring its feinting to an end: such indeed had been the course of his thinking from the first episode, particularly in the text discussed here.

As Mary Dedalus is the focus of Stephen's brooding, so is Caddy Compson that of Quentin's obsessions. The young man is losing his grasp on his consciousness, is becoming *eccentric* by having Caddy, the warm center of his life, escape him because of her promiscuity. That is why he regards all other young men as breaking his exclusive and, as he would have it, immutable hold upon his sister. The thought of the boat race at New London gives rise to the image of Gerald Bland rowing on the Charles River and then to those, superimposed as in a weird photograph, of Dalton Ames, the former lover of Caddy, and Herbert Head, her husband-to-be, whom Quentin hates so much that he wishes him dead, fantasying that he shoots his voice through the floor of Caddy's room, while confronting his sister, dressed in her kimono, leaning by the open window, on the eve of her wedding—just over two months before the "present" day of his suicide. In Quentin's mind, Gerald Bland, Dalton Ames, and Herbert Head, potential or actual lovers of Caddy, are interchangeable, fused into one composite image of Caddy's ravisher, threatening his own impossible stance, as he cannot be at once the guardian of his sister's honor and her despoiler. Those competitors are eminently virile (while Quentin is *unmanned*, rejected into the "background. Something with girls in it"): Gerald's mother (in an incestuous situation that Quentin cannot but recognize) keeps exalting the virility of her son, the "regal" ladykiller; and Herbert's voice keeps asserting itself over the gabble. Those men are also viewed by Quentin as solar, i.e., masculine, beings, fire-annealed: Dalton Ames (who is suntanned and wears khaki shirts) is synonymous with asbestos, and Gerald Bland rows "solemnly up the glinting forenoon," in what later appears a godlike ascension, "up the long bright air like an apotheosis, mounting into a drowsing infinity" (149).

In the two novels, Quentin and Stephen act both as narrators of external events and as reporters of their inner thoughts. But the greater lack of control in Quentin's narrative, evinced by the irrepressible erupting of images into his consciousness, works itself into a writing technique markedly different from that of Joyce, in spite of surface similarities. At the beginning of Faulkner's text, the narrator uses a kind of monologue as little "interior" as possible, aiming at "pure" description of gestures, sights, and thoughts recognized as such and thus controlled: "and *I thought* how it would be nice for them."[7] (The predicate expressed here grammatically ascribes the thinking to a central, controlling I. Later in the text, when the narrator's consciousness begins to frazzle out, precisely, the verb *to think* in the personal form no longer appears.) Quentin tries to make sheer perception fill in the whole of consciousness so as to stop thinking about time and his sister. (Caddy's sex life and her having to marry Herbert Head are, as it were, the irretrievable recognition that she lives *in* time, that her imperfect flesh is controlled by time rhythms, and that everything in life must needs be temporary—a thought [and a word] that is unbearable for the idealist Quentin: his ultimate "conversation" with his father is indeed a desperate denial of the temporariness of life.) However, no description can be "pure" or innocent. Quentin notices precisely what brings him back to his obsessions: the river, another time symbol, which makes him think of the Harvard-Yale boat race a short while ahead, a race he will not attend since he will be dead: "I saw the river and I thought how nice it would be for them down at New London if the weather and Gerald's shell." But breaking off *one* thought and taking another tack does not alter the course of his consciousness: Gerald Bland is associated directly with the river and indirectly with Caddy.

A *double entente* of a sort in Quentin's narrative also shows his failure to block off the return of his obsessions: "I watched it sort of frazzle out into slack tide flats." Apparently, the neutral pronoun indicates the river, though it has not been mentioned yet (Quentin "notices" it only in the next sentence), but this undecided "it" really points to Quentin's own consciousness: his hold upon his thinking, and consequently the sense of his identity, begins to dissolve, so much so that toward the end of the day, when he is about to jump into the Charles River, the central unifying "I" becomes an impotent, anonymous "i," dangling without any predicate.

In Joyce's text, it is even more obvious that the description of the exterior setting indeed points to the narrator's consciousness, even though he is grammatically absent and the first reference to him, in the second paragraph, is in the third person ("It lay behind him"). (In the beginning of Faulkner's text, down to the first italics, the omnipresence of the first person—ten occurrences—manifests the obsessive fear of the loss of identity.) The unquoted, more feminine, end of Yeats's lyric surfaces in the narrative—thus clearly ascribed to a recognizable narrator, since the borrowings from Yeats ("woodshadows," "white breast of the dim sea") imply the presence of a narrator's memory. The setting in the first paragraph is feminine, too, in its color ("white"), its suggestion of serenity and lightness, the soft, flowing, liquid sounds (the recurrence of the "w" sound is remarkable: "woodshadows," "seaward," "where," "water," "whitened," "white," "twining," "wavewhite wedded words"), the incremental rhythm, wavelike, with wedded words (intertwined occurrences of "white," "dim," "twining").[8] The sea being also a phantasmatic equivalent of the mother, this seascape clearly becomes a motherscape: in this context, and with such convergence of effects, the quotation from Yeats, "white breast of the dim sea," sounds almost like a redundancy, and "the twining stresses" of Yeats's line suggest—indeed contain—tresses, a woman's intertwined hair. Finally, the circular shape of Dublin's bay is linked in the narrator's mind with the memory of his dying mother. When the sun disappears, the deep green, cloud-shadowed bay becomes a "bowl of bitter waters," an obvious reminder of the "bowl of white china . . . beside her deathbed holding the green sluggish bile which she had torn up from her rotting liver" (5). As the bay and the dying mother were then directly associated, the "bowl of bitter waters" now immediately brings up to Stephen's memory his singing of Fergus's song to his dying mother. Moreover, the feeling of guilt toward the mother is compounded by a similar feeling toward the mother country (the bitter waters of Dublin's bay), and also toward the Catholic church: Stephen here also thinks of his dying mother in connection with "the sacrament." The trinity Ireland-church-mother is really the one and same demon inhabiting the narrator's conscience: hence the narrowing of his gaze from the circular bay to the bowl of bitter waters that must be drained to the dregs.

Haunted though they both are by their private demons, Stephen's and Quentin's stances as narrators differ markedly. Stephen retains a capacity for detachment that Quentin has all but lost. Stephen can judge himself when he is by his mother's bedside, "silent with awe and pity," whereas Quentin, fantasying that he has shot Herbert's voice through Caddy's bedroom floor, does not view himself with any sort of detachment, though he thinks of himself in the third person. He has no place in his consciousness for anything but his obsessions, and no control whatever over their emergence and recurrence, since even the attempt at seemingly "pure" description brings back to him the desperate dilemma for which the only way out will be to let himself be "heal[ed] out to the sea and the caverns and the grottoes of the sea" (111)—a phantasmal substitute for the lost sister. Conversely, Stephen can to a certain extent control the flow of his memories ("Where now?"), and he knows that recalling sunny memories is just "phantasmal mirth," and that he must eventually confront his guilt. More remarkable is his capacity for word-play, implying a distancing power (e.g., the remembered odor of musk being recalled to qualify his own memorizing, "muskperfumed"); and for twining quotations into the texture of his narrative: his is indeed a *cultivated* narrative, while the mind of the Harvard student is so tightly applied to, and possessed by, the stream of his thoughts that there is no room in it for literature or for verbal enjoyment.

The texture of the two narratives—or should one say the tessitura of the two narrators' voices?—is consequently different. Despite the general lack of conjunctions between the clauses, Joyce's syntax aims at creating logic and continuity, and a sense of identity ("Fergus' song: I sang it alone"; "Her secrets: old feather fans"). Conversely, Faulkner expresses the sense of dissolving identity by fragmenting Quentin's time into discrete units, frantically coordinated by "and"—an attempt to introduce sequence and logic where there is only fragmentation. The surface continuity of Quentin's narrative shows indeed constant breaks in the stream of his thoughts, but paradoxically no blanks, as if Quentin wanted to block off the possibility of unwelcome thoughts or refused to acknowledge their sudden, uncontrollable emergence into his consciousness. In Stephen's narrative, the ellipses are syntactical; in Quentin's, they are of the mind. The paratactic mode of expression in Joyce here creates sequence and an irrefragable sense of identity, whereas the crackups in the narrative's surface together with the spurious coordination manifest in Faulkner's text a paratactic mode of apprehension.

Even though his narrative is made up of perceptions and daydreamings, quotations and memories, word-playing and questionings, it thus appears that the various stresses in Stephen's voice are twined into one rich, continuous, unfrayed, extraordinarily supple cord. Quentin's voice, on the other hand, exposes its frayings, and the broken, untwined strands of its texture. Here, Faulkner makes an original use of italics, laying flat, as it were, the different layers of Quentin's consciousness: the change in type makes up for the inadequacy of the flat page and of the necessarily sequential order of the writing to express the simultaneity and superposition of several images in the consciousness: "I to be one of the . . . background" occurs simultaneously in Quentin's mind with the image of the fire-annealed Dalton Ames and with that of the hated Herbert Head. Similarly, the memory of one of his father's aphorisms, "Women do have . . . an affinity for evil," is concomitant with two traumatic memories of Caddy's wedding (a manifestation of her affinity with evil), i.e., Herbert's voice prevailing over all the other voices, and the first line of John Keble's poem, "Holy Matrimony," sung at the ceremony itself: "The voice that breathed o'er Eden."

The limitations inherent in the order of writing, and of reading, are not all negative, however, for they allow a dual reading of the text: according to contiguity or sequence, and according to grammar, since the images breaking into the surface level of Quentin's consciousness are set apart on the page by italics, the absence of which would make improbable or difficult such "grammatical" reading of a text, which Barthes would then probably call "texte de jouissance." "I to be one of the *Dalton Ames Oh asbestos Quentin has shot*" makes Quentin one of Caddy's despoilers, siding with Dalton and Herbert, which is both wishful thinking and unbearable: hence the phantasm of murder; simultaneously, "I to be one of the . . . background. Something with girls in it" pushes Quentin back into the girls' camp and into inaction—into the impossibility of claiming Caddy for himself. Thus Quentin's dilemma regarding Caddy is represented graphically on the page. One could similarly remark that the second occurrence of italics in the text superimposes three voices that, to Quentin, "breathed an affinity for evil": his father's assertion, Herbert's voice, and the choir that sang at Caddy's wedding ceremony. In the third occurrence, the thought of Gerald the lady-killer, and of male philandering smugly approved of by society, is so outrageous to Quentin that he shoots Herbert the Caddy-killer. Finally, the risqué situation told by Mrs. Bland in a scene imagined (or recalled?) by Quentin brings a series of flash images, cut off as soon as formed, in all of which Caddy is associated with sex—the only passage in the text that really resorts to the stream of consciousness technique, i.e., an immediate discourse, as close as possible to the point where thinking originates, in which the elliptic inarticulateness supposedly representing a prelogical state of the mind has become almost a prerequisite of the technique, at least since Molly's soliloquy.

The commonly used expression "interior monologue" is certainly an unhappy one, applying inadequately to such a versatile type of discourse, made of reporting of actions, descriptions, memories, phantasms, and what can be more strictly termed stream of consciousness. Such Protean plasticity of his medium Faulkner may indeed have learned from Joyce. However, even a textual comparison does not solve the disputed question of influence, but rather, as often happens in comparative work, enables us to point out differences and specificities, beyond general similarities. I would rather argue that Faulkner was spurred by Joyce's *Ulysses* to create for Quentin's monologue in *The Sound and the Fury* a narrative form suiting his particular needs, and that he might not have made it such a versatile medium had it not been for Joyce's example, which indeed Faulkner seems to have had in his mind from his first novel, *Soldiers' Pay*.[9]

This brings the critic back to Faulkner's early statements concerning Joyce—that he had never read *Ulysses*, but that it was "possible that [he] was influenced by what [he] heard"[10]—and to both his lifelong grudging admiration toward Joyce and reservations as to his achievements: "He was electrocuted. He had more talent than he could control."[11] In other words, Faulkner acknowledged that Joyce had been a master,[12] but that, like all gifted disciples, he had outgrown the master, as appears in this text from *The Sound and the Fury*, and as seems confirmed in a declaration of Hamilton Basso concerning Faulkner in 1925, namely that he "had got past Verlaine, Eliot, Pound, and Joyce."[13] At this point, the Faulknerian is sent back to the *Paris Review* interview: "Don't bother just to be better than your contemporaries or predecessors. Try to be better than yourself. . . . The artist is completely amoral in that he will rob, borrow, beg, or steal from anybody and everybody to get the work done."[14]

Notes

1. James Joyce, *Ulysses* (New York: Random House, 1961), pp. 9–10. All subsequent references will be given within parentheses after the quotations.
2. William Faulkner, *The Sound and the Fury* (New York: Knopf, 1929), pp. 129–31. All subsequent references will be given within parentheses after the quotations.
3. See in particular Michael Groden, "Criticism in New Composition: *Ulysses* and *The Sound and the Fury*," *TCL* 21 (1975): 265–77.
4. See my article "Quentin Compson, ou le regard du poète," *Sud* 14–15 (1975): 62–80.
5. *The Collected Poems of W. B. Yeats* (London: Macmillan, 1952), pp. 48–49. See Weldon Thornton, *Allusions in "Ulysses": An Annotated List* (Chapel Hill: University of North Carolina Press, 1968), p. 16, and Don Gifford with Robert J. Seidman, *Notes for Joyce: An Annotation of James Joyce's "Ulysses"* (New York: Dutton, 1974), p. 10.
6. Gifford, p. 15.
7. My italics.
8. The poetic quality of the description has been noted by Bernard Benstock, "Telemachus," in *James Joyce's "Ulysses": Critical Essays*, ed. Clive Hart and David Hayman (Berkeley: University of California Press, 1974), pp. 13–14.
9. See, among others, Michael Millgate, "Starting Out in the Twenties: Reflections on *Soldiers' Pay*," *Mosaic* 7 (1973): 1–14, p. 7; Joseph Blotner, *Faulkner: A Biography* (New York: Random House, 1974), p. 429; Groden, pp. 267–69; Cleanth Brooks, *William Faulkner: Toward Yoknapatawpha and Beyond* (New Haven: Yale University Press, 1978), p. 75. My point about the "influence" of *Ulysses* on *The Sound and the Fury* seems confirmed by this declaration of Faulkner in 1955: "I began

to write before I read *Ulysses*. I read *Ulysses* by the middle 20's and I had been scribbling for several years" (James B. Meriwether and Michael Millgate, eds., *Lion in the Garden: Interviews with William Faulkner, 1926–1962* [New York: Random House, 1968], p. 197). In 1924 Phil Stone indeed gave a copy of *Ulysses* to Faulkner, who autographed it (Blotner, p. 352). That Joyce's novel did not induce an immediate and deliberate borrowing of technical tricks, but slowly helped Faulkner create his own medium, would then appear in the fact that Faulkner wrote his non-Joycean third novel *Flags in the Dust* (published as *Sartoris*) in 1927 and *The Sound and the Fury* between March and September 1928.

10. *Lion in the Garden*, pp. 30–31.
11. Frederick L. Gwynn and Joseph L. Blotner, eds., *Faulkner in the University: Class Conferences at the University of Virginia, 1957–1958* (Charlottesville: University Press of Virginia, 1959), p. 280.
12. *Lion in the Garden*, p. 112.
13. Blotner, p. 418.
14. *Lion in the Garden*, pp. 238–39.

Bloom and Quentin

André Bleikasten

I turned out the light and went into my bedroom, out of the gasoline but I could still smell it. I stood at the window the curtains moved slow out of the darkness touching my face like someone breathing asleep, breathing slow into the darkness again, leaving the touch. *After they had gone up stairs Mother lay back in her chair, the camphor handkerchief to her mouth. Father hadn't moved he still sat beside her holding her hand the bellowing hammering away like no place for it in silence* When I was little there was a picture in one of our books, a dark place into which a single weak ray of light came slanting upon two faces lifted out of the shadow. *You know what I'd do if I were King?* she was never a queen or a fairy she was always a king or a giant or a general *I'd break that place open and drag them out and I'd whip them good* It was torn out, jagged out. I was glad. I'd have to turn back to it until the dungeon was Mother herself she and Father upward into weak light holding hands and us lost somewhere below even them without even a ray of light. Then the honeysuckle got into it. As soon as I turned off the light and tried to go to sleep it would begin to come into the room in waves building and building up until I would have to pant to get any air at all out of it until I would have to get up and feel my way like when I was a little boy *hands can see touching in the mind shaping unseen door Door now nothing hands can see* My nose could see gasoline, the vest on the table, the door. The corridor was still empty of all the feet in sad generations seeking water. *yet the eyes unseeing clenched like teeth not disbelieving doubting even the absence of pain shin ankle knee the long invisible flowing of the stair-railing where a misstep in the darkness filled with sleeping Mother Father Caddy Jason Maury door I am not afraid only Mother Father Caddy Jason Maury getting so far ahead sleeping I will sleep fast when I door Door door* It was empty too, the pipes, the porcelain, the stained quiet walls, the throne of contemplation. I had forgotten the glass, but I could *hands can see cooling fingers invisible swan-throat where less than Moses rod the glass touch tentative not to drumming lean cool throat drumming cooling the metal the glass full overfull cooling the glass the fingers flushing sleep leaving the taste of dampened sleep in the long silence of the throat* I returned up the corridor, waking the lost feet in whispering battalions in the silence, into the gasoline, the watch telling its furious lie on the dark table.[1]

Ba. What is that flying about? Swallow? Bat probably. Thinks I'm a tree, so blind. Have birds no smell? Metempsychosis. They believed you could be changed into a tree from grief. Weeping willow. Ba. There he goes. Funny

100

little beggar. Wonder where he lives. Belfry up there. Very likely. Hanging
by his heels in the odour of sanctity. Bell scared him out, I suppose. Mass
seems to be over. Could hear them all at it. Pray for us. And pray for us. And
pray for us. Good idea the repetition. Same thing with ads. Buy from us.
And buy from us. Yes, there's the light in the priest's house. Their frugal
meal. Remember about the mistake in the valuation when I was in Thom's.
Twentyeight it is. Two houses they have. Gabriel Conroy's brother is
curate. Ba. Again. Wonder why they come out at night like mice. They're a
mixed breed. Birds are like hopping mice. What frightens them, light or
noise? Better sit still. All instinct like the bird in drouth got water out of the
end of a jar by throwing in pebbles. Like a little man in a cloak he is with tiny
hands. Weeny bones. Almost see them shimmering, kind of a bluey white.
Colours depend on the light you see. Stare the sun for example like the eagle
then look at a shoe see a blotch blob yellowish. Wants to stamp his trademark
on everything. Instance, that cat this morning on the staircase. Colour of
brown turf. Say you never see them with three colours. Not true. That half
tabbywhite tortoiseshell in the *City Arms* with the letter em on her forehead.
Body fifty different colours. Howth a while ago amethyst. Glass flashing.
That's how that wise man what's his name with the burning glass. Then the
heather goes on fire. It can't be tourists' matches. What? Perhaps the sticks
dry rub together in the wind and light. Or broken bottles in the furze act as a
burning glass in the sun. Archimedes. I have it! My memory's not so bad.[2]

"The two great men in my time were Mann and Joyce. You should
approach Joyce's *Ulysses* as the illiterate Baptist preacher approaches the
Old Testament: with faith."[3] Joyce was beyond doubt one of the very few
novelists of his time whom Faulkner was willing to acknowledge as writers
of genius.[4] There can be no question either that Joyce had a significant
influence on his work. Yet whether that influence was a "major" one, and
whether there is any justification in calling Faulkner Joyce's American prize
pupil (as so many historians of modern fiction do) remains debatable. The
network of intertextuality in Faulkner's novels is woven of so many threads
as to make it impossible to single out any individual writer as his literary
father. Faulkner's literary fathers were many, and he killed them all—just
as Joyce had done before him.

    If writing is parricide as one of the fine arts, its success depends to a large
extent on the author's ability to dispose of the corpse and to efface all traces
of the murder. As might have been expected, then, Faulkner did his best to
cover up his tracks. When did he start reading Joyce? Which of his works
did he read? In what measure was he familiar with them? To such questions
there can only be conjectural answers. It has been suggested that Faulkner
"saw some or all of the issues of *The Little Review* from March, 1918, to
December, 1920, in which *Ulysses* was serialized, and that he probably read
substantial parts of it as it appeared (with some gaps caused by censorship
difficulties) in that medium."[5] Yet all we know is that in 1924 he had been

given a copy of *Ulysses* by his friend and mentor Phil Stone, and even this piece of information is open to suspicion.[6] As to Faulkner's own statements about his reading of Joyce, it is as if they had been made with the perverse intention of keeping us wondering forever: in 1932, three years after publishing *The Sound and the Fury*, he claimed that he had never read *Ulysses*;[7] in 1955 he admitted having read it in "the middle 20's";[8] in 1958 he told Richard Ellmann that he only read it in 1930 but had known about the book before from excerpts and from conversations with friends.[9]

Internal evidence, however, strongly supports the assumption that Faulkner had begun to read Joyce *before* writing *The Sound and the Fury*, and there is good reason to believe that he discovered him in the early twenties, at the crucial time of his career, when he was turning from poetry to prose. Though not pervasive, Joyce's influence is clearly discernible in the experimental sketches published in New Orleans in the early months of 1925:[10] through the use of first-person narrators, Faulkner attempted impressionistic effects in the Joycean manner, and the technique of some of the longer stories (like "Home" or "Out of Nazareth") foreshadows the "stream of consciousness" of *The Sound and the Fury* and *As I Lay Dying*. Quite Joycean too are the snatches of interior monologue and the scrambled time sequences of *Soldiers' Pay*, Faulkner's first novel (1926), and so, even more conspicuously, are the aesthetic speculations of *Mosquitoes*, his "Portrait of the Artist" (1927), and the "Circe"-like *Walpurgisnacht* with which this novel closes.[11]

There are also occasional echoes of Joyce in *Flags in the Dust/Sartoris* (1929),[12] but neither in the early prose nor in the first three novels is Faulkner's debt to Joyce a large one. Much more was involved, however, in *The Sound and the Fury*, for in this novel Faulkner adopted Joyce's "mythic method"[13] and relied on interior monologue more extensively and more consistently than ever before.[14] This time his very approach to fiction came close to Joyce's. Indeed, with the exception of *As I Lay Dying*, *The Sound and the Fury* is Faulkner's most Joycean novel. Yet it should be remembered that it is also one of his very best: with this work he accomplished his breakthrough to mastery. That this breakthrough coincided with the most Joycean phase of his career is perhaps no accident. To the younger writer, Joyce must have been more than a literary model among others—a unique example of creative freedom and versatility, a dazzling revelation of the boundless possibilities of the language of fiction. Perhaps it was only Joyce's precedent that could fully awaken Faulkner to the potentials of his own genius.

Let me turn now to the passages from *Ulysses* and *The Sound and the Fury* chosen for comparison.

The passage from Quentin Compson's monologue occurs about four pages before the section's ending. It records some of the last moments of Quentin's last day, when his tortured mind is less than ever in control of its thoughts, and his obsession with death (by water) is at its most compelling. In its distraughtness and drivenness alone, it differs markedly from the excerpt from the "Nausicaa" chapter I have been asked to compare it with. Quentin's monologue here points to the disorder and agony of a psyche on the verge of total collapse. Bloom's, on the other hand, seems very close to articulate consciousness: it is almost as if he were talking to himself, and one feels that at any moment he could break into speech. Moreover, his fitful speculations are direct responses to an external stimulus (the sight of a bat), set off, as they are throughout Bloomsday, by "the now, the here" of June 16, 1904. Admittedly, Quentin's stream of consciousness is likewise prompted by present perceptions and actions, but the latter function primarily as memory-triggers: with Quentin, the past encloses and engulfs everything. This absolute primacy of the past lends his monologue what one might call its *vertical* dimension: every present experience is at once overshadowed and overwhelmed by some analogous experience in the past, so that it appears as a *metaphorical* re-presentation or psychodramatic reenactment of the past (as can be seen most plainly in the famous fight scene with Gerald Bland), while, conversely, the past tends to turn into a prefiguration or rehearsal of the present (hence the double—past and present, literal and symbolic—meaning of the phrase "seeking water"). In sharp contrast to this verticality, the movement of Bloom's reverie follows a *metonymic* order, gliding, in glib alliteration, from "ba" to "bat," from "bat" to "belfry," from "belfry" to "bell," from "bell" to "mass." In both cases, of course, we are invited to participate in the seemingly haphazard process of "free association," a process based on both similarities and contiguities, yet in Quentin's monologue—at least at this point—the process becomes so involuted that the reader is at a loss—or would be, had he not come to realize what words like "shadow," "sleep," "honeysuckle," or "door" represent in Quentin's private memories and fantasies.

To make sense of this passage from *The Sound and the Fury* it is essential that we bear in mind the section's major leitmotifs. It goes without saying that in *Ulysses* the reader is likewise expected to heed the manifold connotations of the text: "metempsychosis," for instance, refers back to Molly's question about "met him pike hoses" in the "Calypso" section and is indeed one of the many verbal motifs associated with Bloom.[15] Neither is "bat" without symbolic overtones: the word has occurred twice before in the "Nausicaa" chapter; the bat belongs with the chapter's pervasive bird and flight imagery, and might in addition be a sly hint at Bloom's "seduction" by Gerty MacDowell, Victorian virgin and Victorian vamp(ire).[16] Yet even for the casual reader the passage preserves a large measure of intelligibility. As much could not be said of the final pages of Quentin's monologue: if read out of context, they will dissolve into incoherence.

This is not to say that they offer nothing but unrelieved confusion. Like so many paragraphs in the Quentin section, this one also begins with what looks like straightforward first-person narration: "I turned out the light and went into my bedroom." The opening consists of two "kernel clauses" joined by the connective "and." In its stark simplicity, it reminds one of the reduced syntax of Benjy's idiolect in the previous section. Yet this is only the beginning, and we might note that in the next sentence there is no longer coordination between clauses, nor even a comma to make their juxtaposition perceptible: "I stood at the window the curtain moved slow out of the darkness." Furthermore, the clauses are weighted by three loosely appended groups with the typically Faulknerian *-ing* forms ("touching," "breathing," "leaving"). So there is already a shift toward indeterminacy in the second sentence, and the further we get in the text, the more incoherent it becomes (except for the last two lines, which take us back to the beginning, i.e., to the scene of present action). As happens quite often in Quentin's monologue, what began as orderly narration ends in fevered logorrhea.

And the less control Quentin has over his thoughts, the more he yields to the fascination of the past. The shift from present to past is signaled here by the change from roman type to italics: "*After they had gone upstairs.*" A childhood memory wells up (significantly related to the parental couple and to Benjy's "bellowing"), which in turn induces vivid recollections of earlier or later times: the picture in the book, its revealingly contrasted interpretations by Quentin and Caddy (the latter being much more defiant and "manly" in her response); honeysuckle, the haunting symbol of sisterly sex; memories of himself as little boy getting up at night to go to the bathroom; the invisible bodies of his parents and other members of the family before which he would pass in the sleep-filled darkness; the door. With reference to Quentin's imminent suicide, all these disjointed memories become emblematic of his present condition, pointing as they do to his extreme anguish and sense of helpless lostness, most tellingly epitomized by the poignant vision of the children imprisoned in the lightless mother-"dungeon." Quentin is drawn into a nightmare world, an ominous, shadowy world of slumbering shapes that he is afraid to awaken. In his regressive revery he identifies totally with the fearful little boy he has in fact never ceased to be, while in his present actions he attempts to fight off his anxiety by a futile insistence on order.[17]

In reading the first half of the passage, most readers will have difficulty in identifying the time sequences to which the narrative fragments belong. As their succession conforms neither to chrono-logical order nor to the established laws of discursive logic, we must necessarily look for another principle of intelligibility, a principle only to be sought in the assumed functioning, or rather dysfunctioning, of Quentin's neurotic mind. Yet although the fragments are presented in increasingly random fashion, they still form recognizable units of meaning. After "*yet the eyes*," however, the process of dislocation is taken a step further, if not in the narrative of Quentin's actions (which remains fairly easy to follow), then in the italicized record of his mental agitation. To borrow from Roland Barthes's terminology, the text now shifts from the *lisible* (the readable or readerly) to the *scriptible* (what can be written, but not read, at least not in terms of traditional models): to incongruous word-strings, with neither punctuation nor syntactic order. The signifiers still throb with meaning, yet their differential relations have become purely potential. There are predicates and subjects, but as they are all adrift, one hesitates at every turn between several possibilities ("I can see"/"hands can see"; "can see cooling fingers"/"can see invisible swan-throat"). The collapse of syntax is complete; the laws of communicative language no longer obtain. Interpretation then becomes an extremely aleatory business. What shall we make, for example, of the cryptic allusion to Moses' rod? Readers with a knowledge of the Bible will recognize the rod with which Moses smote the rock to bring forth water (Exod. 17:6), and so will account for the scriptural reference in terms of the water motif. On the other hand, in a section where phallic symbols are aplenty, one might also speculate about the Freudian implications of the magic rod. As Julia Kristeva has suggested,[18] Moses, the archetypal father figure, seems to be here an oblique reminder of the Law or, to put it in Lacanian terms, of the Symbolic Order into which Quentin has failed to enter. Repetition of sounds and words, inversions, displacements, condensations, sexual symbols—it is indeed tempting to read the whole sequence as a dream text about castration, the unconscious equivalent of death. Dissolution of language and dissolution of self appear here as complementary aspects of a single process, in the course of which even the speaking subject vanishes in "the long silence of the throat."

In Bloom's monologue we are obviously in less deep and less troubled waters, waters in which subjectivity is still buoyantly alive. There is no onrush of half-forgotten memories, no unraveling of language and self. Bloom is not the patient of his discourse and, much like Stephen, he brings an active intelligence to bear upon the impressions that come flooding in on him. His alert and nimble mind records motions, shapes, and colors, asks questions, gives tentative answers (often modalized assertions: "probably," "Very likely"), ventures into generalizations and evaluations ("Good idea the repetition"), and assesses its own performances ("My memory's not so bad"). And while Quentin's solipsistic brooding ends in agonized confusion, Bloom's quasi-scientific speculations lead to the slightly comic triumph of a *eureka* ("I have it"). The emphasis here is on perception and cognition rather than affect. However erratic, Bloom's thought processes do not slip altogether out of control; however idiosyncratic, they are not self-enclosed in the dark, devious way Quentin's are and seem to indicate a rather fair balance between inner and outer worlds.

What, then, do the two passages have in common? Both present themselves as direct, immediate renderings of unsorted, unuttered thoughts, without any narrator to mediate between character and reader, and in both the discontinuities and shortcuts of "free association" are suggested by truncated syntax. In other words, both are indeed "interior monologues." But if Joyce and Faulkner use the same literary convention, they use it in strikingly different ways. With Joyce, interior monologue, as exemplified by Bloom's speech, functions as a kind of mental shorthand, and as soon as we have grown familiar with its elliptical code, its difficulties can be mastered without too much effort. Faulkner, on the contrary, seems more concerned with extreme states of mind, seems to pay more attention to the "primary processes" of the unconscious, and so takes language to the critical point where it falls apart. It would be utterly mistaken, however, to infer from these observations that in *The Sound and the Fury* the technique of stream of consciousness is used more daringly than in *Ulysses*. For it would have been quite easy to switch comments if other passages had been retained for comparison. In *The Sound and the Fury*, especially in the Jason section, one could easily find passages of interior monologue very similar in texture to what we have discovered in the fragment of Bloom's speech. Conversely, in *Ulysses*, whenever a character's deeper desires and anxieties are involved, interior monologue moves toward the kind of throbbing opacity that characterizes so much of the Quentin section. Consider, for example, the following passage at the close of the "Nausicaa" chapter:

> O sweety all your little girlwhite up I saw dirty bracegirdle made me do love sticky we two naughty Grace darling she him half past the bed met him pike hoses frillies for Raoul to perfume your wife black hair heave under embon *señorita* young eyes Mulvey plump years dreams return tail end Agendath swoony lovey showed me her next year in drawers return next in her next her next. (P. 382)

With Bloom's dozing off, his monologue turns into the seemingly directionless, alogical language of a dream sequence. It is a far cry from the mild obscenity of Bloom's fetishistic fantasies to the pathos of Quentin's obsessions, yet when it comes to evoking the twilight of consciousness (Bloom falling asleep, Quentin on the threshold of death), the disruptive procedures used by Joyce and Faulkner are surprisingly alike.

To Joyce as well as to Faulkner "interior monologue" was a flexible instrument, adaptable to many functions, and neither used it only in the restrictive sense that equates it with the dubious notion of "stream of consciousness." As can be seen from the two excerpts we have been considering, interior monologue in their fiction covers a wide spectrum of mental processes, ranging from more or less "controlled" thinking to the puzzling arabesques of "free" association, and the verbalization of these processes is accordingly modulated from elliptical but still fairly ordered prose to word arrangements that, apparently, make no sense at all. The phrase "stream of consciousness" refers to the latter, to what are supposed to be the linguistic equivalents of the random flux of spontaneous thought. In *Ulysses* Joyce frequently uses interior monologue, but the final "Penelope" episode, with its eight long unpunctuated "sentences," is in fact the only one in which the effect of stream of consciousness is sustained throughout. As to Faulkner, he resorts to interior monologue in the first three sections of *The Sound and the Fury* and in *As I Lay Dying*, but in these instances too stream of consciousness proper is only used sporadically. The term seems hardly adequate for the Benjy section, a unique verbal construct ruled by conventions of its own, nor does it apply to Jason's speech, which would be more aptly defined as dramatic soliloquy, and the stream of consciousness one finds in Quentin's monologue, though predominant in its final pages (except the very last page, which Faulkner added after he had completed his manuscript), is subtly counterpointed with past-tense, first-person narration and remembered dialogue. In *As I Lay Dying* stream of consciousness effects are likewise limited: they occur only in the sections attributed to Darl, Dewey Dell, and Vardaman, and the extremely fragmented, almost playlike structure of this novel prevents prolonged identification with any of the speakers.

To find "pure" stream of consciousness, we might turn to Edouard Dujardin, but who, apart from the Joyceans, cares to remember Dujardin? *Les Lauriers sont coupés* is a dead novel, as all novels patterned on rigid preconceptions are bound to be. If Joyce and Faulkner were much more successful in their uses of interior monologue, it was because of their capacity to exploit fully the many possibilities it had opened up for fiction, but also because of their skill in combining it with other—innovative and traditional—fictional procedures. Without worrying unduly about purity of method, they used all the tools that were at hand. Their practice as craftsmen had taught them that purity is no virtue for novelists.

Notes

1. *The Sound and the Fury* (New York: Random House, 1946), pp. 191–92.
2. *Ulysses* (New York: Random House, 1961), pp. 377–78. Further references in parentheses in text.
3. "Interview with Jean Stein vanden Heuvel" (1955), in James B. Meriwether and Michael Millgate, eds., *Lion in the Garden: Interviews with William Faulkner 1926–1962* (New York: Random House, 1968), p. 250.
4. See also statements on Joyce in Frederick L. Gwynn and Joseph L. Blotner, eds., *Faulkner in the University: Class Conferences at the University of Virginia, 1957–1958* (Charlottesville, Va.: University Press of Virginia, 1959), pp. 53, 280.
5. Richard P. Adams, "The Apprenticeship of William Faulkner," *Tulane Studies in English* XII (1962): 139.
6. See Michael Millgate, *The Achievement of William Faulkner* (New York: Random House, 1966), p. 15; Joseph Blotner, *Faulkner: A Biography* (New York: Random House, 1974), p. 253.
7. See Henry Nash Smith, "Writing Right Smart Fun, Says Faulkner," *Dallas Morning News*, Feb. 14, 1932, Sec. IV, 2. Repr. in *Lion in the Garden*, p. 30.
8. See *Lion in the Garden*, p. 197.
9. See *James Joyce* (New York: Oxford University Press, 1959), p. 308n.
10. All these pieces have been reprinted in Carvel Collins, ed., *William Faulkner: New Orleans Sketches* (New Brunswick, N.J.: Rutgers University Press, 1958).
11. For specific parallels, see Robert M. Slabey, "Faulkner's 'Mosquitos' and Joyce's 'Ulysses,' " *Revue des Langues Vivantes* XXVIII (Sept.–Oct. 1963): 435–37; Joyce W. Warren, "Faulkner's 'Portrait of the Artist,' " *Mississippi Quarterly* XIX (Summer 1966): 121–31; Cleanth Brooks, *William Faulkner: Toward Yoknapatawpha and Beyond* (New Haven and London: Yale University Press, 1978), pp. 129–51.
12. See *Toward Yoknapatawpha and Beyond*, p. 371.
13. Before reading *Ulysses*, Faulkner may have read T. S. Eliot's discussion of Joyce's method in "Ulysses, Order, and Myth," which had appeared in *The Dial* in November 1923.
14. In the first three sections, but not in the final one, where Faulkner adopts the broader (though not omniscient) point of view of an impersonal narrator.
15. See Richard M. Kain, *Fabulous Voyager: A Study of James Joyce's Ulysses* (New York: Viking Press, 1959), p. 281.
16. As W. Y. Tindall points out, the bat is one of Joyce's recurrent symbols, one he had already used with suggestions of the vampire in one of the love poems of *Chamber Music*. See *James Joyce: His Way of Interpreting the Modern World* (New York: Scribner's, 1950), pp. 117–18.
17. On Quentin's anal compulsion for order, see James C. Cowan, "Dream-work in the Quentin Section of *The Sound and the Fury*," *Literature and Psychology* XXIV, 3 (1974): 97.
18. See *Polylogue* (Paris: Editions du Seuil, 1977), p. 353.

Stephen and Quentin

Nancy Walker

He went out. The door closed. His feet went down the corridor. Then I could hear the watch again. I quit moving around and went to the window and drew the curtains aside and watched them running for chapel, the same ones fighting the same heaving coat-sleeves, the same books and flapping collars flushing past like debris on a flood, and Spoade. Calling Shreve my husband. Ah let him alone, Shreve said, if he's got better sense than to chase after the little dirty sluts, whose business. In the South you are ashamed of being a virgin. Boys. Men. They lie about it. Because it means less to women, Father said. He said it was men invented virginity not women. Father said it's like death: only a state in which the others are left and I said, But to believe it doesn't matter and he said, That's what's so sad about anything: not only virginity, and I said, Why couldn't it have been me and not her who is unvirgin and he said, That's why that's sad too; nothing is even worth the changing of it, and Shreve said if he's got better sense than to chase after the little dirty sluts and I said Did you ever have a sister? Did you? Did you? (*The Sound and the Fury* [New York: Modern Library, 1946], pp. 97–98.)

He had come nearer the edge of the sea and wet sand slapped his boots. The new air greeted him, harping in wild nerves, wind of wild air of seeds of brightness. Here, I am not walking out to the Kish lightship, am I? He stood suddenly, his feet beginning to sink slowly in the quaking soil. Turn back.

Turning, he scanned the shore south, his feet sinking again slowly in new sockets. The cold domed room of the tower waits. Through the barbicans the shafts of light are moving ever, slowly ever as my feet are sinking, creeping duskward over the dial floor. Blue dusk, nightfall, deep blue night. In the darkness of the dome they wait, their pushedback chairs, my obelisk valise, around a board of abandoned platters. Who to clear it? He has the key. I will not sleep there when this night comes. A shut door of a silent tower entombing their blind bodies, the panthersahib and his pointer. Call: no answer. He lifted his feet up from the suck and turned back by the mole of boulders. Take all, keep all. My soul walks with me, form of forms. So in the moon's midwatches I pace the path above the rocks, in sable silvered, hearing Elsinore's tempting flood.

The flood is following me. I can watch it flow past from here. Get back then by the Poolbeg road to the strand there. He climbed over the sedge and eely oarweeds and sat on a stool of rock, resting his ashplant in a grike. (*Ulysses* [New York: Random House, 1961], p. 44.)

The task of tracing the influence of one author upon another is a frustrating and tentative one at best. The works of James Joyce and William Faulkner do share some stylistic similarities, and it has been well established that Faulkner knew Joyce's works and admired them. However, the two authors had very different concerns and employed different stylistic techniques, and a comparison between these two passages, one from the second chapter of *The Sound and the Fury* and the other from the third chapter ("Proteus") of *Ulysses*, serves primarily to convince the reader of how well each author adapted style to the demands of subject matter.

Both Faulkner and Joyce are concerned in these passages with presenting characters in moments of particular stress, and both, of course, are adept at rendering that stress in a way that allows the reader to enter a complicated emotional world. However, that entry is difficult—more so in the passage from *Ulysses* than in that from *The Sound and the Fury*—because of the privacy of the characters' emotional states and the referential nature of their thoughts. Both passages begin in a standard third-person narrative style with the first-person narrator (Quentin and Stephen, respectively) entering quickly to establish the controlling consciousness. The first part of each passage is descriptive, placing Quentin at the window of his room in Cambridge and Stephen at the seashore.

One reference in both passages is clear and universal, and that is the "flood" image. Quentin sees his fellow students going by his window as "debris on a flood," and Stephen, on the edge of the sea, speaks of "Elsinore's tempting flood." Faulkner frequently uses water in the traditional sense to represent rebirth, regeneration, sexuality. And it is this last reference which has particular meaning for Quentin. Water appears in many contexts in *The Sound and the Fury*, but it is always connected somehow to Caddy and her sexuality—from Benjy's elemental conection, "Caddy. Water," to Quentin's washing the mud from Caddy's drawers, and ultimately to Quentin's suicide by drowning, at once a denial of and a submersion in sexuality.

However, for Faulkner, the concept of a flood goes beyond ordinary literary associations with water. The flood is chaos, uncontrolled and threatening. It is also associated with women, as Faulkner demonstrates most overtly in *Old Man*, in which the young convict is forced by the Mississippi River flood of 1927 to rescue and travel with a woman, a pregnant woman at that, who reminds him of a world that has betrayed him. In a similar way, Quentin's woman, Caddy, has betrayed him by losing her virginity, and when he sees the "flood" of his classmates going by he thinks of another uncontrollable element in his life: Spoade, who has called Shreve his (Quentin's) "husband" in mockery of their friendship. This reminds Quentin of Shreve's remark about "little dirty sluts," which sets off another in a series of reminiscences of conversations between Quentin and his father about virginity, most of which follows a rather straightforward "I said, Father said" format. The sequence of thoughts, in other words, is logical, given our knowledge of prior events.

Stephen is confronted by water in much the same way in the passage from chapter 3 of *Ulysses*. The first part is almost pure narrative, in which Stephen nears the sea, his feet begin to sink in the mud, and he retreats. The sea—water—here is not so much chaos as trap, the sucking of the mud at Stephen's boots, in the same way that the tower is a trap to which he will not return. Water, here identified as "Elsinore's tempting flood," is as inexorable a force as Quentin's flood, reaching and tempting, but ultimately destructive and threatening.

The other dominant image is time. Quentin is preoccupied with watches, clocks, all symbols of time, because he wants to stop time, to turn back the clock, to undo the past. Because he cannot do this in life, he chooses to stop his own time by stopping his own life. Stephen, too, on Sandymount strand, is preoccupied with the passage of time, and he imagines the "shafts of light" moving over the "dial floor" toward evening—an evening he had determined not to spend in the tower.

In the use of dominant imagery, then, revealing the emotional states of their characters, Faulkner and Joyce use quite similar and traditional techniques. But in terms of more specific stylistic devices, the two passages are far more striking for their differences than for their similarities. Faulkner's technique might be described as "cinematic," flashing one conversational confrontation after another before the reader's mind, whereas Joyce's style is more purely stream of consciousness, featuring highly allusive language and unidentified pronoun references, a style that might be called "literary."

Faulkner uses an almost pure first-person narrative, with Quentin replaying "tapes" of past conversations in his head. Joyce uses a more complex technique, with an alternation of speakers. Joyce's "fluid succession of presents" involves faster, more subtle shifts from one reference point to another than does Faulkner's passage, and the language becomes that of dream or nightmare rather than Quentin's obsessive memories. Quentin and Stephen are both haunted young men, but Quentin is haunted by the past, so that there is really no present, and certainly no future for him, whereas Stephen is plagued by several present realities and is constantly aware of the flood of time that is his future.

Faulkner uses interior monologue in the passage from *The Sound and the Fury*. Quentin is talking to himself, replaying conversations with Spoade, Shreve, and his father, all on the subject of virginity and sisters. The reader has little difficulty determining who the speaker is at any point, because of both the usual conversational signals ("Shreve said, I said") and the common subject matter. The pieces of former conversations are reproduced almost exactly as they were originally stated, most in complete sentences. The gaps that the reader must fill in are those of time: what Shreve said in the recent past and what Quentin's father said in the more distant past—and in a different place—are all one past to Quentin, and that past is his only reality.

Joyce, in "Proteus," more nearly approaches stream of consciousness, though not so nearly as he does later in the novel. Stephen is talking to himself, as is Quentin, but there are two important differences. One is the intrusion of apparently random images, such as "Blue dusk" and "A shut door of a silent tower," which are not immediately related to the sequence of the monologue. Whereas Quentin's is a single-track mind, Stephen's is shown to be ranging from past to future, from fantasy to reality, in a sequence determined only by the wanderings of his mind. Second, the narrative voice continually shifts from third person ("He had come nearer the edge of the sea") to first person ("Here, I am not walking out to the Kish lightship, am I?") and even to second person ("Turn back") as the narrative enters and leaves Stephen's persepective.

Finally, there are linguistic differences between the two passages. Faulkner's language here is conversational, even colloquial ("if he's got better sense than to chase after the little dirty sluts"). The references are internal, that is, to events and concerns within the novel itself: Spoade's remark about Quentin and Shreve, Caddy's loss of virginity, Quentin's frustration with a world that seems to take lightly what is so vitally important to him. Quentin cannot see or imagine, at this moment, beyond his own obsessions; he has no future, only a past.

In the passage from "Proteus," however, Joyce reinforces Stephen's own dramatic sense of himself by using an elevated diction and rather stately sentence structure, as in, "I will not sleep there when this night comes." In part this is a reproduction of Irish syntax; in part it is Stephen's self-mocking irony, his sense of himself as an actor in a tragicomedy, which is heightened by the Shakespearean references: "So in the morn's midwatches I pace the path above the rocks, in sable silvered, hearing Elsinore's tempting flood." That this is a fantasy, an actor on a stage, is underscored by the reader's knowledge that the scene takes place at 11:00 in the morning and our understanding that Stephen is imagining that it is night because he has determined not to sleep in the tower and does not know where he will spend the night. Whereas Quentin cannot think beyond the moment, Stephen is trying in these early chapters of *Ulysses* to plan his future and is able to see his situation with some humor and dramatic flair, to achieve some distance from himself.

Both Joyce and Faulkner attempted with some considerable success to present the thoughts and emotions of characters with little structuring or interference by traditional narrative technique. A comparison of fragments from each author's work is obviously insufficient to produce a definitive statement, but on the basis of these two passages we can begin to see the ways in which narrative technique can be manipulated to reveal character.

PART V

Dubliners as "Looking-Glass":
Reality or Illusion

A Book of Signs and Symbols:
The Protagonist

Florence L. Walzl

For a generation Joyce scholars have been greatly concerned with the nature of words and images and their possible symbolism in the *Dubliners* stories. Numerous studies have confirmed Fritz Senn's statement that in *Dubliners* Joyce wrote in a "most complex, heavily allusive style," different only in degree from the "later convoluted intricacies of *Ulysses* and *Finnegans Wake*," and that from the beginning he "seemed incapable of using words in one single bare sense only."[1] For example, there are now over one hundred studies analyzing individual *Dubliners* stories. In these explications it is common to find major images of the tales treated as metaphors carrying literary, historical, or psychological overtones. Moreover, in various thematic-structural studies of *Dubliners* as a collection of fifteen linked stories—an approach pioneered by Brewster Ghiselin's extraordinary article on "The Unity of Joyce's *Dubliners*" in *Accent* in 1956[2]—there is confirmation of the use of such recurrent motifs as movement-stasis, presence-absence, and vitality-inanition, and of repeated effects of light-dark, warmth-cold, and water-sterility in unmistakable life-death connotations. Patterns of directions, colors, designs, and shapes, of virtues and vices, and of certain historical, literary, and religious allusions are also evident. Finally, recent studies of the three terms "paralysis," "gnomon," and "simony," which Joyce inserted into the opening of the final version of "The Sisters," the initial story of *Dubliners*, indicate that these were added to project emblematically three main themes of the book, paralysis—the inability of the characters to act meaningfully; the gnomon—their stunted development and incompleteness as individuals; and simony—their selling of themselves and others for mercenary reasons. The great weight of this evidence supports the view that the ultimate meaning of the *Dubliners* collection depends significantly on a unitary stylistic level, which exemplifies the central ideas of the book in various images, symbols, and even verbal ambiguities.

One aspect of *Dubliners* that has had much less critical attention is the nature of the "protagonist." Though each tale has a different main charac-

117

ter, essentially all seem to be variants of a central everyman figure. My aim is to identify this figure and make observations about its origin. I believe this "protagonist" is a composite figure deriving from classical and Christian archetypes and also reflecting Celtic myth and Irish nationalism. Since such an approach is comprehensive, in this study I will discuss chiefly the Christian prototypes.

Two suppositions: Since Dublin is the subject of this book, it seems valid to begin by saying that the protagonist is the Dubliner; moreover, since Joyce himself stated that in this "moral history" of the Irish people he was grouping the stories in four stages, "childhood, adolescence, maturity and public life," one can presume also that an implicit life history is at the center of the book. Technically, Joyce went to a great deal of trouble to incorporate such a concept into the structure of *Dubliners*. For example, in the first eleven chronological stories, every main character—with one exception in "A Little Cloud"—is either specifically or inferentially made older than the one in the previous tale.[3] Also there is extraordinary patterning within the story groups that suggests the presence of a universal central figure. For instance, the three boys of the tales of childhood, all orphans, are made isolated figures seeking meaning and values in three common crises of early life; in short, they seem a type. The two quartets of tales of adolescence and maturity alternate female and male central characters in paired stories involving life choices and their effects. Each of the four final stories dealing with public life depicts the individual reactions of a member of a cohesive Irish cultural group. Throughout all these stories, details of plot and characterization oppose contrasting and complementary characters in like and unlike situations. The effect is a projection of universal man and of the human condition—despite the distinctively Irish settings and the naturalistic style.

Beyond the realistic fictional level of this Dublin everyman loom figures of larger dimensions. The protagonist of *Dubliners* is essentially mythic. Of the greatest importance thematically is Joyce's evocation of Christian archetypes—great shadowy background figures on Joyce's fictional stage, against which his modern men and women play out their roles. Such an approach to character and situation is very old in the literature of Western Europe. Its origins are in the medieval concept of Biblical exegesis, which looked at characters and events of the Old Testament as foreshadowing Christ and his career. In this concept there were four well-recognized levels of interpretation: the first, a literal level of interpretation; the other three, symbolic or allegorical.

On the first, *literal* level, the event of Old Testament history was regarded as historical actuality and was interpreted realistically. A second level was the *typological* level, in which some personage of this Old Testament event was seen as foreshadowing Christ in his actions. For example, Melchisedech in his sacrifice of bread and wine was viewed as prefiguring Christ at the Last Supper. Another level was *tropological* or moral level, involving specific choices of virtues or vices and other matters of Christian doctrine. The final level was the *anagogical* or mystical: a foreshadowing of the union of God with the beatified members of his church at the end of time, often in an apocalyptic setting.

It is a commonplace that this exegetical scheme had a profound influence on the work of English Renaissance writers, particularly Spenser's *The Faerie Queene* in the sixteenth century and John Bunyan's *Pilgrim's Progress* in the seventeenth century. In fact, Book I of *The Faerie Queene* reflects these four levels obviously. At the literal, fictional level the Red Cross Knight is a knight on a quest for his lady. At the moral, tropological level he is holiness, who must meet and defeat all the seven deadly sins, and eventually be united with truth. He is also a recognizable type of Christ, and his great three-day battle with the dragon (Satan) is his crucifixion. At the end his betrothal to Una, the one true faith, represents the mystical marriage of Christ to his Church and foreshadows the blessed end of the world for the Redeemed. There is also a political level of allegory, for the Red Cross Knight is also St. George, the patron saint of England, and a century of Tudor history is presented in disguised form. Joyce too was to complicate his typology by introducing Irish national figures. However, the great influence on Joyce in the use of this approach to character is overridingly Dante.

Such a multileveled view of human action was intensified in Joyce by his admiration for Dante and close study of the *Divine Comedy*. In a prefatory letter Dante explained how his epic should be read, defining in detail a first "literal" meaning and three others termed "allegorical or mystical."[4] Joyce demonstrated that he understood the Dantean structure well, when in 1905 he wrote "Grace," the story that at that date he expected to be the climactic ending of *Dubliners*. He modelled it on the three parts of the *Divine Comedy*, *Inferno*, *Purgatorio*, and *Paradiso*. Perhaps not so well realized is the fact that the four levels of allegorical interpretation of the action were also adhered to, as Father Robert Boyle showed graphically in 1969 in an article published in the *James Joyce Quarterly*.[5] It is very significant that in this important story Joyce used Dante's structures, but equally significant that he changed the thematic approach. Joyce's method is parody. Mr. Kernan's *Inferno* is a drunkard's fall down a lavatory stairs; his *Purgatorio* is his reluctant consent to make a retreat; and his *Paradiso* is his attendance at the retreat, where a sorry group of businessmen—politicians, pawnbrokers, and pubkeepers— listen to a sermon by a materialistic priest on the cash register values of Christian virtue. Joyce parodies the Dantean structure, satirizes the action, and offers ironic inversions of the characters and themes. Thus "Grace" offers one key to Joyce's method in handling his protagonists: ironic parallels and contrasts.

It should be emphasized, however, that in pietistic Catholic Ireland one did not need to be a reader of Dante to have some sense of the vast scale of man's spiritual pilgrimage. This view of cosmic history so pervaded religious thinking for centuries that a set of Christian commonplaces developed for the everyday man. Each Christian must be a type of Christ in himself, must make a deliberate choice of virtue, and must carry his cross. Girls were to emulate the Virgin Mary or virgin saints, and families were to look to the Holy Family of Nazareth as models. Above this earthly hierarchy were the angels and God the Father united with the Son and Holy Spirit in the Trinity. The devout Christian was accustomed to compare himself to prototypes of virtue, which he should emulate, and of evil, which he should abhor. That is the way the *Dubliners* characters think of themselves and the way Joyce often presents them. But in this "looking-glass" Joyce holds up to the Irish people, the image is often ironic and satiric.

Some examples. In "The Boarding House," Polly Mooney connives with her formidable mother to trap a reluctant suitor into matrimony—even if Polly must plead a pregnancy. In the story she is called a "little perverse madonna," and there is repeated confessional and reparation imagery throughout. In the story "Eveline," a young girl contemplates elopement overseas with a sailor in order to escape her life of loveless drudgery. As she tries to decide, she glances at a picture of the Sacred Heart revealing His promises to St. Margaret Mary Alacoque. Eveline's motives contrast ironically with this image of divine love and sacrifice, and the fact that St. Margaret Mary was a paralyzed nun foreshadows Eveline's own psychological paralysis at the gangplank. Her name signifies "little Eve," and it evokes a typal figure of temptation.

In "Clay," the story of a little old spinster, the narrative modulates between Maria as a Virgin Mary figure—a "peacemaker" and loving "mother" to those she works with—and the figure of a Celtic witch in her physcial appearance and troublemaking. In "Two Gallants," a story dealing with the seduction of a servant girl, the betrayal of Christ is reenacted by Corley, who is called "conqueror" and "master" and who delivers "final judgments." His passive partner in the seduction, Lenehan, is described as his "disciple." The ironic inversion of Scripture is unmistakable when Corley holds up the gold coin he has extracted from the girl. The girl herself combines Christian and nationalistic types. She wears blue, the Virgin's colors, but as a slavey in a rich man's house, she recalls the legendary Cathleen ni Houlihan, the figure of Ireland, serving her English conquerors and betrayers. She is also associated with a harp, the emblem of Ireland, on which patriotic tunes are played, but significantly it is a harp whose "coverings" have "fallen" and that seems "weary alike of the eyes of strangers and of her master's hands." These few instances can only suggest the richness of the archetypal groups and ironic parallels.

This everyman approach to the characters affected greatly the handling of the father figures in *Dubliners* and established the complex concept of fatherhood that appears in all of Joyce's later works. At the literal level of the fiction, fathers or surrogate fathers most often tend to be blustering, drunken authoritarians who quickly turn to violence when crossed. Less often they are timid ineffectuals who bow to domineering wives and mothers. Then there is the gallery of Joyce's priestly fathers, infirm, venal, hypocritical, paretic, or mad. With them is associated a set of sacramental symbols related to the powers of the priesthood. There are also the father figures for the nation, notably Parnell. Finally there is the ultimate prototype of God the Father, both hangman God and loving Creator, both Blake's Nobodaddy and Celestial Wisdom.

For example, all the stories of childhood are pilgrimage-quest narratives, in which boys seek father figures to give meaning and reality to their lives. But the quests all end in disillusionment. The little boy of "The Sisters" seeks faith and authority from a dying priest, but at his wake he finds only defect and emptiness in the priest's life and death. The boy of "An Encounter" at the end of his day of quest for "real adventures" meets a psychotic pederast from whom he must flee as for his life. The conclusions of the paired stories of maturity, "A Little Cloud" and "Counterparts," contrast fathers and sons as religious archetypes. As Little Chandler tries to soothe his screaming baby and his angry wife glares at her ineffectual husband, the child, already a source of contention, is called "lambabaun . . . little lamb of the world." This Christ-child image climaxes the ironic inversion of the Holy Family. In "Counterparts" Farrington, a frustrated, drunken father, arrives home late after an evening of pubcrawling and beats his little son. The tableau of the furious father raining blows on the hapless child who is kneeling and praying a *Hail Mary* for him is a savage God-the-Father and Son irony.

Because Joyce aimed at his book's being a "moral history" of Ireland, it was essential also that he he should have a nationalistic level throughout, presenting life as it molds Dublin youth and offering also a cross-section of the society in its various cultural aspects. One argument that *Dubliners* is truly a realistic "looking-glass" for the Irish people is based on his sociological sketches of Dublin life. Yet there are problems and conflicts between the naturalistic and the analogical levels. For example, in "Two Gallants" one must ask who are the betrayers and who the betrayed. The story is a chain of betrayal. The slavey seduced and cheated may in turn be cheating her employer. Corley, the master and lord, is also the Judas. At the end of "Ivy Day in the Committee Room," when Hynes, the only man who has been faithful to the memory of Parnell, recites his sentimental poem on Parnell's death—a poem full of martyr-crucifixion images—one wonders if Joyce intended the ending to be serious or to be bitterly satiric of Ireland's bombastic patriotism and long history of political betrayals.

One thing seems clear. The protagonist in *Dubliners* is an everyman figure: child, youth, or adult, he stands firmly in Joyce's Dublin hierarchy. If "Grace" had ended *Dubliners*, as Joyce originally intended, the book would have concluded with an impression of social realism. But that is not the final impression, for the book ends with "The Dead," a story written later and one of larger scope. True, it has a picture of a party that is a cross-section of Dublin provinciality, but its conclusion looks at the nature of being from a broader view. Traditionally works such as Dante's, presenting multileveled, cosmic views of mankind, tend to have a messianic climax, a scene of the righteous at the end of time. I suggest *Dubliners* has such a conclusion in Gabriel Conroy's vision of the cemetery, where snow falls "like the descent of their last end, upon all the living and the dead." In this vision central motifs reappear, and the archetypes that have haunted the background of the book emerge more perceptibly.

"The Dead" is both a study of a dead society and of the one man who realizes that fact about his culture and himself. He is caught, paralyzed in the prison of self and society. Even Michael Furey, his rival for his wife Gretta's tenderest emotion, is dead—a ghost. But Michael is a ghost that lives vibrantly in Gretta's consciousness as her living husband does not, because he was willing to die for love. The main themes—the need for escape, the necessity of sacrifice that liberation entails, and the importance of understanding—all find expression in the final vision. Archetypal figures representative of sacrificial love also cluster in the vision. The two rivals are namesakes of great archangels: St. Gabriel is the angel of Annunciation, in the Old Testament to Daniel and in the New Testament to Mary and Elizabeth, and St. Michael is the guardian angel of the Last Judgment. For Gretta the greatest moment of realization in her life is the memory of Michael come from his sickbed to say farewell to her, and standing in the cold under a tree in a garden. "I think he died for me," Gretta tells Gabriel. In this evocation, the young Irish lover, St. Michael the Commanding Angel of the Final Judgment, and Christ, who died for all on the tree of the Cross, all merge—and with them merges also a remembered hero from Yeats's *Cathleen ni Houlihan*. In this play the Poor Old Woman who is Cathleen (Ireland) in disguise speaks of one of the many martyrs for Ireland's freedom. "He died for love of me," she concluded. All the archetypes unite in this symbology of sacrificial love.

In contrast, Gabriel's great moment of epiphany is his personal vision of the cemetery in Oughterard. There the snow is falling upon "the lonely churchyard on the hill where Michael Furey lay buried. It lay thickly drifted on the crooked crosses and headstones, on the spears of the little gate, on the barren thorns"—*crosses*, *spears*, and *thorns* are all evocations of Christ's sacrifice. This moment of epiphanic insight is the climax of the story and the book, and its reality is that of an individual consciousness. But the final sentence of *Dubliners* takes us from this rational reality to dream consciousness: Gabriel's "soul swooned slowly as he heard the snow falling faintly through the universe and faintly falling, like the descent of their last end, upon all the living and the dead." Is Gabriel's swoon an acceptance of death or is it the prelude to a new life—a realization that one must die to live? The question of quintessential reality or illusion remains unanswered in this conclusion.

Notes

1. "'He Was Too Scrupulous Always': Joyce's 'The Sisters,'" *JJQ* 2 (Winter 1965): 66.

2. See *Accent* (Spring–Summer 1956), pp. 76–78 and 207–12.

3. The age patterns in Joyce's four life spans are adopted from Roman typology. See my article "The Life Chronology of *Dubliners*," *JJQ* 14 (Summer 1977): 408–15.

4. As quoted in the "Introduction," *The Comedy of Dante Alighieri*, trans. Dorothy L. Sayers (New York: Basic Books, 1962), Vol. I, pp. 14–15.

5. "Swiftian Allegory and Dantean Parody in Joyce's 'Grace,'" *JJQ* 7 (Fall 1969): 11–19.

The Dantean Design of Joyce's *Dubliners*

Mary T. Reynolds

The early critics of *Dubliners* saw the book as an example of realism, and the stories as typically *tranche de vie* writing. Gradually, however, it becomes clear that Joyce, as John Kelleher says, "may have regarded the surface story with an even more uncompromising realism than his critics have allowed," at the same time that he created successive levels of meaning by insistent symbolism. *Dubliners* was the first of Joyce's books to carry a suggestion of Dantean structure. The stories were written in the mood and manner of Dante's abrasive denunciations of faction-ridden Florence, the city Dante describes as "piena d'invidia," "full of envy" and every sort of iniquity. "Rejoice, O Florence," says Dante in the canto on Ulysses (*Inferno* 26), "in being so great that thy name resounds throughout Hell" (*Inf.* 26:1–3, trans. Singleton). Joyce's term "paralysis" is his metaphor for the "static lifelessness of unrelieved viciousness" that Samuel Beckett, writing under Joyce's inspiration, describes as the essence of Dante's Hell.[1] *Dubliners* became Joyce's version of Dante's *Inferno*.

When Joyce sent the manuscript to Grant Richards in late November 1905, the first story, "The Sisters," was still in the form of its first publication in a Dublin paper edited by George Russell ("AE"), *The Irish Homestead*. But in the published version, as Jackson Cope discovered, the first story opens with the words that Dante set above the gate of Hell in *Inferno* 3: "There was no hope." Moreover, the final story, "The Dead," concludes with a vision of a frozen Ireland, a reminiscence of Dante's image of that frozen world "where the shades were wholly covered" ("la dove l'ombre tutte eran coperte"), from the final canto of the *Inferno* (34:11).[2] The book's last sentence and its first sentence were written, as Professor Cope comments, in deliberate emulation of the *Divine Comedy*. The closing sentence of "The Dead" recalls frozen Cocytus, Dante's last image of despair: "His soul swooned slowly as he heard the snow falling faintly through the universe and faintly falling, like the descent of their last end, upon all the living and the dead" (*D* 224). From *Dubliners* on, each of Joyce's works would carry a Dantean pattern.

The first of the *Dubliners* stories to be written were the three published in Russell's *Irish Homestead*: "The Sisters" in its first version, "Eveline," and

"After the Race." The revision of "The Sisters" came very much later. Whatever Dantesque implications we find in the themes and arrangement of the stories must reckon with the belatedness of that revision, which made the theme of simony the central focus of the book as a whole. The fourth story was "Hallow Eve," for which no manuscript has been found except in the final form as "Clay." However, there was an earlier form of this story for which we do have the manuscript fragment that indicates the story's central focus to be a family gathering at holiday time. The discarded story carried the title "Christmas Eve." The first appearance of a Dantesque pattern in *Dubliners* is—whether by deliberate design or by a chance inspiration later amplified—in this change. Joyce discarded Christmas and gave his new story the ambiance of Halloween, thus introducing a fortune-telling motif that reflects Dante's *Inferno* 20, the canto of the soothsayers. The parallel is present not only in the predicting of future events in "Clay" but also in the witchlike appearance of Maria, which clearly owes something to the presence of another virgin in *Inferno* 20, the prophetess Manto, "la vergine cruda" (*Inf.* 20:82). Joyce took a new direction, it is now clear, with the writing of the fifth and sixth stories. Thereafter he wrote very fast, and brought the collection to its first-stage conclusion by December 4, when the complete manuscript was first sent to Grant Richards.[3]

It seems, however, that the Dantean conception as such—the realization that his stories put together might form a narrative pattern similar to the scheme that makes Dante's *Inferno* a drama of passion and action, shaped as a moral critique of society—first entered his mind as early as March 1905. This was the month in which he finished chapter 18 of *Stephen Hero*. As originally written this chapter began with an episode deliberately constructed as a detailed parallel to *Inferno* 15, a parody of Dante's portrayal of Brunetto Latini. This has been thought of as a separate chapter, having been so labeled by Theodore Spencer because of a misinterpretation of Joyce's markings in the manuscript at MS pages 609 and 610.[4] Joyce at this time apparently intended to use his pastiche of *Inferno* 15 as an episode in the final chapter of the revised *Portrait of the Artist*. At some time after 1907, and probably closer to 1911–12, he wrote in red crayon at the bottom of the page, obscuring four lines of his manuscript, "End of second Episode of V." (He also added the four lines to the margin of the next page, writing "Chapter XVIII" at the top of the page.) Thus when he says he has finished chapter 18, in a letter of March 15, 1905,[5] Joyce is referring to a much longer piece of work. Significantly, this was a chapter of *Stephen Hero* that dealt with Dante and Aquinas, and it described a work, a critique of society, to be written by Stephen Daedalus. The terms used fit both the *Inferno* and *Dubliners*.

It is thus possible to say with confidence that Joyce's symbolic mode, which appeared in published form for the first time in *Dubliners*, must be recognized as an aesthetic decision closely connected with his judgment in favor of a Dantean matrix. When the titles are set in parallel columns showing both the order Joyce assigned to the stories in the book and the order of their composition, a new light is thrown on the last six stories Joyce wrote for the book. They are, in order: "Araby," "Grace," "Two Gallants," "A Little Cloud," "The Dead," and finally the massive revision of "The Sisters." These are the stories most plainly and specifically associated with cantos of Dante's *Inferno*, although each of the fifteen stories has its Dantean counterpart.

Another set of parallel columns, showing the order in which Dante placed sins and sinners in his *Inferno*, will allow the titles of the *Dubliners* stories to be arranged to show the Dantean moral order of Joyce's book. It is not Dante's precise order, but it shows a very close "fit" of the stories to the stages in his moral hierarchy. The result is a catalog of moral death, every story in *Dubliners* being matched with an episode in the *Inferno* either by subject matter or incident.

Let us examine this Dantean order of the stories. Joyce specifically described his ordering principle as a chronology from childhood to "public life." There is in "Araby," the third story, a strong reminiscence of Dante's *Vita Nuova*; the story thus becomes preeminently a little narrative of love, and its position at such an early stage in the book is surely related to the comparable position of the immortal Francesca in Dante's great love story in *Inferno* 5. Eveline, the heroine of the fourth story, is an indecisive character incapable of making a positive decision; she thus would fit the lukewarm sluggard who made the great refusal, "il gran rifuto," and was thereby condemend forever to the vestibule of Hell in Canto 3. An example of prodigal waste, which Dante the pilgrim saw paired with avarice in *Inferno* 7, is found in Joyce's fifth story, "After the Race."

The story "Counterparts" is Joyce's equivalent of *Inferno* 8, the canto that depicts Dante's Fifth Circle and its wrathful sinners. Farrington is the epitome of the violent man: "A spasm of rage gripped his throat," "His heart swelled with fury," "His fury nearly choked him." At the end of the tale we find that "he jumped up furiously," seized a walking stick, and beat his child, "striking at him viciously" (*D* 87, 97, 98). No one is killed, but in his raging frenzy Farrington would also qualify for the Seventh Circle of the murderers, *Inferno* 12:49.

The mortal crime of suicide, punished in *Inferno* 13, has its turn in "A Painful Case." Sodomy, the matter of Dante's fourteenth and fifteenth cantos, is the subject of "An Encounter." With "The Boarding House," which was the first story written as an element in the Dantean pattern, we enter Joyce's equivalent of Malebolge, that vast expanse of hell where the fraudulent are found. Mrs. Mooney, the "Madam" who "deals with moral problems as a cleaver deals with meat" (*D* 63), is quite clearly one of the panders of *Inferno* 18. In "Two Gallants" the seducers of *Inferno* 18 are seen in action, and the pairing of Joyce's two stories in the sequence of *Dubliners* seems to be an intentional reflection of Dante's linking of these two groups of sinners.

The simoniacs of *Inferno* 19 are represented in *Dubliners* by two stories, first in the new version of "The Sisters," with its explicit and fearful vision of the simoniac priest enticing the young boy into "some pleasant and vicious region" (*D* 11). The story "Grace" is Joyce's classic portrayal of simony. It is a dramatic and unambiguous statement of the Irish clergy's exchange of spiritual benefits for worldliness and gain.

As we have noted, the story of Maria, the heroine of "Clay," turns on fortune-telling, a parallel to Dante's description of the soothsayers in Canto 20. "Ivy Day in the Committee Room" deals with grafters, the Dublin ward heelers whose corrupt maneuvers are the equivalent of the evil for which the barrators are punished in *Inferno* 21.

The eighth story, "A Little Cloud," takes its title from *Inferno* 26:39: "si come nuvoletta." This is Dante's simile of the little cloud, by which he describes the flame hiding Ulysses and other false counselors found in this region of hell. Ignatius Gallaher, whose fraudulence is stressed and whose bad counsel has helped to damage the life of Little Chandler, is described as similarly hidden, "emerging after some time from the clouds of smoke in which he had taken refuge" (*D* 78). The story of Gallaher, suitably adjusted by Joyce, resembles a capsule history of the protagonist of *Inferno* 26: "Of course he did mix with a rakish set of fellows at that time, drank freely and borrowed money on all sides. In the end he had got mixed up in some shady affair, some money transaction: *at least that was one version of his flight*" (italics mine). The last words remind the reader that Dante in this canto invented a new version of the story of Ulysses. This was a sequel to the Homeric account, a last voyage that Dante describes as a "mad flight," "il folle volo," in *Inferno* 26:125, and then again as "il varco folle," "the mad flight," in *Paradiso* 27:82.

The thirteenth of Joyce's stories, "A Mother," shows the disruption created by the greedy Mrs. Kearney. Her quarrelsome nature makes her a classic example of the fomenters of discord whom Dante placed in *Inferno* 28.

The last story of *Dubliners*, "The Dead," has its correlative in the final cantos of the *Inferno*, where we find the traitors buried in the eternal cold of frozen Cocytus. Dante shows us examples of traitors to family, traitors to guests, traitors to benefactors, traitors to their country: all aspects of betrayal that can be found in the thoughts and actions of the protagonist of

"The Dead," Gabriel Conroy. Joyce's setting, a Christmas feast, makes play with food as dramatically as Dante's tale of Ugolino portrays starvation, thus suggesting an ironical inversion of *Inferno* 33. The central figure at the feast is Gabriel, and Gabriel is punished, in the final incident with his wife that climaxes the story, as a reprisal for having sinned against his kinfolk and his country.[6] The story, as John Kelleher has shown, is a ghost story. Gabriel ridicules his middle-class forefathers, to whom he owes his education and his present position as a well-to-do Catholic teacher in Protestant-dominated Ireland; they punish him for his unthinking temerity. He denies his country: "Well, said Gabriel, if it comes to that, you know, Irish is not my language" (*D* 189). When baited by one of the guests, Miss Ivors, he retorts in a similar vein but even more strongly: "O, to tell you the truth . . . I'm sick of my own country, sick of it!" As these indiscretions continue and multiply, Gabriel makes a disrespectful salute to the statue of Daniel O'Connell, who compelled the repeal of the Catholic penal laws. Such a denial of Gabriel's origins is a spiritual betrayal, which is seen also in his contemptuous thoughts of his aunts and his family. Most unforgivable is his disdainful jest about the hard-working ancestor whose starch mill brought the Conroy family to the economic security that Gabriel carelessly takes as his due—the middle-class respectability of a house in the very sanctum of Protestant Ascendancy Dublin, Usher's Island. Gabriel's joking account makes everyone laugh at the old man's horse, plodding round and round the hated statue of King Billy—William of Orange, conqueror at the Battle of the Boyne—just as the subject Irish for so many centuries were forced to trudge and toil in a meaningless round under their masters' rule (*D* 208). Thus, after his humiliating rejection by his wife, we find that Gabriel's soul "swooned slowly" in a vision of himself and all Ireland covered with falling snow.

Joyce has followed Dante in creating a moral structure that is not a precise reflection of Catholic doctrine. Dante used the seven deadly sins as the structure of his Purgatory, but not in his Hell. There are striking omissions from the Dantean list of sins, and his ordering of distinctions in the gravity of moral error, while not in conflict with doctrine, is his own. He considers flattery a graver moral fault than seduction, and simony more serious than either; he gives but little attention to pride and envy. Joyce saw that Dante had taken a moral and philosophical (basically Aristotelian) pattern, rather than a strictly doctrinal pattern or even a purely religious basis for his structure. Both Dante and Joyce see their inferno in the nonsectarian terms with which Father Foster describes the structure of the *Inferno*, "mainly as an outline of *human* evil drawn by human wit" (italics mine).[7] Only the heretics and simoniacs in Dante's hell are "Christian" sinners, in the sense that their transgression implies the standards of a

specifically Christian world—and even here, the chosen heresy is Epi-
cureanism, a form of unbelief that does not necessarily presuppose Christianity.

In some such reading of the *Divine Comedy* Joyce must have found his
warrant for creating his own imaginative pattern and his own hierarchy of
moral depravity. His *Dubliners* comes closest to Dante's *Inferno* in the strong
emphasis that Joyce places on the antisocial quality of injustice in human
malice and fraud. Joyce's idea of *"frode,"* fraud, which is the governing
design of thirteen cantos, is a close reflection of Dante's. Joyce's stories
emphasize malicious injury *to one's fellow man*. A central element of his
design is the dispostion to inflict injustice and injury, which is found
somewhere in every story and is dominant in several.

But Joyce also follows Dante in allowing his narrative skills free rein.
Joyce wishes to call the attention of his city to its moral condition, and to do
this he produces a vigorous play of personality and dramatic action. Hence
the mixture in his stories of good and evil, faults and mere weaknesses,
humor and anger and pathos. They are full of ambiguities, such as the
plight of Maria in "Clay," which is rendered through a fortune-telling game
that is harmless in itself and dangerous only when a whole society falls prey
to superstition.

The fifteen stories are epiphanies of frustration, "broadening from private to public scope," in the words of Harry Levin.[8] Joyce's tripartite
structure presents his city under the aspect of childhood, youth, and
maturity, with three additional stories representing, as he said, "public life"
in Dublin, and ending with the longer novella, "The Dead." Such a
chronological arrangement permits Joyce to suggest, as Dante also does, a
progression from the less culpable forms of moral failure to the most
unregenerate evil. In Joyce's view, the evils of "public life" under Dublin's
institutional masters represented a moral failure far more culpable because
it was unconscious of wrongdoing and quite self-confident. The last four
stories of the book are suffused with complacence. A venal ruling establishment is portrayed throughout the book, operating under clerical guidance
in a simoniacal pattern that becomes increasingly explicit. Dublin life has
become a frozen conformity under this perverted control. This is the angry
vision that issued in Joyce's Dantean arrangement of the stories of *Dubliners*.

Notes

1. Samuel Beckett, "Dante . . . Bruno, Vico . . Joyce," in *Our Exagmination Round
His Factification for Incamination of Work in Progress* (New York: New Directions,
1942), p. 22.

2. Jackson I. Cope, "An Epigraph for *Dubliners*," *James Joyce Quarterly* 7 (1970): 362–64.

3. *The James Joyce Archive* (New York: Garland Publishing Co., 1979), Vol. 4: *Dubliners: A Facsimile of Drafts and Manuscripts*, general editor Michael Groden; preface by Hans Walter Gabler, pp. xxv–xxxi.

4. Ibid., Vol. 8: *The Manuscript of Stephen Hero*, prefaced and edited by Hans Walter Gabler, pp. 239, 241.

5. *Selected Letters of James Joyce*, ed. Richard Ellmann (New York: Viking Press, 1975), p. 58.

6. John V. Kelleher, "Irish History and Mythology in James Joyce's 'The Dead,'" *Review of Politics* 27 (1965): 414–33; at p. 416.

7. Kenelm Foster, O.P., "The Theology of the Inferno," (Cambridge: Black-friars, 1957), pp. 51–52.

8. Harry Levin, *James Joyce: A Critical Introduction* (Norfolk, Conn.: New Directions, 1941), p. 30.

Structure and Meaning in Joyce's "The Sisters"

Phillip Herring

I

JOYCE'S GNOMONIC VISION

In an important article on James Joyce's *Dubliners* story "The Sisters," Burton A. Waisbren and Florence L. Walzl argue convincingly that Father Flynn suffered from paresis, otherwise know as syphilis of the central nervous system, and that Joyce took some care to describe numerous symptoms of this disease while calling it simply, though ambiguously, *paralysis.*[1] This explains much—why the priest is surrounded by an air of mystery that his young friend cannot comprehend, why he seems to have been "defrocked," why adults in the story are so uneasy about their friendship. By hinting at syphilis without using a more specific term, Joyce could shock readers, especially those attuned to the implications, while escaping censorship. Surely the "truth" about Father Flynn has been discovered.

Evidence to contradict the Waisbren-Walzl thesis is unlikely to surface, but it could be attacked on grounds of relevance. The story was carefully constructed so that the point is precisely that neither the boy nor the reader can know the truth they seek; that all appears inscrutable is hence a *donnée* of "The Sisters." How useful, then, is extratextual evidence such as Joyce's interest in syphilis (as seen in the *Letters*) and the fact that *paralysis* was a common euphemism for syphilis in Joyce's day? We begin with this example because at issue here is not merely how we interpret one short story, but rather whether or not it is possible to interpret Joyce at all with any degree of validity, for to illustrate the general ambiguity of Joycean texts is to effectively sabotage Joyce scholarship. What more could a scholar show us than how such a text arrived in its final, ambiguous form? This is the central issue in Joyce criticism today, and one that was hotly debated in recent symposia. On one side are the traditional scholars, who do research, study manuscripts, and cite evidence, and on the other side are practitioners of contemporary literary theory, who are skeptical about language and what it can do.

Although my own work has been "scholarly," and in my two books I have taken pains to show Joyce's debts to his predecessors and how, like a scholar, he did research on his subjects, in this paper I wish to show that Joyce intended to give aid and comfort to the enemy, that he generated structures and meanings in a precociously experimental way as early as the first story of *Dubliners*.

On numerous occasions Joyce provided guideposts to interpretation,[2] but it has not been generally accepted that "The Sisters" itself functions in that capacity. Still, on one level, the story is about ambiguity, about the impossibility of reaching certainty. His seemingly contradictory strategy of producing both ambiguous texts and the keys to interpreting them may have had the effect of keeping the professors busy, one of Joyce's stated purposes, but it also shows his early skepticism about our ability to get at the truth except in fragments, to understand finally and completely the impressions that our senses bring us, to analyze and interpret experience with a high degree of certainty, and to express ourselves unambiguously in eel-slippery language.

The reader of "The Sisters" encounters several barriers to understanding: the text is full of elliptical language filtered through the consciousness of a bewildered youth who broods over the deceased Father Flynn and the meaning of their friendship. Readers are easily deceived into thinking that the boy is merely naïve, and that greater maturity would be an advantage to him in wrestling with the holes in meaning, an illusion that should be dispelled at the story's end, when we are denied access to the boy's final thoughts. His reaction to new and probably decisive information is cloaked in ellipses, while the reader is left to fill in the gaps. If the truth about Father Flynn has been left to the reader, can it not be said that this truth is of necessity relative?

The opening lines of the early version of the story, published in *The Irish Homestead* in 1904 (*D* 243), illustrate that indeterminacy was no late addition (italics mine):

> Three nights in succession I had found myself in Great Britain Street at that hour, as if by *providence*. Three nights I had raised my eyes to that lighted square of window and *speculated*. *I seemed to understand* that it would occur at night. But in spite of the providence which had led my feet and in spite of the reverent curiosity of my eyes *I had discovered nothing*.

This theme of uncertainty, reminiscent of Conrad's *Heart of Darkness*, was reinforced in the story's final version with the addition of three words widely accepted as keys to interpretation in *Dubliners* as well as "The Sisters." Here the boy's interpretative difficulty, first attributed to fickle

Providence and human frailties, is now located in language itself: "Every night as I gazed up at the window I said softly to myself the word *paralysis*. It had always sounded strangely in my ears, like the word *gnomon* in the Euclid and the word *simony* in the Catechism" (*D* 9). No logic binds these three italicized words together—only the strangeness of their sounds in the boy's ear. To him the meanings are private ones, perhaps only loosely connected, if at all, to dictionary definitions. The words seem to cast a spell over him and, at the same time, point to many interpretive possibilities about which the sensitive reader may speculate. Father Flynn was a paralytic; what do *gnomon* and *simony* have to do with him? Can these terms be applied to anyone or anything else? Yet the reader, like the boy, is impelled to seek a truth he can never find: the three words neither lead them toward illumination nor can they be dismissed as meaningless. This is the dilemma of following the lead of the author-critic-tease who provides keys to understanding an ambiguous text. My essay is about how it is possible to use one term—*gnomon*—as an instrument of interpretation within this curious epistemological framework.

Let us take a closer look at the key words. In *A Portrait* young Stephen Dedalus says, "Words which he did not understand he said over and over to himself till he had learned them by heart: and through them he had glimpses of the real world about him" (*AP* 62).[3] The comprehension of key concepts is also the primary means of orientation for the boy in "The Sisters," who, with the reader, may see that the magical word that has preoccupied him—*paralysis*—describes considerably more than Father Flynn's physical debility. In the final story of *Dubliners*, "The Dead," the word "dead"—that final paralysis—may refer not only to those faithful departed, but to their survivors; in this first story *paralysis* is applicable both to the priest (it has become his *rigor mortis*) and to those who mourn him, perhaps even his young friend in his interpretive dilemma or even the reader. Upon reflection we are meant to see that it is epidemic in Ireland's capital.[4]

Like most of Joyce's work, "The Sisters" is about transcendence, in this case how a young boy wishes to elude the authority of elders who unwittingly inhibit his spiritual and intellectual growth, who are instructive only as negative examples. His impatience indicates that his uncle and Mr. Cotter are antagonists, a class eventually to be joined by the sisters of Father Flynn and perhaps the priest himself. More than age, what distinguishes the boy from the others is a condition of mind: the boy knows he knows little and seeks to arrive at understanding through inquiry, while the others think they know and obviously do not, long ago having given up the search for meaning. He is open to learning and experience; they are not. A condition of mind such as the elders have could be called *paralysis*, though, ironically, he will approach no nearer the truth than they. Still, his struggle to interpret is more noble than their acquiescence.

Gnomon is the second key word on the first page of "The Sisters," meaning, as the *OED* tells us, both a parallelogram with a smaller parallelogram missing in the upper right-hand corner and, second, the pillar of a sundial, which tells time by casting part of a circle into shadow.[5] One should give more credence to Euclidean usage, since the boy's understanding is probably restricted to that, but Joyce surely knew that in both definitions the missing part is what is important, either as a space that defines a geometric shape or as a shadow that indicates the time of day. For this word *gnomon* I claim more than my predecessors, because by perceiving gnomonic principles at work, readers can gain new insight into character, structure, and narrative technique—not in all of Joyce's texts necessarily, but in enough of them to warrant systematic examination of these principles. Joyce probably knew that in Greek the word means "indicator."

Upon reflection, a reader might first be struck with the gnomonic nature of the story's language: it is elliptical, evasive, sometimes mysterious. A mystery is there to be uncovered, but boy and reader will be frustrated by language in their attempts to solve it. We do know that it concerns the priest's vocation, his apparently forced retirement due to the effects of paralysis (however that is defined), and the exact nature of his friendship with the boy, for whom all this is an area of experience perpetually cast in shadow. He seems totally dependent for information on his elders (who won't knowingly cooperate), just as the reader is on the text. Candlelight on a darkened blind (a geometrical form partially cast in light) may tell the boy that the priest is dead, but that will hardly be an issue. Too many pieces are missing from the puzzle for him to see the picture clearly. Even when important pieces are filled in, such as at the story's end, neither boy nor reader is party to any epiphany.

Gnomonic language works as follows: if the boy eschews dictionary meanings, unsympathetic characters in "The Sisters" misuse words and fracture sentence structure. Associated with their narrative style is the ellipsis, which presents hiatuses of meaning that can only be filled in by readers or listeners.[6] The tiresome, pipe-puffing Mr. Cotter, speaking of the dead priest, says there was "something queer . . . there was something uncanny about him. I'll tell you my opinion . . ." (*D* 10), thus producing spaces in meaning while he hints at a clerical weakness he cannot or will not articulate. Even the boy falters at one point, when comparing the atmosphere of his mysterious dream to Persia. Like us, he is baffled by these holes in meaning: "I puzzled my head to extract meaning from his [Cotter's] unfinished sentences" (*D* 11).

Questing characters in *Dubliners* are frequently assaulted by something I call a "tyranny of triteness," that is, the vacuous language or malapropisms associated with the people who await them at their destinations. In "The Sisters" the boy hears ritual dialogue and misnomers like "the *Freeman's General*" for "the *Freeman's Journal*," "rheumatic" for "pneumatic" wheels. These signs of defective language are appropriate to the conversation's subject—a defective priest. Father Flynn "was too scrupulous always," Eliza says. "The duties of the priesthood was too much for him. And then his life was, you might say, crossed." (These hollow phrases, pumped so long for meaning by the critics, are meant to evoke laughter in the reader as they must have in Joyce.) Speaking at cross purposes, the aunt says, "He was a disappointed man. You could see that" (*D* 17).

This exchange occurs as part of a ritual dialogue of condolence that Joyce must have heard at funerals or wakes.[7] It is the gesture that is important, for the ritual words themselves are not really vehicles for communication. The dialogue begins (*D* 15) with the aunt saying, "Ah, well, he's gone to a better world." One expects to learn nothing, yet the shocker comes when the sisters deviate from traditional inanity to reveal information about their brother that the priest would have wished left unsaid. This the boy must try to evaluate, but the story's final ellipses prevent readers from gauging his success.

So far we have discussed "gnomonic" language: ellipses, hiatuses in meaning, significant silences, empty, ritualistic dialogue. *Gnomon* is also the primary negating force in *Dubliners*, which is why there is continual emphasis on emptiness, incompletion, solitude, loneliness, shadow, darkness, and failure, which so affect the lives of the characters and allows subtle expression of Joyce's political views. Dubliners seek to fly by nets erected to keep them down. Here one of the chief advantages of textual ambiguity emerges: stories may achieve greater depth and complexity and yet seem simple enough to have broad, popular appeal. But by employing the subtle symbolist technique of suggestion rather than commentary, Joyce also could better fulfill his mission as a subversive artist. Readers alerted to the theme of ambiguity from the first page of *Dubliners*, "trained" to read the stories skeptically, could feel more deeply the political impact they contain. In theory the author then need not fear censorship because libelous thoughts are in the reader's mind, not in the text. Gnomonic ambiguity thus has the effect of enlisting a reader as co-creator in the production of meanings that are in harmony with the author's political intentions. This subtle alliance of politics and language helped Joyce to evoke the odor of corruption that hangs over his stories, to point the finger at the forces of oppression, and still to evade the consequences.[8] *Dubliners* is often most eloquent in its silences.

Joyce must have been well instructed in the dictionary meanings of *gnomon*, because the concept is relevant to most of the major concerns of *Dubliners*. It points to what is missing, suggesting that these missing things are characteristic of the whole of Dublin life at a significant *time* in its history. (Here the sundial meaning of the word is applicable.) Readers are thus urged to examine the implications of what is missing, an approach taken with rewarding results by Hugh Kenner and Wolfgang Iser.[9] In general, *gnomon* indicates how selective examples, such as the characters of *Dubliners*, define life in their city, how shadows illuminate presences, how abnormality can define the normal. The first sentence of "The Sisters" describes the hopelessness of Father Flynn's physical condition by saying that his time is growing short: "it was the third stroke." Immediately thereafter we are told that the school term is over—"it was vacation time," which here denotes free time within a school calendar and may hint at the story's theme of freedom and bondage. In the night a rectangular window is lighted in the priest's house, and if he is dead two candles will illuminate his head, while his feet are cast in relative darkness. If some words or silences are significant, clichés like "*I am not long for this world*" are thought "idle," gnomonic in their vacancy of meaning, just as the priest was partly dead in his life. All this play on light and shadow, presence and absence, is set forth in the first half page of "The Sisters."

As we read along, the word *gnomon* suggests additional possibilities: the boy lacks direction and guidance; he is told to box his corner as if his life had geometric shape; like the story his dream is open-ended; he usually sits in the corner of the priest's room. Father Flynn lacks a whole chalice, an intact vocation, muscular coordination, a confessor to absolve him, an appropriate vehicle in which to revisit the house of his youth. His mourners "gazed at the empty fireplace" in his room (*D* 15); the fallen chalice contained nothing. An obsolete meaning of *gnomon* is "nose" (*OED*), the cavities of which Father Flynn attempts to fill with snuff, though the greater part falls on his vestments. Boy and priest are counterparts as failed clerics, a small corner in the geometric shape of the church in Ireland, but one of real significance. Like their fellow Dubliners, they are gnomonic in their needs, gnomonic in their representativeness, and their story is gnomonic in that the precise description of their problems and the remedies thereof are left to the reader.

The third key word in the opening paragraph of "The Sisters" is *simony*, the buying and selling of ecclesiastical preferment. If *paralysis* describes the moral and physical condition of Dubliners, given their need for freedom, transcendence, and fulfillment, and *gnomon* reemphasizes these absences at a particular time in history, then *simony* too must be stretched to relevance. It points to corruption in high places and illegitimate ecclesiastical authority as primary obstacles hindering the peoples' fulfillment. Thus the first two terms describe the condition, telling the reader how to arrive at meanings deeper than the textual surface, while the word *simony* places the blame squarely where Joyce thought it belonged—on institutions and their representatives who barter what is a sacred right. Ambition, energy, free will, revolutionary zeal—these forces played no role, and could not, Joyce thought, in a city and country where centuries of political and religious oppression had caused a general paralysis of mind and will. Transcendence came only through death or emigration.

Simony reinforces *gnomon* and *paralysis* as a thematic key for understanding the story's central problem—what the boy and priest meant to each other. The term may be a broad paintbrush for church walls in Ireland, but it also works on the individual level. Father Flynn's own indoctrination program could in part have had personal gain as its motive; having cracked a chalice and lost a vocation, whatever guilt he might suffer could possibly be expiated by providing a clerical replacement. Spiritually, says Thomas E. Connolly, Father Flynn "has become a remainder after something else is removed, a gnomon."[10] If, in addition, he is "not all there"—mentally as well as physically incapable of coordination—this defective priest, who is, after all, defined in terms of vocation, might from impure motives be capable of seeking a replacement for himself. The boy's preoccupation with *simony* might indicate an awareness that this trap has been evaded, but he too suffers from a kind of gnomonic vacancy in terms of vocation and experience.

The boy's dream of the priest trying to confess to him may be the beginning of the boy's awareness of impropriety. To hear the priest's confession is to accept the priestly vocation. Though this happens in a dream, he is aware of coercion and feels his "soul receding into some pleasant and vicious region" (*D* 11), where, unwanted, the priest follows. We cannot know whether or not the priest has committed the sin of simony, but his young friend is definitely suspicious that he has been coerced by an old teacher who, at the least, has charged a tuition in snuff.

If "The Sisters" is seen as a geometric structure, then one part of it will always remain in shadow. Indeed, the elusive title suggests that meaning will be displaced. Gnomonic interpretation must thus involve speculation about textual meaning, and what follows is mine: If Father Flynn has sought to bind his novice, he has probably freed him instead; if he has wished to indoctrinate him, it is surely the example of what he became that made the more lasting impression. Whatever transcendence the youth has gained, it involves not religion but a deeper knowledge of what it is to know. Like the boys in "An Encounter," and "Araby," or Little Chandler in "A Little Cloud," the price he pays for such rude instruction will be a sense of humiliation that will not soon fade. All of them have sought light, positive images, and have been taught by negatives, shadows, the incomplete geometric shape instead of the whole one. The last sentence of "The Sisters" describes Father Flynn in the confession box; like the coffin that will contain him, it is a rectangular shape now in shadow, now in light. The door is opened to reveal him laughing to himself, but what precisely causes this laughter, what it means, or what its consequences are for his vocation will remain forever in doubt. The story's final ellipses do leave space for our minds to focus on unspoken implications, but if the reader must supply the missing pieces, can the picture ever look quite the same to any two observers?

II

AFTER "THE SISTERS"

In *The Riddles of "Finnegans Wake,"* Patrick McCarthy says, "Again and again Joyce returns to the idea that the artist is a riddler, a constructor of verbal mazes. . . ."[11] As with his last work, so also with the first, and most of the in-between. The reason lies, again, in his idea of incomplete form; the concept affects characterization, structure, imagery, and meaning in general. A few examples should suffice. Given the political and sociological realities of Joyce's Dublin, his characters typically lack some vital ingredient for happiness—love, freedom of various kinds, the generosity and benevolence of other people, including figures of authority. Consequently, there seem to be no happy people in Joyce's work, no instances of harmonious relationships, and, given Joyce's epistemological and linguistic skepticism, few instances of trouble-free communication between people. James Duffy and Mrs. Sinico misunderstand each other; so do Stephen and Cranly, Richard Rowan and Bertha, Bloom and Stephen. Dubliners seem to suffer as much from isolating communication barriers as from the oppression of church and state. By implication, then, they communicate with each other as Joyce does with his readers—incompletely—and with less happy results.

The most interesting structural technique Joyce consistently used was the enigmatic or open ending, another example of incomplete form. Contrary to popular belief, such endings were not the invention of modernist writers, but can be traced back at least as far as *Tristram Shandy*. The idea has always been to deny readers the orderly closure consistent with their generic expectations. According to my definition, the use of such endings would, in Joyce's case, be part of an overall pattern of gnomonic incompletion. Literary texts are, of course, sequential as geometric forms are not, but to imagine a text as gnomonic is to see it as a shape with a missing corner of meaning (the ending), which a reader is invited to complete. Whereas the gnomon must always be completed in the same way, with lines intersecting at a given point, a gnomonic ending invites speculation. By definition no one shape fits so well as to exclude other possible endings, though the range of possibilities is limited.

It appears that Joyce simply lopped off the ending of "The Sisters" and substituted ellipses just at the moment when, as in "Araby," boy and reader might have shared an epiphany. Given the endings of the later stories, it seems safe to say that this is the structure that fits, though the precise nature of the epiphany would be a matter of speculation. Sandwiched between these stories is "An Encounter," where the boy seems on the verge of an epiphany at the end but is still quite confused.

It scarcely needs to be demonstrated that enigmatic endings are the rule rather than the exception in *Dubliners*, with each story building toward that magical moment where Gabriel Conroy experiences a kind of egotistical death and transfiguration in an open ending of a considerably more sophisticated kind than in any previous *Dubliners* story. Whereas in "A Painful Case" James Duffy's epiphanic moment changes the nature of his consciousness, in "The Dead" Joyce goes a step further and shows Gabriel Conroy having a mystical experience as a result of such a moment, one that threatens to obliterate his identity.

In *A Portrait of the Artist*, the epiphanic moment is expanded into what I call a visionary ending, where Stephen Dedalus's awareness of vocation causes him to stand on an imaginary Mount Pisgah to behold a Promised Land of the future that can never exist for him. Ironically, for Moses it is the homeland that cannot be entered, while for Stephen it is the homeland that must be left.

Ulysses and *Finnegans Wake* offer open endings that are frequently discussed and need not be treated here. They defy reader expectations, show the incompatibility of major characters, and affirm a vision that is confused at best. By this point Joyce's gnomonic techniques have become at the same time highly experimental and rather predictable, affecting all aspects of literary form, meaning, and character. Obscurantism has become a trademark.

III

THE LIMITS OF AMBIGUITY

Returning to "The Sisters" as a paradigm of interpretation, we may repeat the question posed at the end of the first section: "if the reader must supply the missing pieces, can the picture ever look quite the same to any

two observers?" Essentially the question involves discussing where meaning resides in such a process and how it occurs—whether predominantly in
the text, or in the reader's mind, or in the dialectical interrelationship.

Recently Colin MacCabe has said of *Dubliners*, "There is no single
message inscribed in the code and the meaning of the text is produced by
the reader's own activity. . . ." Furthermore, "The splitting of the subject
is achieved through the accentuation of the split between enunciation and
enounced. This is effected in the text of *Dubliners* by those moments when
the reader is no longer assured in his position in the enounced and thus
experiences his own discourses as enunciation, as a process of production."[12] Although MacCabe approaches this subject from an angle different from mine, he seems essentially correct in describing what Joyce
probably thought he was doing in his experiment with meaning.

Jacques Derrida and J. Hillis Miller hold similarly skeptical views about
the possibility of meaning occurring in reading. Miller has said: "all language is figurative at the beginning. The notion of a literal or referential use
of language is only an illusion born of the forgetting of the metaphorical
'roots' of language. Language is from the start fictive, illusory, displaced
from any direct reference to things as they are."[13] All readings are thus
misreadings; we are left with fragments of a truth we can never see whole.
We cannot therefore speak of validity in interpretation, but only of the
persuasiveness of readings, a relative concept. Although Miller does not
write about the first page of *Dubliners*, he would probably sympathize with
Joyce's strategy for teaching skepticism there, noting that the italicized key
words are basically indecipherable because they have private meanings and
associations as well as dictionary definitions that are slippery and loose.

In opposition to deconstruction is E. D. Hirsch, Jr., who made an
important distinction between "meaning" and "significance" in *Validity in
Interpretation*: that textual meaning cannot be separated from authorial
intention, whereas significance may vary with the reader; in *The Aims of
Interpretation* he reaffirms that "a text cannot be *interpreted* from a perspective different from the original author's. Meaning is understood from the
perspective that lends existence to meaning. Any other procedure is not
interpretation but authorship." Hirsch goes on to say that "Every act of
interpretation involves, therefore, at least two perspectives, that of the
author and that of the interpreter. The perspectives are entertained both at
once, as in normal binocular vision. Far from being an extraordinary or
illusory feat, this entertaining of two perspectives at once is the ground of
all human intercourse. . . ."[14]

Hirsch is persuasive in his defense of the traditional scholarly methods
used to determine authorial intention. However, he seems not to have had

Joyce in mind, for the central question for us here remains: Is critical relativism not justified where authorial intention can seldom be established and where the author himself subscribes to relativism? Yet even if Joyce favored textual ambiguity, it would of course be a mistake to conclude that authorial intention can never be established, or that Joyce never had a dominant message in mind in any particular statement, or that evidence, logic, authoritative reasoning, and judgment can do no more than reinforce our own perspectives.

This brings us to a consideration of what seem to be problems in advocating the position that Joyce's texts were generally designed to reflect multiple meanings. One problem is that of authority. If interpreters of Joyce are caught up simply in MacCabe's "process of production," reading texts such as we have described from ever differing perspectives, how is it possible to distinguish between more or less plausible interpretations? Is it ever possible to state categorically that a Joyce text means *x* or *y*, or must one continually be diffident about meaning?

As early as 1965 Fritz Senn attached importance to the opening of "The Sisters" as forecasting the experimentalism to come in Joyce's work.[15] Recently, in an important article, he emphasized the necessity of skepticism in reading, questioning "how we, as Joyce readers, when we could benefit from such a unique education in applied skepticism [as is found in Joyce's texts], can still be as dogmatic in our own practical performances as in fact we are."[16] Senn urges critics to become less assertive, more aware that whatever evidence can be found for one interpretation, equally forceful evidence can always be found to contradict it. Among other things this suggests that no real progress has been made in understanding Joyce's texts since their publication; that criticism is only a game where no player really has an advantage; that all we can hope for is a fresh, interesting perspective in a discipline (?) where little or nothing of importance can ever be known.

But common sense tells us this is false, that we are much more knowledgeable, more sophisticated readers of Joyce than ever before, in large part thanks to the scholarship and rigor of traditionalists, and in part thanks to progress in the editing and publication of manuscripts and definitive texts. No other term but *progress* will do to describe that process by which we are continually able to learn new things about writers such as Joyce. The more we learn, the greater is our authority as readers and the more likely it is that our dogmatism will on occasion be justified. If Fritz Senn were to assume a dogmatic tone, I would listen respectfully.

The issues raised here about how meaning occurs in Joyce will never be settled to the satisfaction of many interpreters of texts, but they should be considered in depth by those who advocate an easy relativism, perhaps not

having worked their way through the subtleties of works like Wolfgang
Iser's *The Act of Reading*.

Joyce surely taught us to be skeptical about language, addressing the
question most directly and humorously in *Finnegans Wake*, where, with
mock seriousness, he says that although we "may have irremovable doubts
as to the whole sense of the lot, the interpretation of any phrase in the
whole, the meaning of every word of a phrase so far deciphered out of it [the
hen's letter], . . . we must vaunt no idle dubiosity as to its genuine authorship and holusbolus authoritativeness."[17] But in the face of this persistent attitude toward meaning, and our uneasy feeling that too much depends upon our response to the text and too little on the text itself or
authorial intention, readers have no alternative but to be skeptical about
Joyce's skepticism and to attempt to avoid the fallacy of imitative form in
interpretation. We know intuitively that "The Sisters" is not about life in an
Eskimo village, but at what point would we become intolerant of a brilliant
espousal of that thesis? Obviously we have no recourse but to attempt to
limit the range of possible meanings; good interpretation has to reject
implausibility. Fortunately, Joyce helps us to do that too. Returning to the
paradigm of our story, *gnomon* indicates that meaning is open-ended, but
paralysis and *simony* are important keys to thematic limitation in interpretation.

Boy and reader in "The Sisters" seem to follow a parallel course in their
struggle with meaning, but this is actually an illusion. The boy interprets
the world as text and the reader the text as world. A sophisticated reader,
recognizing the self-reflexive qualities of the story, can also read the text as
text and consider its playfulness, but whereas there is no limit to the range
of readers who may read the story, there is only one boy, and his level of
sophistication can be established within a narrow compass. Though he
narrates, he cannot read the text, nor can he be responsible for the range of
possible meanings there. Though obliged to read the world as text, he
cannot read the world as world, and, denied a glimpse at that epiphanic
moment, the reader cannot know at the story's end how much the boy has
learned about his world or even what the maturer narrator knows. Even if
both decipher, the nature of their ignorance differs because of a time gap
and the struggle of narration, differing as well from that of any reader.

In the end, a potential advantage lies with the reader, for the words of the
text, regardless of slippery etymologies, do not change, while the boy-
narrator must deal with shifting impressions based on incomplete information about a forbidden subject. Consciously or unconsciously, the narrator
provides the reader with signposts to meaning, even if nobody in the text's
world seems willing to render him a similar service.

Notes

1. "Paresis and the Priest: James Joyce's Symbolic Use of Syphilis in 'The Sisters,'" *Annals of Internal Medicine* 80 (June 1974): 758–62. See also Joyce's *Letters*, II, 192, and *The Complete Dublin Diary of Stanislaus Joyce*, ed. George Harris Healey (Ithaca: Cornell University Press, 1962), p. 51, on Joyce's interest in this disease. All references to *Dubliners* (abbreviated *D*) are to the Viking Critical Edition (New York, 1969), edited by Robert Scholes and A. Walton Litz.

2. Cf. my *Joyce's Notes and Early Drafts for Ulysses: Selections from the Buffalo Collection* (Charlottesville: University of Virginia Press, 1977), pp. 121–23.

3. *A Portrait of the Artist as a Young Man*, Viking Critical Edition, edited by Chester G. Anderson (New York, 1968).

4. See *D* 269; *Letters*, I, 55; II, 134.

5. See Euclid's *Elements* (Book II, Definition 2) on *gnomon*, and also Thomas E. Connolly, "Joyce's 'The Sisters,': A Pennyworth of Snuff," *College English* 27 (December 1965): 195, on the edition of Euclid Joyce probably used. The most authoritative article on *gnomon* and one to which I am indebted for several ideas, is Gerhard Friedrich's "The Gnomonic Clue to James Joyce's *Dubliners*," *Modern Language Notes* 72 (June 1957): 421–24. Friedrich says that "'paralysis' means literally a loosening or weakening at the side . . . parallelograms that are non-rectangular may be thought of as loosened at the side; and the Euclidean gnomon has moreover the appearance of an impaired, cutaway parallelogram" (p. 422). See also David R. Fabian, "Joyce's 'The Sisters': Gnomon, Gnomic, Gnome," in *Studies in Short Fiction* 5 (Winter 1968): 187–89; and Robert Adams Day, "Joyce's Gnomons, Lenehan, and the Persistence of an Image," *Novel* XIV (Fall 1980): 5–19.

6. Ellipses are a prominent feature of the epiphanies collected in Robert Scholes and Richard M. Kain, eds., *The Workshop of Daedalus* (Evanston: Northwestern University Press, 1965) and other *Dubliners* stories, where they often function merely as pauses in narration.

7. On the decorum of wake visits, see pages 379–80 of the very thorough article by Florence Walzl, "Joyce's 'The Sisters': A Development," in *James Joyce Quarterly* 10 (Summer 1973): 375–421.

8. If this was Joyce's assumption, it turned out to be false. His publisher Grant Richards and the printer were to demand excisions of essential pieces that would mar his carefully completed texts; i.e., their gnomonic strategy wasn't Joyce's.

9. See Kenner, "Molly's Masterstroke," *JJQ* 10 (Fall 1972), 19–28 (see also *JJQ*, 14 [Summer 1977]); "The Rhetoric of Silence," ibid., 382–94; Iser, *The Act of Reading* (Baltimore: Johns Hopkins University Press, 1978), 168–69.

10. Connolly, "Joyce's 'The Sisters,'" p. 195.

11. (Rutherford, N.J.: Farleigh Dickinson University Press, 1981), p. 153.

12. *James Joyce and the Revolution of the Word* (London: Macmillan, 1978), p. 36; cf. pp. 29, 67; 80. MacCabe emphasizes the difference between Joyce's texts and those of realists such as George Eliot, who attempted to fix their "subject in reality," and, through commentary, to restrict the range of possible readings. J. Hillis Miller would not approve this distinction. He shows the deconstructive nature of Eliot's *Middlemarch* in "Narrative and History," *ELH* 41 (Fall 1974): 455–73.

13. "Tradition and Difference," a review of *Natural Supernaturalism* by M. H. Abrams, *Diacritics* 2 (Winter 1972): 11. Quoted in Vincent B. Leitch, "The Lateral Dance: The Deconstructive Criticism of J. Hillis Miller," *Critical Inquiry* 6 (Sum-

mer 1980): 597. This is an excellent summary of Miller's developing views on deconstruction.

14. (Chicago: University of Chicago Press, 1976), p. 49.

15. "'He Was Too Scrupulous Always': Joyce's 'The Sisters,'" *James Joyce Quarterly* 2 (Winter 1965): 66–72. Senn makes the important point (p. 68) that the boy confuses the word *paralysis* with its referent.

16. "Dogmad or dubliboused?" *JJQ* 17 (Spring 1980): 238.

17. (New York: Viking Press, 1939), pp. 117–18.

PART VI

Legitimate and False Correspondences: Symbols and Images in *Ulysses*

Introduction

Zack Bowen

The question under consideration is twofold: Does our pat-
tern-hunt have a purpose, and, if it does, which are the meaningful patterns
and which are not? Are, as many of us claim in print, Joyce's patterns
crystal clear and unambiguous, or does meaning lie in confusion itself?

The significance of patterns is much easier to see in *Portrait* because
everything in the novel has meaning for its central consciousness, Stephen
Dedalus; the patterns are his and the ultimate meanings his to assemble into
the final portrait of himself as artist. *Ulysses* is a more encompassing book in
composition and structure, and in the development of Joyce's artistic
design. The novel has a farther-reaching series of meanings and correspondences than those of which Stephen has cognizance, and it subsumes
his view of the world as only one of a number of multiple perspectives. In
fact, where judgmental errors in Stephen's perspective are only hinted at in
Portrait, they are blatantly apparent in *Ulysses*. For instance, in "Scylla and
Charybdis," when Stephen stands on the library steps where he stood in
Portrait, again looking for omens, portents, and symbols, he is virtually told
by Mulligan that the father figure for whom he has been searching is passing
before him. Mulligan speaks in mocking terms about the prospective relationship between the two, and Stephen fails to see any correspondence or
take any notice of the man the reader has early consigned to the role of
surrogate father.

The narrative consciousness of *Ulysses* contains clues, correspondences,
and subsequent ambiguities that are not even a part of Stephen's ken. The
range of experiences of *Ulysses* is greater than the individual consciousness
of a character can make them. Yet these clues and correspondences have a
tantalizing similarity to the diverse experiences of other characters in the
book.

The major motif of structure and composition involves, on the ecclesiastical level, the recurring concepts of transubstantiation and consubstantia-
tion, or the similarities between situations experienced by one character
and others in the novel. This process results in a transformation of major
characters until each, in a metaphoric sense, assumes the identity of
another. Hence the Stoom and Blephen reference. When two characters

147

undergo similar or related experiences they become consubstantial in the communal experience while having simultaneous individual existences. The third metaphoric term for the confluence of experience, theme, and image—metempsychosis, Molly's term about the transmigration of souls—deals with the interchangeability of identity even after death, placing the concept in a linear perspective.

Finally Bloom's preoccupation with parallax provides a concept from physics for the interchangeability of circumstance and theme, which allows us to look at two characters or situations from different perspectives, so that, although we appear to be looking at different things, we are viewing the same phenomenon. Bloom's preoccupation with the term *parallax* is central to the structure of *Ulysses*. As it links similar motifs and experiences and provides us with a metaphoric perspective to account for the similar-ities, while at the same time accounting for the differences, parallax informs the basic pattern for the several structures of the novel. In short, what appear to be isolated fragments and false correspondences might from another perspective be a part of the central matrix of the book. This blending of motifs and commonality, of course, is a direct prefiguration of *Finnegans Wake*. Thus Joyce has progressed in his novels from a single consciousness defining its own meaning in *Portrait* through the multiple consciousness of *Ulysses* to the all-inclusive consciousness of *Finnegans Wake*, where there are no such things as false leads and patterns, since everything is possible and perhaps intentional. If all of this sounds like the idea that similarities might be found that make almost anything a lead, or symbolic of something because it is related to everything else, that is precisely my thesis.

So far, however, we have only discussed those themes arising directly out of the text. In keeping with the new Booth philosophy, I would like to turn to the dimension supplied by the quirky and not so quirky readers, who impose themes, plots, and meaning on the ambiguities of *Ulysses*. For one person I encountered several years ago, the question of whether Stephen and Bloom would ever form a permanent alliance, or whether Molly's "Yes" is positive or negative, had little meaning. He simply saw his entire life recorded in the pages of *Ulysses*. Tickets, stubs, bills, legal papers, and mathematical formulae provided the marginalia in his copy. There simply was not a page that did not appear to him to be directly related to corresponding events in his life.

The correspondence hunt is an intellectual exercise, but the value of the novel, and the reason we keep coming back to *Ulysses*, is its humanity, its affinity with universal human conditions. Indeed, it might be argued that we may easily go off the deep idiosyncratic end in our zeal. Critics read morality and immorality, right wing or leftist positions, etc., out of every work of art, as their reading becomes a part of the process of composition. *Ulysses*, unique in its plethora of details leading to monumental ambiguities, cries out to be reassembled into meaningful patterns. As some readers seek correspondences that fit their own lives and those of the three main characters, and others try to make sense of the same material, we begin to hope that Stephen will somehow put it all together into a book like *Ulysses*, or that Bloom will finally compose his "experiences in a cabman's shelter." Like Stencil in *V*, Stephen and Bloom grope for the meaning of events as we, like Pynchon's readers, monitor the situation and provide our own structure and meaning. Like Barth's Giles we discover that passéd is passéd and flunkéd, that there are no right and wrong answers, no such things as false correspondences; far-fetched, maybe, but *Ulysses* is at once a work of art that duplicates the chaotic condition of existence and one on which we seek to impose order, symbolism, proportion, and finally meaning.

Legitimate and False Correspondences

Morton P. Levitt

It is the pleasure of finding correspondences—of isolating motifs, tracing connections among them, and elaborating on their thematic potential—that initially attracts many serious readers to *Ulysses*. This is especially true of those harmlessly anal types who also love crossword and jigsaw puzzles and who may come to love *Finnegans Wake*. As a lover of puzzles and correspondences, both literary and non-, I would like to suggest that this may also be one of the great dangers of Joyce criticism, that this seemingly innocent pursuit may too often detract from the far more significant human aspects of the novel. It is just this capability which those critics hostile to Joyce (the English, in particular) have cited when attacking him as antihumanist. They are obviously wrong, we all know, but we may well be giving them too much ammunition for their attack.

Most of us would agree, I think, at least in principle, that we should be wary of symbol-hunting, those imaginative tricks by which a Tindall turns a Mulligan into a messenger of the gods (perhaps Athene herself), or a cup of cocoa into a godhead-granting communion. I would like to warn also against the dangers of more innocent symbolic and even metaphoric readings—of working out, that is, all the potential correspondences with which Joyce challenges us. This is not to deny the metaphoric structure of the novel; it would be as foolish to argue that the sole reality of *Ulysses* is its surface reality as to accept the old canard that Joyce is a faker. We know well the richness and wonders of his fiction; but its very richness may act at times against its larger purposes. And this may be true even where Joyce encourages our search for correspondences—perhaps especially where he does so. For critic and novelist alike, *Ulysses*—not to speak of the *Wake*—may offer too much potential for self-gratification, may too often turn pleasurable puzzle-solving quests into negative constructs.

As truth is no absolute legal defense against libel, so too the fact that a correspondence is true—true according to Joyce's stated intentions or to the strictest New Critical reading—does not mean that it must be followed through, that it will not interfere with the author's larger human concerns. We sometimes libel his work, with his complicity, even when we are truthful. What do we make of the fact, for example, that both Stephen and

Bloom are keyless? More importantly, what can this tell us about them and their enterprise? That they are devoid of identity or roots? That they are Manxmen or advertising men or musicians or home rulers? That they will never enter the kingdom of . . . whatever? The possibilities are as many as they are foolish. And what about the multiple periods of the women in the novel: a sign of fertility or of infertility, of some form of creative, authorial stasis, or all or none of the above?

We can easily understand the Parable of the Plums in symbolic terms: the sterility of modern-day Ireland juxtaposed against the borrowed fertility of John F. Taylor's Israel/Ireland speech, as recited by J.J. O'Molloy. (But the Palestinian wasteland of Agendath Netaim, as Bloom visualizes it, does seem to undercut this reading.) Still, consistent or not, none of this makes Stephen's performance very convincing. His tale is inept and unfunny, and we are as likely to be bewildered by its telling as are his listeners. The episode does tell us something, however, of Stephen's intellectual intractability—the state of the would-be artist as a not-quite-so-young man, of the intended exile back again at home—although it may do so despite and not because of its labored correspondences.

And what about the alleged, oft-celebrated Homeric analogues: do such passing phrases as "Usurper" ("Telemachus," p. 23), "Seadeath" ("Proteus," p. 50), the "wise shoulders" of Mr. Deasy ("Nestor," p. 36), the action of Bloom "to close and chain the door" ("Ithaca," p. 669) really entitle us to see correspondences, even ironic correspondences, to Bronze Age Greece? Do such references serve as more than crutches for inadequate undergraduate readings (or teachings) of the novel?

A more serious problem of function and form is "Oxen of the Sun"— some of the richest workings in *Ulysses* and some of the thinnest material— inducing readings as ingenious and unnecessary as Huge Kenner's filling in of times and spaces. My own preference is to trust Joyce's omissions and to assume that that's the way life sometimes is, that we cannot in literature any more than in life make all the connections. Had Joyce wanted to fill in the gaps for us he would have been Dickens. I tend to fear that if we hurry with Kenner to make the last train to Kingstown, we just may trample Bloom in our rush.

Bloom's human vulnerability is perhaps most apparent in a scene whose correspondences are unquestionably legitimate: his memory of lovemaking with Molly on the Hill of Howth. It is a wonderfully lyrical scene as he recalls it in "Lestrygonians": somewhat comic perhaps, but erotic and wondering, and we may learn more about Bloom from this memory than from perhaps any other on this day. "Me. And me now," he concludes (p. 176), and we understand for the first time something of the depth of his loss and of his awareness of that loss. It is no coincidence that Molly concludes her memory in "Penelope" with the same scene. Looking on from outside, we may view the lovemaking on Howth as a mine of correspondences: it is Bloom who is "Ravished," Bloom to whom the seedcake is passed in an act both ironic and revealing. To this point, the potential correspondences are perfectly consistent with the human center of the scene.

But if we follow the goat who intrudes on the lovers and attribute to him all his potential symbolic properties—all of them seemingly quite appropriate in a scene of love—we may too easily find ourselves lured away from Molly and Bloom, turning from sentiment to comedy, from humans to symbols, distorting one of the most profoundly revealing scenes of the novel. In such a case, the relatively harmless, totally understandable exercise of tracing correspondences can prove harmful indeed. Like the unwary reader who follows Swift's hero into his stable at the end of Book IV of *Gulliver's Travels*, the critic of Joyce is in danger of becoming the victim of his own innocent ingenuity unless he is exceedingly wary in conducting his correspondences.

Following a Suffix into the Maze

James F. Carens

"For this, O dearly beloved, is the genuine Christine" (*U* 3: 22).[1] With these words, and particularly with the suffix he attaches to "Christ," the blasphemous Buck Mulligan reveals himself as a priest of science for whom the eucharist is no more than one member of a class of chemical substances. How different he seems from the brooding Stephen who can reflect in "Proteus" that there is but one body of Christ no matter how often or simultaneously the act of transubstantiation is performed (*U* 40: 9–18). This difference fades, however, a moment later, when Stephen mocks himself: "Cousin Stephen, you will never be a saint" (*U* 40: 19). Yet Mulligan's "Christine" has prepared the way for other motifs that emerge in *Ulysses*.

One character who has no significant bearing on the events of the novel and no fictional association with any of the major characters is linked to Mulligan by this suffix. In "Wandering Rocks," the Reverend Hugh C. Love visits St. Mary's Abbey, where, according to Ned Lambert, he is pursuing his research on a book about the Fitzgerald clan (*U* 230–31). Indeed, as Love traverses the streets of Dublin, he is "attended by Gerald-ines tall and personable" (*U* 245: 10). He is, like Mulligan, capable of discerning a class but not an essence. Joyce's ironic counterpoint contrasts Love and his foolish fantasies with Tom Rochford, a real life "hero" who, according to Lenehan and McCoy, rescued men from sewer gas (*U* 232–33). Unwilling to allow such a correspondence to develop without paradox, irony, and reversal, Joyce has already indicated that the usurping Mulligan, like Thomas Fitzgerald, is one of a group of historic pretenders (*U* 45: 25–30), but also, like Rochford, he has saved lives (*U* 4: 49, 45: 30).

In the case of the suffix attached to "Christ" and "Gerald," we cannot help being teased into reflecting on its feminine ending, as well as Joyce's method of creating correspondences from buried, almost trivial details, which contribute to a pattern of meaning. In this case the feminizing of the names attaches a quality of effeminacy to Mulligan and to the Reverend Love. Compelled by Joyce's fabric of associations and correspondences, we also recognize this same link between the Protestant clergyman and Leopold Bloom. Also, the element of effeminacy in Stephen's association

153

with Mulligan is implicit early, when the Buck flippantly addresses him as
"my love" (*U* 4: 12)—later to become, in Stephen's mind, "his dearmylove"
(*U* 202: 18). This latent homosexuality in Stephen's association with Mulligan is again intimated when Stephen responds to Mulligan's touch, "Cranly's arm. His arm" (*U* 7: 14). It becomes unavoidably explicit by "Proteus,"
when Stephen reflects of Mulligan, "Staunch friend, a brother soul: Wilde's
love that dare not speak its name" (*U* 49: 22–23). The feminine element in
Bloom's nature and the element of latent homosexuality in him are also
implied early in the novel, but the full identification of Bloom with femininity and homosexuality is withheld until "Circe." There Bloom's link to
Hugh C. Love is established following Bella Cohen's description of Bloom
swooning in transvestite fantasy. It is then that Bloom admits how Gerald,
"dear Gerald," "dearest Gerald," converted him in high school to the cult of
the beautiful (*U* 536–37).

   Having come thus far in suggesting a series of correspondences that link
Bloom, the Rev. Love, Mulligan, and Stephen to femininity and latent
homosexuality, I have to admit that when I find the Mesdames Gerald and
Stanislaus Moran of Roebuck among the fox-hunting pack that pursues
Bloom from Bella Cohen's brothel (*U* 586: 39), I do not know quite what I
am to do. The method of the novel has compelled me to attend to brothers,
to Geralds and Geraldines. Should I assume that Joyce is associating his
actual brother Stanislaus with femininity and homosexuality? Is Roebuck
Hill, an estate in Dundrum,[2] intended to lead me to that "brother soul"
Buck Mulligan? But, if so, where can I possibly go with the name Moran? I
have encountered sheer puzzle that seems to compromise the way I have
been reading.

   There is no doubt at all, however, as to the implication, a few pages later,
in another catalogue, found in the midst of "Circe" 's Black Mass, of a pair
of names that constitutes a ribald pun. The combatant brothers Lord
Edward Fitzgerald and Lord Gerald Fitzedward (*U* 599: 6) prepare us for
the love-hate nexus in the campy celebration of the Mass by Father Malachi
O'Flynn and the Reverend Mr. Hugh C. Haines Love. This passage has
been thoroughly explicated by a number of writers,[3] and I am concerned
only with certain of its symbolic details. Joyce derived the "grey bare hairy
buttocks" of Haines Love (*U* 599: 28) from the more romantically rendered
bare-buttocked, grey form of Father Oliver Gogarty in George Moore's *The
Lake*.[4] So one is led by a centrifugal allusion to the point where one may
conclude that for Joyce, at least, the two celebrants here are Gogarty-
Mulligan-O'Flynn and Gogarty-Mulligan-Haines-Trench-Boylan-Love.
(Bloom's rival is Hugh C. "Blazes" Boylan, and Richard Ellmann has
established the relationship between the character Haines and Oliver
Gogarty's visitor, S. C. Trench.[5] It may be noted that the rival opposites

tend to merge as well as to conflict in *Ulysses*, as they were to do in *Finnegans Wake*.)

When Haines Love offers prayer "To the devil which hath made glad my young days" (*U* 599: 23), we are made to recognize that the homosexual love-hate celebrated here is but the obverse of Stephen's heterosexual attachment to the "Lecherous lynx, . . . *la belle dame sans merci*, Georgina Johnson, *ad deam qui laetificat juventutem meam*" (*U* 433: 8–9)—the whore who has delighted his youth. The name Georgina surely evokes again Christine and the Geraldines. I suspect, too, that for Joyce she had something to do with George A. Jackson (*U* 678: 33–34), a real-life analogue for Joyce's dead brother, George, and for Gogarty, too, through association with Sinbad the Sailor. (Jackson made the scenery for the pantomime *Sinbad the Sailor*, 1892;[6] Gogarty, as Joyce well knew, had produced a long bawdy poem about Sinbad.) Probably Georgina then also has something to do with J. A. Jackson (*U* 237: 17)—a real-life analogue for James A. Joyce himself and, as a Trinity cyclist, for Gogarty, who cycled at Trinity. I am being spun centrifugally by biography away from what is most pertinent to the text, I know. Indeed, if I pursue the matter further, I should be able to account for Georgina Simpson (*U* 742: 38), whose open house the Blooms attended during their courtship. From correspondences and the expectations they create, I have been led entirely into the realm of puzzle and uncertainty once again. If it can be said that all of this pursuit of associations is making academic nonsense out of incidental fictional detail, then I believe it should be argued that in *Ulysses* incidental fictional detail is meant to puzzle us.

What can be said with assurance is that Georgina Johnson, who, according to Stephen, is "dead and married" (*U* 559: 21–22), will lead me back to the man in the macintosh who "loves a lady who is dead" (*U* 333: 32–33) and to the nexus of contraception associated with him, and also to the identification of marriage or union with death and that "other world" Martha Clifford does not like (*U* 77: 37).

Despite the comic importance of correspondences to the *Odyssey*, despite the formal significance of the elements of the schema Joyce provided Budgen, and despite the confusions of the maze, the kinds of correspondence I have briefly pursued seem important thematically. The particular correspondences I have mentioned lead, first of all, to central motifs in the novel; second, to blind alleys and uncertainties that cause one to question even those correspondences that seem to make sense; and, third, to James Joyce himself, who has created patterns of symbolic and, at times, entirely personal meanings that, like life itself are sometimes significant, sometimes totally perplexing.

Notes

1. This and all other citations of *Ulysses* are from the edition by Random House, New York, 1961.

2. Don Gifford and Robert J. Seidman, *Notes for Joyce* (New York: E. P. Dutton, 1974), p. 425.

3. See, for instance, Robert Martin Adams, *Surface and Symbol* (New York: Oxford University Press, 1967), pp. 29–35.

4. George Moore, *The Lake* (London: Heinemann, 1921), p. 270.

5. Richard Ellmann, *James Joyce* (New York: Oxford University Press, 1959), pp. 177–78.

6. See Adams, pp. xv–xvi.

Deacon Dedalus: The Text of the *Exultet* and Its Implications for *Ulysses*

Robert Adams Day

Most Joyceans think of Stephen Dedalus as a would-be priest of eternal imagination, not a deacon, and despite the amount of work that has been done on Joyce and the liturgy, they know the *Exultet* (unless they are devout or fairly devout Catholics) only as something mentioned a couple of times in notes to *Ulysses* and *Finnegans Wake*. But I propose that this ancient chant and its symbolism, fitted, so to speak, into the jigsaw puzzle of "Ithaca," settles the never-ending argument about what, if anything, will happen to Stephen as a result of his encounter with Bloom. Few of us, surely, want to join certain early critics of Joyce in asserting that their meeting means nothing at all;[1] but equally few would declare that the puling esthete Stephen, transformed by looking into a mirror with Bloom and seeing Shakespeare, comparing Gaelic and Hebrew in Bloom's kitchen, and drinking the creature cocoa, sits down on June 17, 1904, takes up his pen, and writes, "Stately, plump Buck Mulligan. . . ." Sudden and total conversions or Pauline experiences are as rare in realistic art as they are in daily life, and in this connection it makes sense to remember the whore Zoe's proverbial remark, reading Stephen's palm, that Thursday's child has far to go. But how far, and in what direction?

I suggest that the *Exultet* is to be seen as occupying a midpoint in the Joycean symbolic cosmos between Joyce's perpetual mythologizing of himself and his adventures and his creation of Stephen as an independent being, like yet unlike his creator. And I should say at this point, by way of introduction, that I am entirely in agreement with the view of Walton Litz in his essay on "Ithaca"; he accepts Mary Reynolds's interpretation of the powerful echoes from Dante found in the scene in Bloom's back garden, and writes:

> [T]he meeting of Stephen and Bloom has provided a release from bondage
> . . . on the figurative level they take on heroic and creative possibilities.
> Having confined himself to a realistic time-scheme which made impossible
> the actual dramatization of that dynamic growth of personality so character-
> istic of the conventional novel, Joyce vested this element in his symbolic
> structures. . . . *Ulysses* is mock-heroic in immediacy, but heroic in

157

> perspective. . . . [When] they urinate . . . this is the moment of symbolic
> union, and the fact that it is richly comic in the manner of Sterne does not
> detract from its ultimate seriousness. [They part] with their futures adum-
> brated but not dramatized. . . .[2]

I intend to go further and demonstrate that the shadows of that adumbra-
tion are very sharp and precise; that in the dark garden Father Bloom and
Deacon Dedalus are celebrating, in comic-symbolic mode, the Vigil of
Easter; that the text of the *Exultet* shows us this; and also that Joyce had
planned a fairly strict itinerary for Stephen on his way toward acquiring the
power of "transmuting the daily bread of experience into the radiant body
of everliving life" (*P* 221). The services of Holy Week had beyond their
traditional symbolism a special and personal significance for Joyce, and I
contend that in his early work he alluded specifically to them, intending a
parallel significance for Stephen.

There is abundant evidence for the consuming interest—or obsession—
of Joyce the unbeliever throughout his life concerning the rituals that
commemorate the Passion. Carola Giedion-Welcker noted that "Joyce wore
a lilac necktie—a color that he loved and whose Passional significance the
former Jesuit student believed in."[3] Alessandro Francini Bruni recorded of
the early Trieste years that

> You had better not look for Joyce during the week before Easter because he is
> not available to anyone. On the morning of Palm Sunday, then during the
> four days that follow Wednesday of Holy Week, and *especially during all the
> hours of those great symbolic rituals at the early morning service* [the Easter Vigil],[4]
> Joyce is at church, entirely without prejudice and in complete control of
> himself, sitting in full view and *close to the officiants so that he won't miss a single
> syllable of what is said*, following the liturgy attentively in his book of the Holy
> Week services, and *often joining in the singing of the choir.*[5]

Joyce told Jacques Mercanton that he went every year to the services of
Good Friday (the Mass of the Presanctified) and Holy Saturday (the Easter
Vigil). As late as 1938 he was still attending; Mercanton got up at five in the
morning and arrived at St. Francis Xavier's at the moment of the blessing of
the fonts to find Joyce already there. "He was following the ritual from very
close." The two, with Mercanton guiding Joyce, accompanied the proces-
sion to the altar. Then, as the Mass began, "he made a nervous, impatient
gesture and murmured in English, 'I have seen the rebirth of fire and of
water. Enough until next year. The rest is without interest'." And the two
went away "while the Gloria burst out from the bell-towers."[6]

So much for Joyce's lifelong and consuming interest in the Easter Vigil;
but is it echoed in Stephen Dedalus? We think of the youthful Stephen of

the *Portrait* as proud—proud as Lucifer, and, like him, doomed to fall from the sky; but young Stephen has some curious views on deacons and their place in the liturgy. These, I think, are prophetic; at least they reveal an unexpected streak of humility in this yet unruined archangel. As the Jesuit director dangles before the youthful sodality prefect the alluring vision of priestly power, Stephen remembers "his own proud musings":

> And *above all it had pleased him to fill the second place* in those dim scenes of his imagining. He shrank from the dignity of celebrant because it displeased him to imagine that all the vague pomp should end in his own person or that the ritual should assign to him so clear and final an office. He longed for the minor sacred offices . . . to stand *as deacon* in a dalmatic of cloth of gold on the step below the celebrant, his hands joined and his face toward the people, and sing the chant *Ite, missa est*. . . . In vague sacrificial or sacramental acts alone his will seemed drawn *to go forth to encounter reality;* and it was partly *the absence of an appointed rite* which had always constrained him to inaction whether he had allowed silence to cover his anger or pride *or had suffered only an embrace he longed to give.* (P 158–59; emphases added.)

We have reason to remember the phrase "to go forth to encounter reality" as significant, if only because Joyce makes Stephen echo it on the last page of the *Portrait*. There we can find it ironic if we look ahead to *Ulysses* and see how little Stephen has made of his first attempt to encounter reality. But in Bloom's garden the somewhat older Stephen will find an "appointed rite," comic and earthy, that will pull down his pride and free him to offer embraces.

After he has decided to reject the priest's offer, young Stephen, knowing that "the oils of ordination would never anoint his body," feels nonetheless that "the end he had been born to serve" offers "a new adventure . . . like music . . . like triplebranching flames" (P 165). Those triple flames point directly to the diaconate and the *Exultet*.

Non-Catholics tend to ignore, and lay Catholics to forget, what Joyce and Stephen knew well—that the priesthood is attained only after the imposition of the lesser orders—doorkeeper, reader, exorcist, acolyte, and finally subdeacon and deacon. Nowadays the minor orders (the first four) are usually conferred together while the candidate is still a seminarian, the major ones soon afterward; anciently the process could take much time. A deacon says or sings, "Go, the Mass is finished," closing the rite; he reads or sings the Gospel (the Epistle being allotted to the subdeacon); he is technically permitted to preach and baptize, and he may distribute Communion; but his major and unique contribution to the liturgical year, his "big moment," so to speak, comes during the Easter Vigil, when he has his sole remaining ritual task: he sings the *Exultet*.

The Easter Vigil, celebrated in antiquity in the depth of night on Holy Saturday, moved gradually backward through the centuries, until by Joyce's day it was being celebrated early in the morning; it was restored to the original time and the ritual somewhat condensed by Pius XII in 1951.[7] The rite as Joyce knew it, however, accorded a different role (and larger than at present) to the deacon.[8] It is "the most important moment in the entire liturgical year; it is then that Christians celebrate their 'passing over,' by baptism . . . from slavery to the Devil to the freedom of the children of God." It is "in two main parts: a festival of light, and a festival of baptismal water and of baptism itself" (*LM* 492). At the Tenebrae service on Holy Thursday (which we know Joyce also attended whenever he could and which he had attended at Notre Dame [*JJ* 133] a few hours before receiving the telegram "Mother dying"), the altar has been stripped in commemoration of the stripping and scourging of Christ and the lights put out one by one, leaving the church in darkness. The Easter Vigil begins, if possible, outside the church in the gloom of night. Charcoal, ignited from fire kindled by striking flint and steel, is blessed; then the deacon, wearing a white dalmatic, takes a triple candle (reminiscent of Stephen's "triplebranching flames"), lights one branch, enters the church, goes halfway to the altar, lights a second branch, reaches the altar, and lights the third (*MR* 187). He then sings the *Exultet*, during which he pauses to trace the monogram Chi-Rho, for Christ, on the four- or five-foot-long paschal candle, and inserts in it five grains of incense; it thus becomes a symbol of the body of Christ with its five wounds. This candle is then lighted from the triple one, and the baptismal water is blessed and prepared for use during the ensuing year by a decidedly phallic progressive insertion of the paschal candle into it in three stages—touching the surface, halfway down, and touching the bottom of the vessel—with appropriate prayers. Before this last ceremony, all the lights of the darkened church are turned on or ignited.

The *Exultet*, a floridly figurative hymn of praise to the paschal candle, which may date from as early as the fourth century, was certainly well known to Joyce and to Stephen. For not only is it the most probable source of the paradox *felix culpa* ("happy fault" or "fortunate sin"), ubiquitous in the *Wake*,[9] but Stephen remembers one of its concluding phrases on Sandymount strand: "Allbright he falls, proud lightning of the intellect. *Lucifer, dico, qui nescit occasum*" ("Lucifer, I say, who knows no fall"; *U* 50). Moreover, unless Joyce is being supersubtle, not only Stephen but his creator has committed the phrase to memory and has remembered it wrong: the Missal has "*Ille Lucifer*' ("*that* Lucifer," i. e., Christ or the light of Christ) and has the less emphatic word *inquam* for "I say," not *dico*, "I assert" (*MR*, 194). Further, the phrase is a late addition, coming after the *Egoist* version and thus forming part of Joyce's crucial thematic overlay of the early chapters.[10]

These facts, however, do not prove that Joyce was thinking of the *Exultet* when he wrote the scene in Bloom's garden. The particular part that concerns us, though, running from Bloom and Stephen's leaving the kitchen to their vision of the "heaventree of stars," is also an afterthought, having been inserted in two stages in the Harvard and Texas proofs.[11] It is this passage, with its Dantean echoes, that has furnished most of the evidence for the view of Mary Reynolds and Walton Litz concerning Stephen's transformation through Bloom. Briefly, their reading of the scene runs thus: the two emerge from the basement with the first light of dawn, just as Dante and Vergil emerged from Hell on the shores of Purgatory (Canto I). Joyce's interrogator echoes Cato's question to the pilgrims, "Who has guided you?" The pair glimpse the stars, like Dante and Vergil; the "commemorative" 113th Psalm, intoned *secreto* by Stephen, is the one that Dante used to illustrate his fourfold meaning and is sung by the redeemed souls as they approach Purgatory (Canto II); it commemorates the transit of the Red Sea by the children of Israel, the confounding of their enemies, and the parallel redemption of Christians from sin and Satan through Christ's victorious ascent from Hell. These are the "symbolic structures" of which Litz speaks.[12] (Parenthetically, Dante's quitting Vergil in Cantos XXVII and XXX of the *Purgatorio* is not much less abrupt or unsentimental than Stephen's leaving Bloom—each has higher things to think of.)

No one has noticed, though, that the text of the *Exultet* also reinforces all these parallels and, furthermore, touches problems that Dantean references do not solve. Why do we have "order of precedence," "attendant ceremony," "wilderness of inhabitation"? Why does Bloom, carrying a lighted candle, "set the candlestick on the floor"? Why a *diaconal* hat, of all things? Why are we told with seemingly unnecessary elaboration, that Stephen put the hat "on his head"? Why do Stephen and Bloom regard the "visible luminous sign," the "splendid sign," Molly's lamp? Why, unless Joyce is being gratuitously grotesque, do they urinate? Why does Stephen Jesuitically quibble, while he pisses, over the hyperduly or perhaps latria due to Christ's foreskin? And why, finally, do they hear the churchbells, and why do the bells make Stephen think (his last recorded thought in *Ulysses*) of his obsessive *liliata rutilantium*? Because what the two are doing is a parodic and structural transformation, in the homeliest and grossest terms, of a rite whose symbolism Joyce takes very seriously—the Vigil of Easter, with the *Exultet*. (In this connection we should not forget that Bloom's humblest actions during the day are turned into Hebrew priestly rituals—burnt offering, rite of Melchizedec, etc. [*U* 728–29]—and that his privy in the garden is the Holy of Holies, which the High Priest must enter alone—Levites or deacons not admitted.)

The *Exultet* begins with the deacon calling on the hosts of heaven (*Angelica turba caelorum*) and earth to rejoice at Christ's victory over darkness, and on the faithful to join them; he thanks God for numbering him among the deacons (*intra Levitarum numerum*) so that he may praise the candle. Christ is the lamb whose blood sanctifies the doorposts of the faithful so that the Angel of Death will pass over (*MR* 187–89). The second part of the hymn hypnotically repeats the phrase *haec nox est*—"this is the night" when God brought our fathers out of Egypt to cross the Red Sea dryshod; this is the night when the fiery pillar swept away sin; this is the night when Christ broke the bonds of death. *O felix culpa*, to merit so great a redeemer. This is the night that shall be resplendent as day. The candle with its many (figurative) flames does not suffer lessening of its light (*MR* 190–93).

At this point the paschal candle is marked to represent the body of Christ, and lighted. The deacon goes on to sing: this is the night when heaven and earth, the human and the divine, are joined. He ends with the prayer that Lucifer may find the light burning still—Lucifer as the rising morning star and as Christ who knows no setting and who rose from death (*MR* 193–94).

After the hymn come prayers for those in power, lessons from Scripture, and the blessing of the baptismal water by a progressive triple insertion of the paschal candle, as we noted before. At this point comes, as the revised or modern missal says, "the most suitable time of the whole year for baptism," or spiritual rebirth (*LM* 518),[13] and the church is now fully illuminated.

It is, of course, arguing in a circle to ask rhetorically whether the liturgy contains any ceremony better suited to symbolize a turning point toward freedom and redemption in a man's life, whether religious or psychological-artistic. But when we see that the *Exultet* reenacts the biblical and Dantean parallels that have long been noticed in "Ithaca," that it is performed by a deacon and priest or a father figure and a man in a "diaconal hat" who had wanted to be a deacon, that it involves a movement between indoors and outdoors, at night, with the morning star about to appear, and that the deacon and his creator evidently remember at least two crucial phrases from it, the argument seems less circular.

But is the symbolism really consistent and without conflict? And above all, why a deacon, not a priest?

First, a reversal. When Bloom and Stephen go from the house into the garden, from the "house of bondage" (Egypt) into the "wilderness of inhabitation" (Sinai), they might seem to be *leaving* the church, since they quit a building. But if Bloom's garden contains the Holy of Holies or privy, and abuts on Eccles Street (for *ecclesia* or church), the garden *is* the church, and the candle has been properly lighted without, a pause being made at the door for the *Exultet* to begin, as Bloom sets the candlestick on the *floor* or threshold.[14] (The paschal candle stands on the steps of the altar.) A number of scholars have discussed Joycean hats as symbols of power or maturity; so, perhaps, by putting a diaconal hat on one's head one becomes a deacon.[15] (We ought also to remember how, after having traversed Purgatory and achieved victory over his own frailties, Dante in Canto XXVII is "crowned and mitred" by Vergil in token of his new priesthood and kingship.) It is fitting for celebrant to precede deacon in the "attendant ceremony," while the candidate for the priesthood quietly repeats a psalm about crossing the Red Sea. The hour is appropriate, with the morning star about to appear, and the visible luminous or splendid sign of Molly's lamp is fitting for the female deity of Joyce's truly perceived world, firmly rooted in the flesh and not transcending it except verbally. Moreover, the Book of Common Prayer tells us that an "outward and *visible sign*" represents "an inward and spiritual grace."[16] The blessing of the waters is concelebrated by Bloom and Stephen. The sexual symbolism of candle and font having been perceived, Joyceans at least should not be too sensitive about urination as creation, consecration, or baptism; nor should they be puzzled further about Stephen's association of his own penis with that of Christ triumphant. The bells ring in rejoicing as the ceremony ends, and since the *Exultet* begins with a rejoicing angelic *turba* or throng together with sparkling or rutilant lights, *liliata rutilantium turma* should not be very far from Stephen's thoughts. Stephen, as a dedicated would-be artist who has consciously rejected the church, does not need to be freed from sin, but he does need freedom from guilt and the consequent freedom of firm confidence in his own worth, his plans, his future; and *liliata rutilantium* reassures him that his mother is being welcomed by rejoicing confessors and virgins in heaven.

A wilderness of inhabitation may seem like a contradiction in terms, but a wilderness there must be. The Israelites did not attain the Promised Land until they had completed forty years of suffering and false starts in Sinai. They needed to be perfected in their faith by tribulation, and for Stephen, Dublin, even at its highest point, can afford but a Pisgah-sight of Palestine. Purgatory likewise is figuratively a wandering in the wilderness for the same purpose; it takes much time and labor for Dante to get to the Earthly Paradise, even though he has been released from the hopelessness of Hell and is confident of powerful assistance. Stephen can hardly be expected to head for a literal desert, but for a true artist the cities of men must forever be a wilderness, however populous; one's trials there perfect one's faith and dedication to one's art. Not only do the techniques of *Ulysses* forbid a depiction of Stephen's trials in the desert, as Litz has noted, but if Joyce is a Blake in his symbolism and a Defoe in his realism, the Defoe aspect must

prescribe a very long, very tedious, and very muddled purgation, tentative
and fitful—certainly not a melodramatic conversion, and certainly never to
be depicted by an artist who has progressed beyond *Dubliners* and who has
said that he is tired of Stephen anyway.[17]

This is all very well, some may say, but why must Stephen be a *deacon*?
Why wouldn't symbolic ordination at once as priest do just as well, since
ordination is also the beginning of a long and painful road? There are
reasons—symbolic, biographical, and cogent—that should lead us further
to favor the diaconate. "And let you, Stephen," says the director, "make a
novena to your holy patron saint, the first martyr, who is very powerful
with God, that God may enlighten your mind" (*P* 159–60). I think that St.
Stephen did this favor for Joyce; not only was he the first martyr, but he
was also the first *deacon*, made such by the Apostles as a helper or minis-
trant, not a priest.[18] In the martyrology he heads both the class of martyrs
and that of deacons.[19] His powerful defense of his faith before the Sanhe-
drin caused that body to cast him forth to be stoned to death at the
Damascus Gate of Jerusalem. His chief persecutor was Saul of Tarsus, who
shortly thereafter went out of the Damascus Gate to have the experience
that converted him into the Apostle Paul.[20] St. Stephen's Day is December
26, on which, in Ireland and northern England, boys used to kill a wren and
go about with it begging for pennies with the chant, "The wren, the wren,
the king of all birds," used in *Ulysses* (*U* 481) and immortalized in many
guises in *Finnegans Wake*.[21] *Stephanos* is "he who is crowned"—either with a
diadem or with a wreath of laurel, so that he may represent king and artist at
once. In any case, a young man whose patron is the archetype of deacons
and martyrs is not unlikely to fantasize about himself as a deacon, especially
if he is also obsessed with regarding himself as a perpetual martyr. The
young Stephen (or Joyce) in Paris, passing arduous evenings in the Bibliothèque Ste. Geneviève, was reminded of the identification on entering or
leaving that temple of learning, for his eyes could not have escaped the
beautiful façade of the church of St. Stephen the Martyr just across the
square, next to the Pantheon.

Lastly, the canons of the church and the events of Joyce's own life
provide revealing information. The diaconate is not to be conferred until
the candidate has reached the age of twenty-two,[22] and both Joyce and
Stephen (as we are carefully told in *Ulysses*) were twenty-two in 1904. We
remember that Joyce had attended Tenebrae at Notre Dame just before he
received the fatal telegram; we might therefore suppose that the rites of
Easter would be appropriate to a liberation from the season of mourning
and self-doubt that Tenebrae had inaugurated. And it is pretty clear that
Molly (or one of her avatars) for Stephen, and certainly Nora for Joyce,
were the *ewige weibliche* that brought final liberation and thus conferred

priestly orders and therefore supernatural powers on the artist-as-priest. But Joyce first "walked out with" Nora on the day of *Ulysses*, June 16, 1904, and one might suppose that that took care of the matter. However, there was an impediment. Joyce did not achieve total union with his earthly goddess—what he would have called complete carnal intercourse, *cum ejaculatione seminis in vas naturale*—until they got to Zurich in October (*JJ* 190, 775 n. 4). But a few weeks before this, still in Dublin, and exactly three months after their first meeting, on September 16, 1904, Joyce wrote Nora a letter in "oddly formal diction," in which, as Ellmann says, "he suggested his recognition of the perhaps irrevocable decision they had just made" (*JJ* 182). In it he says, "Are you sure you are not under any misapprehension about me? . . . The fact that you can choose to stand beside me in this way in my hazardous life fills me with great pride and joy. I hope you are not breaking all before you today" (*Letters*, II, 53).

"But you must be quite sure, Stephen," says the director,

> that you have a vocation because it would be terrible if you found afterwards you had none. . . . the sacrament of Holy Orders . . . imprints on the soul an indelible spiritual mark which can never be effaced. It is before you must weigh well, not after. It is a solemn question, Stephen, because on it may depend the salvation of your eternal soul. (*P* 160)

Three months to the day after Bloomsday, the irrevocable decision was taken and the director's portentous sentiments echoed by Stephen's future creator; and the canons of the church tell us that before a deacon can be ordained as a priest there must elapse an interval of—three months.[23]

Notes

1. For an informative survey of the history of critical opinion on this controversial question, see Richard M. Kain, "The Significance of Stephen's Meeting Bloom: A Survey of Interpretations," in *"Ulysses": Fifty Years*, ed. Thomas Staley (Bloomington: Indiana University Press, 1964), pp. 146–60.
2. "Ithaca," in *James Joyce's "Ulysses": Critical Essays*, ed. Clive Hart and David Hayman (Berkeley: University of California Press, 1974), pp. 400–401.
3. "Meetings with Joyce," in *Portraits of the Artist in Exile*, ed. Willard Potts (Seattle: University of Washington Press, 1979), p. 260.
4. See the discussion below: during Joyce's lifetime the Vigil of Easter was commonly celebrated early in the morning of Holy Saturday.
5. "Joyce Stripped Naked in the Piazza," in *Portraits*, ed. Potts, pp. 35–36, 38n. Emphases added.
6. "The Hours of James Joyce," in *Portraits*, ed. Potts, pp. 214–15.
7. *The Layman's Missal*, hereafter cited parenthetically in the text as *LM* (Baltimore: Helicon Press, 1962), p. 492.

8. For the official text of the earlier version, I have used the *Missale Romanum*, hereafter cited parenthetically in the text as *MR* (Mechliniae: H. Dessain, 1921), pp. 187–97.

9. Niall Montgomery, "The Pervigilium Phoenicis," *New Mexico Quarterly* 23 (1953): 437–72, finds twenty transformations of the phrase in the *Wake*.

10. I have used the transcriptions of the MSS; proofs; and the *Egoist* and *Little Review* versions in Robert E. Hurley, "The Proteus Episode of James Joyce's *Ulysses*" (Ph.D. diss., Columbia University, 1963), pp. 183, 211.

11. See Joseph Prescott, *Exploring James Joyce* (Carbondale: Southern Illinois University Press, 1964), pp. 67, 144.

12. See Litz, pp. 399–402, and Mary T. Reynolds, "Joyce's Planetary Music: His Debt to Dante," *Sewanee Review* 76 (1968): 456–58.

13. The answerer's voice in "Ithaca," locating Bloomsday in Bloom's reflections, places it "at the critical turning-point of human existence" (*U* 696), emphasizing the same idea and echoing Dante's *nel mezzo del cammin*.

14. The reversal is perhaps anticipated in Bloom's muddled recollection of the Haggadah in "Eolus," where he thinks, led us "*into* the house of bondage" (*U* 122; emphasis added). Bloom's house has been a place of bondage for him; the basement kitchen equates with Hell.

15. See Edmund L. Epstein, *The Ordeal of Stephen Dedalus* (Carbondale: Southern Illinois University Press, 1971), pp. 85–87, 193, for the most important references.

16. In the Catechism, explaining the meaning of the word "sacrament."

17. Frank Budgen, *James Joyce and the Making of "Ulysses"* (Bloomington: Indiana University Press, 1960), p. 105. See Robert Boyle, S. J., *Joyce's Pauline Vision: A Catholic Exposition* (Carbondale: Southern Illinois University Press, 1978), pp. 50–51 and elsewhere, for significant insights into the implications of Bloom's mass and Stephen's symbolic conversion and assumption of holy orders.

18. Acts 6:2–6.

19. Sabine Baring-Gould, *The Lives of the Saints*, 16 vols. (New York: Longmans, Green, 1898), XV, 296–99.

20. Acts 6:8–8:3, 9:1–9.

21. See the references in Matthew J. C. Hodgart and Mabel P. Worthington, *Song in the Works of James Joyce* (New York: Columbia University Press, 1959).

22. Canon 975; see Stanislaus Woywod, OFM, *A Practical Commentary on the Code of Canon Law*, 2 vols. (New York: Joseph F. Wagner, 1939), I. 515.

23. Canons 977, 978; Woywod, I, 517.

PART VII

The *Finnegans Wake* Workshop

Prefatory Note

Mary T. Reynolds

Explication has many faces but a single purpose: to produce
an increase of understanding. The *Finnegans Wake* Workshop panel sought
to demonstrate, by maneuvering in depth within one short passage of the
book, some of the manifold inventions and techniques that Joyce brought to
the construction of his text in *Finnegans Wake* as a whole. The passage
chosen was *Finnegans Wake* 34:30–36:34, the meeting of HCE with the Cad
in the Park. After an introductory exegesis, each member of the panel
presented his chosen approach to the text. The chairman, after introducing
the panel members, began the discussion with a brief review of the manuscript evidence of Joyce's revisions of the Cad episode.

Finnegans Wake 34:30–36:34

We can't do without them. Wives, rush to the restyours! Ofman will
toman while led is the lol. Zessid's our kadem, villapleach, vollapluck.
Fikup, for flesh nelly, el mundo nov, zole flen! If she's a lilyth, pull early!
Pauline, allow! And malers abushed, keep black, keep black! Guiltless of
much laid to him he was clearly for once at least he clearly expressed himself
as being with still a trace of his erstwhile burr and hence it has been received
of us that it is true. They tell the story (an amalgam as absorbing as calcium
chloereydes and hydrophobe sponges could make it) how one happygogusty
Ides-of-April morning (the anniversary, as it fell out, of his first assumption
of his mirthday suit and rights in appurtenance to the confusioning of human
races) ages and ages after the alleged misdemeanour when the tried friend of
all creation, tigerwood roadstaff to his stay, was billowing across the wide
expanse of our greatest park in his caoutchouc kepi and great belt and
hideinsacks and his blaufunx fustian and ironsides jackboots and Bhagafat
gaiters and his rubberised inverness, he met a cad with a pipe. The latter, the
luciferant not the oriuolate (who, the odds are, is still berting dagabout in the
same straw bamer, carryin his overgoat under his schulder, sheepside out, so
as to look more like a coumfry gentleman and signing the pledge as gaily as
you please) hardly accosted him with: Guinness thaw tool in jew me dinner
ouzel fin? (a nice how-do-you-do in Poolblack at the time as some of our
olddaisers may still tremblingly recall) to ask could he tell him how much a
clock it was that the clock struck had he any idea by cock's luck as his watch

was bradys. Hesitency was clearly to be evitated. Execration as cleverly to be
honnisoid. The Earwicker of that spurring instant, realising on fundamental
liberal principles the supreme importance, nexally and noxally, of physical
life (the nearest help relay being pingping K. O. Sempatrick's Day and the
fenian rising) and unwishful as he felt of being hurled into eternity right
then, plugged by a soft-nosed bullet from the sap, halted, quick on the draw,
and replyin that he was feelin tipstaff, cue, prodooced from his gunpocket his
Jurgensen's shrapnel waterbury, ours by communionism, his by usucap-
ture, but, on the same stroke, hearing above the skirling of harsh Mother East
old Fox Goodman, the bellmaster, over the wastes to south, at work upon the
ten ton tonuant thunderous tenor toller in the speckled church (Couhounin's
call!) told the inquiring kidder, by Jehova, it was twelve of em sidereal and
tankard time, adding, buttall, as he bended deeply with smoked sardinish
breath to give more pondus to the copperstick he presented, (though this
seems in some cumfusium with the chapstuck ginger which, as being of
sours, acids, salts, sweets and bitters compompounded, we know him to
have used as chawchaw for bone, muscle, blood, flesh and vimvital,) that
whereas the hakusay accusation againstm had been made, what was known
in high quarters as was stood stated in Morganspost, by a creature in youman
form who was quite beneath parr and several degrees lower than yore
triplehydrad snake. In greater support of his word (it, quaint anticipation of a
famous phrase, has been reconstricted out of oral style into the verbal for all
time with ritual rhythmics, in quiritary quietude, and toosammenstucked
from successive accounts by Noah Webster in the redaction known as the
Sayings Attributive of H. C. Earwicker, prize on schillings, postlots free),
the flaxen Gygas tapped his chronometrum drumdrum and, now standing
full erect, above the ambijacent floodplain, scene of its happening, with one
Berlin gauntlet chopstuck in the hough of his ellboge (by ancientest signlore
his gesture meaning: ∃!) pointed at an angle of thirty-two degrees towards his
duc de Fer's overgrown milestone as fellow to his gage and after a rendypresent
pause averred with solemn emotion's fire: Shsh shake, co-comeraid! Me
only, them five ones, he is equal combat. I have won straight. Hence my
nonation wide hotel and creamery establishments which for the honours of
our mewmew mutual daughters, credit me, I am woowoo willing to take my
stand, sir, upon the monument, that sign of our ruru redemption, any
hygienic day to this hour and to make my hoath to my sinnfinners, even if I
get life for it, upon the Open Bible and before the Great Taskmaster's (I lift
my hat!) and in the presence of the Deity Itself andwell of Bishop and Mrs
Michan of High Church of England as of all such of said my immediate
withdwellers and of every living sohole in every corner wheresoever of this
globe in general which useth of my British to my backbone tongue and
commutative justice that there is not one tittle of truth, allow me to tell you,
in that purest of fibfib fabrications.

The Narrative Thread in the Cad Episode

Nathan Halper

The encounter of HCE and the Cad is that of the Father and Son. The son asks the father how he is today. It is a greeting—but the father, who does not understand the language that the son is speaking, takes it as a threat. He thinks that the son is asking the time and this, in turn, is a statement that it is time for the father to move on. He sees the watch as a lethal weapon controlled by a time-mechanism. This, indeed, is what shrapnel is. It is a Waterbury: water—symbol of flowing time; bury—sign of death. The cad is a cadet, i.e., he is young. But also a *cad*—a threat to the father's status quo.

The father is John Joyce or Simon Dedalus. He is "billowing" (bill owing) across the Park. John Joyce was actually stopped by a young man in the Park (he spoke of him as a Cad) who asked him the time. The father is also Joyce himself. The watch is a Jurgenson. Jurgen is a Swiss-German form of George, the name of Joyce's son. The cad looks like a country gentleman, a farmer, which is the meaning of "George." The year is 1922. Giorgio is seventeen, a time when the father might expect him to make his move.

In that year, too, English government in Ireland is threatened by the young rebellious Irish. The Cad is speaking Gaelic. The clothes that Earwicker is wearing resemble those of the Royal Irish Constabulary. Tipstaff and copperstick are consonant with this meaning. At the time, many members of the constabulary were being assassinated in different parts of Ireland.

England is also being threatened by the United States, "New England." American slang—e.g., "sap"—is used to describe the cad. In Russia too, the father figure was being killed. HCE is called Sweatogor—an aging giant in a Russian epic poem who is stopped by a young man who asks him the time.

In 1922 the literary establishment was also being challenged by T. S. Eliot and by Joyce. HCE's clothing is associated with William Butler Yeats. The Gaelic and the American slang are to be associated with these young challengers. (The Cad's question is an echo of the famous question that Joyce is reported to have asked Yeats.) At the time, Joyce and Eliot were literally accused of being Bolsheviks: another reference to the Sweatogor theme.

Notice, finally, that the Father was once a Son himself. The old man is a Gyges: a giant. But Gyges, in Herodotus, killed the king, the father figure, and then married the mother figure, the queen. A basic structure of Joyce's book is thus adumbrated in this passage.

Parsing Rhetorics: The Cad As Prolegomena to the Readings of *Finnegans Wake*

Seán Golden

The passage begins with a matrix of Woman/Mother allied to Language. The necessity for wives (*We can't do without them*) and the role of procreation (here indicated by contraception—*if a lilyth pull early*) are linked with words for sex (*lol*) and sexual innuendo (*fikup*). A matrix of birth, sex, common origins, and instinctual desires is linked to Language with examples of attempts at reunifying the human race (post-Babel) with artificially invented universal languages (Volapük) and with the arcanum allied to Arcadia/Eden (*Zessid's our kadem*), a language of body and nature and mystery which unifies.

At the same time the passage is *confusioning*. Individual puns, as seems to be the rule in *Finnegans Wake*, contain mutually and simultaneously contradictory meanings. The syntax also confuses. *Ofman will toman while led is the lol* seems to be a symmetrically balanced phrase hinging on *while*. While implies two activities occurring simultaneously. The use of the verb "to be" on both sides of *while* seems to indicate the role of the copula as identifying equality: *ofman:toman::led:lol*. But *Ofman* suggests *of Man*, perhaps implying that which comes of Man, man-made, etc., while *toman* invites speculation about what returns to Man or will return to Man. Joyce's prepositions have turned what appear to be nouns into verbal units suggestive of actions, i.e., verbs. This is reinforced by the future tense. *Ofman* (subject) *will toman* (verbal phrase). The incomplete verb "to be" (*will*) makes *toman* the verb, while the balance of the phrase suggested *toman* was a noun. Is it an object as well? Is it transitive or intransitive?

Meanwhile, *led is the lol* suggests a definitive affinity between *led* and *lol*. *Led = the lol*. But *led* could be a verb, in which case *the lol* is *led* while *ofman will toman*. Parsing the sentence this way reveals a fundamental syntactical ambiguity operating independently of any meanings we may assign to the individual puns. Our sense of English grammar is sufficient to allow this parsing without knowing what the words mean (cf. Twas brillig and the slithy toves, etc.). Thus my general rule about the mutually and simultaneously contradictory nature of the puns (cf. *the abnihilisation of the etym*) may apply as well to the syntax, and parsing corroborates the implications of wordlists and exegesis. "Reading" the rhythms and phonic implications of phrases will also work this way often enough to be considerable. Like Gertrude Stein, Joyce manipulates our fundamental sense of grammatical relationships by violating our sense of grammatical propriety.

Volapükian language emphasizes the role of vocabulary. Ambivalent syntax emphasizes the role of grammar. The value of sound, the phonic dimension, is emphasized by homophones (*fikup*) and rhythms (cf. *Lilli-bulero bullenalaw, lilyth pull early! Pauline, allow!*). We respond to the passage on many levels in several areas of perception, including semantics, syntax, and sound, as well as literary and biblical allusion, folk song, and sexual innuendo, and have as a result a constellation of meanings and responses that are differentiable to an extent (i.e., they are not undifferentiated random noises, letters, etc.), but not totally differentiable, and our response to the phrases is in solution. The passage is the solution.

As the passage unfolds the syntax becomes more and more problematical, strained by parenthetical interruption and confused antecedents, culminating in total syntactical breakdown just at the point when a statement seems to have been made (i.e., the reader has the impression that something has been said, which the syntax of the statement totally undercuts). This may be a fundamental rule of grammar in *Finnegans Wake*—that the syntax quite often contradicts the content of the sentence so that singularized meaning cannot exist.

The sentence beginning "Guiltless" has usually been interpreted as HCE's claiming innocence of his crime, yet parsing the sentence reveals an equally valid and opposite reading. *Guiltless of much laid to him he was clearly for once*—i.e., whatever doubt may exist about other occasions, here at least he was clearly guiltless. Or he was guiltless of much (but note, not all) laid to him clearly for once. But, *Guiltless of much laid to him, he _was_ clearly for once*—i.e., while he may often be guiltless of much laid to him, he was clearly guilty for once. *At least he clearly expressed himself as being*, although his attempt to express himself clearly (or the impossibility of doing so?) obfuscates matters. What then does he clearly express? That he was *Guiltless of much laid to him*? Or that he is *being still with a trace of his erstwhile burr* (onetime Irish? onetime Scots burr?)? Then, what *has been received of us that it is true*? That he is guiltless? Guilty? Or that he still has a trace of his *erstwhile* burr? And why has it been received as true? Because it was clearly expressed?

This matrix also contains elements of Irish history and culture and Anglo-Irish relations. *Lillibulero*'s rhythm animates the passage. It's a northern Irish song with Orange connotations, which hopes for Jacobite rescue of Ireland but concludes that Gaelic Ireland will be ruled by an ass and a dog. Some versions are quite viciously anti-Papist. On the other hand, *Ofman will toman* suggests *True men like you men* from *The Memory of the Dead*, a nationalist ballad (and a symptom of the cult of the dead Fenian martyrs that animated Patrick Pearse and the Easter Rising). The confrontation with the Cad takes place within a context of Irish pluralism and divided loyalties, which is the legacy of the English adventure in Ireland. Both ballads are Irish. They are utterly opposed to each other.

Received tradition occupies more of the passage: *They tell the story. . . .* The story is described parenthetically as an *amalgam* (originally an alchemical term) as absorbing as calcium chloride (a drying agent) and hydrophobe sponges (?) can make it, i.e. the opposite of absorbing. (And, if calcium chloride plus water would create hydrochloric acid, a self-destructive amalgam.) Joyce's syntax apparently says that it is absorbing, while his words say it is not. Syntax and sense are at odds. The story takes place one day, which is also parenthetically described as an anniversary, but it is unclear what the anniversary is of, and Roman civil law (the donning of the *toga liberalis* or *virilis*) joins Babel in another contradictory phrase: law attempts to order the confusioning of human races, yet confusioning is the existential situation that defeats Man's attempts at ordering, or attaining to order. Stated simply, They tell the story how one morning he met a cad with a pipe. The rest of this long sentence (and the sentences are growing in length) is qualification of this statement, or aspects of this statement. Here simple syntax is being overwhelmed by detailed qualifications, the details themselves contradictory and confusioning.

The latter hardly accosted him with [How-do-you-do] to ask could he tell him [the time]. This simple statement is complicated by qualifications on top of qualifications and a fundamental contradiction in content (the Irish for how-do-you-do does not mean what-time-is-it). *Latter* is modified by *the luciferant not the oriuolate* (the match-bearing pipe smoker *cum* Lucifer *cum* Lucifer-maker, etc., vs. the time-bearing time-crier). Then there is a parenthetical qualifier that modifies *oriuolate* (some readers assign it to *The latter*). The parenthesis indicates that HCE is still attempting something, presenting himself as something other than what he is. Irish folklore speaks of "going astray," an experience similar to *jamais vu*, often an experience of being lost in a misty and/or boggy place. The solution is to take off coat and cap, turn them inside out, then put them on again to change perception and recover one's senses. HCE seems to be caught in such a situation (and still caught). Two short sentences reinforce the presence of *H, C, & E* before the name Earwicker clarifies the matter.

The syntactical juggling act of the next sentence disguises the fact that it is incomplete: Earwicker . . . realising the . . . importance . . . of physical life . . . prodooced . . . his . . . waterbury . . . but . . . hearing . . . the

. . . toller in the speckled church . . . told the inquiring kidder . . . it was twelve . . . adding . . . that whereas the . . . accusation againstm had been made, what was known in high quarters as was stood stated in Morgans-post, by a creature. . . . Here syntax breaks down completely under the onslaught of modifiers, modifications, rhetorical adjustments, and uncon-scious emotional forces. The modifying phrases and details are enriching in terms of the matrix of the passage, and to the semantic, syntactic, and phonic levels of the text have been added visual codes, the letters H, C, E, and references to ∃ as an ideogram or as E rotated, and as the sigla in the Doodles family for HCE. The politics of the Irish situation have been enmeshed again in Roman law and updated to include communism and actual revolutionary situations, such as the Paris Commune, so that the context of the Easter Rising, the resurgence under a banner of Gaelic Catholic Ireland of an atavistic nationalism that ignores history and the pluralism developed over centuries in Ireland, into an international context of history and political theory. HCE's stammer begins to emerge, a sign of guilt, despite his attempts to clearly express not only his guiltlessness but his allegiance to the cause of the Rising. This attempt undermines him utterly. In support of his word (i.e., his native Irish allegiance to Gaelic Catholic Ireland) he swears upon Wellington's Monument (a symbol of the Anglo-Irishry, the enemy). Moreover his gesture is obscene. At whom is the obscenity directed? The Wellington he swears upon? The Cad? *His* oath? Is it a denial of his oath?

HCE's gesture and oaths are contradictory of what he wants to say—*Me only* instead of *sinn fein*, comrade (Bolshevik) as much as *comráidhe* (or *come raid*: Judas, informer). He allies himself with the Sinn Fein party and its self-help-for-Ireland schemes, but his attempt at an oath leads him to identify with the Anglo-Irish, the Church of England, English justice and law, the Empire, saying he is British to his backbone tongue, and that there is no truth in the lying fabrications (of the accusations made against him), none of which have been raised against him by the Cad to whom he is speaking.

Syntax and sense at odds in ways similar to the divisions within colonized Ireland as a paradigm for syntax and sense being at odds fundamentally and existentially throughout human history and into the present: As it was, so shall it be? Movement from a matrix of sex and source, wives and mothers, through language to lexicography and fabrication: Mother as Verb? Father as syntax? Futility of Order? Delusion of ordering? Neither the sound nor the sense nor the syntax of the passage will precipitate into constituent elements. The solution is in the solution. Language is a constituent element of the social material process, a means of production, implicated in base as well as superstructure, hegemonizer and hegemonized. But in Joyce's linguistic Universe, field, or complex plane of *Finnegans Wake*, Language is neither hegemonizer nor hegemonized (hence Phillippe Sollers's declaration that *Finnegans Wake* is the greatest antifascist document of the twentieth century, because in deconstructing syntax it deconstructs the structures of the State and Family that reinforce the State). Joyce was acutely aware of *the backbone tongue*, of the role of the Mother tongue in molding the man. An English speaker is British to his backbone tongue.

Ireland's "long vicefreegal existence": A Context for *Finnegans Wake* 34–36

Riana O'Dwyer

Joyce in exile was forever Irish. The Irish in Ireland were forever afraid of being foreign, and yet they were unavoidably so. The strands of past arrivals are so tangled in Ireland that any one individual is on a perpetual tightrope of identity, and in this chapter of *Finnegans Wake* the penalty for falling off the tightrope, by identifying with the wrong strand from the past, could be "a softnosed bullet from the sap" (35.25–26).

Throughout *Finnegans Wake* identities for HCE are proposed, from his association with the "Earwickers of Sidlesham in the Hundred of Manhood" (30.7–8) in England; or the presentation of him as "offsprout of vikings" (30.8–9) who founded the city of Dublin; or "poor old Roderick O'Conor Rex, the auspicious waterproof monarch of all Ireland" (380.33–34), last High King; or Leary (610.9), the High King who reigned when Patrick came to Ireland; or Finn Mac Cumhail, representative of all heroic virtues and embodiment of Celtic ideals; to your man Finnegan, the hod-carrier, archetypal in another way, in the way that an average man represents all the people who make up the population, have ever done so, or will ever do so.

The searcher for an identity can never reach quest's end, because there is no end. There is no definitive Irishman because Irishness is part of a process that has gone on before and will continue past the present moment. What we are presented with in this passage is a demand, with violence, that HCE choose a definitive identity, that he select some strand out of the tapestry of the historical process that has made him, and define himself irrevocably by reference to that strand alone.

What are the historical elements immediately implicit in the context of this passage? First, there is the idea of conquest and subjugation. This has just been explored in a juxtaposition of the Norman Conquests of England (A.D. 1066) and Ireland (A.D. 1170) in which the defeat of Harold of England by William the Conqueror becomes the same event as the conquest of Ireland by Strongbow and the Norman lords acting for Henry II one hundred years later (*FW* 30–33). Harold, the former King of England,

becomes subject to William, the new King, or Roderick O'Conor, the last
High King of Ireland, becomes the subject of Henry II; in either case we
witness the fall that "is retaled early in bed and later on life down through all
christian minstrelsy" (3.17–18). I should say here that the events that
history relates of the great men who came to history's notice also take place
in *Finnegans Wake* in regard to everyday men whom nobody notices,
expressing the historical precedents for everyday events.

In Ireland after the Norman Conquest most of the Irish chiefs were left
undisturbed in their spheres of authority, but they were encouraged to
make formal submission to Henry II, in return for which he gave them
English titles. Thus HCE becomes "good Dook Umphrey" (32.15). These
Irish dukes and lords held their authority from the King of England and
began a period of "long vicefreegal existence" (33.30). The chief representative of the king later lived in the Vice-Regal lodge in the Phoenix Park in
Dublin, and it is in the Phoenix Park, near the Wellington Monument, that
HCE meets the "cad with a pipe" (35.11). "The wide expanse of our
greatest park" (35.7–8) was also the scene for the Invincibles' attack that
became known as the Phoenix Park Murders. In May 1882, Lord Caven-
dish and Mr. Thomas Henry Burke were stabbed to death publicly in the
park. Two cyclists rode past them without realizing what was happening.[1]
The actual stabbing was done by a man called Brady, who lurks also in the
cad's request to HCE for the right time: "his watch was bradys" (35.20).
This combines the Greek word for slow with the murderer's surname.

The reminder of the Phoenix Park murders underlines the threatening
nature of the encounter. The Cad addresses HCE in Irish. (35.15–16), a
kind of test, to see if he is one of them, a supporter of "the Fenian rising"
(35.24), or a British sympathizer. It is also reminiscent of the kind of test
that recruits to the original Fianna Eireann had to undergo in the days of
Cormac Mac Art, when riddling, an ability to ferret out the significance of
obscure clues and verses, was one of the necessities for acceptance—the
intellectual test that complemented their physical feats of strength, speed,
and endurance. The menace implied in an apparently simple question is
emphasized in the passage. There are clear indications that the reader is not
to regard it as merely indicative of HCE's paranoia, in particular the
comment: "a nice how-do-you-do in Poolblack at the time as some of our
olddaisers may still tremblingly recall" (35.16–18). It is literally a question
of life and death, and the challenged HCE, "unwishful as he felt of being
hurled into eternity right then," (35.24–25) wished to defend himself.

It might seem that, when faced with the necessity of choosing an identity
upon pain of death, the pragmatic solution would be to opt for that identity
which would please the challenger and so avoid the fate of no longer having
any identity at all. However, even for the pragmatist, life was not so simple

in the period immediately following the Phoenix Park murders, as Dublin was alive with spies and informers. The challenger might be one of those seeking to identify Fenian sympathizers, in which case identification with the Fenian cause would sign the death warrant.

Charles Stewart Parnell, "who was perhaps the most formidable man that ever led the Irish, but in whose veins there was not even a drop of Celtic blood,"[2] was one of those for whom the Phoenix Park murders posed such a crisis of identity. His exertions to achieve the passage of a Land Act, and particularly to ensure fair rents for tenants through use of a boycott against those who took possession of land from which others had been evicted, landed him in jail in October 1881. He had only just been released when the murders took place. Parnell was committed to the use of constitutional means to effect improvements in conditions in Ireland and thus found himself unpopular both in England, because of his success in having the Land Act passed, and with the Fenians, because of his opposition to violence. He almost decided to leave public life at this time, because he felt, with some justification, that he himself was a target for Fenian assassination.[3] Does he speak here, with HCE, answering the Cad with "my British to my backbone tongue" (36. 31–32)?

Though Parnell was persuaded to continue his work for Land Reform and Home Rule, and though the Phoenix Park murderers were arrested and tried in 1883, the matter did not rest there. In 1887 the London *Times* published a series of articles called "Parnellism and Crime," alleging Parnell's support and encouragement for the conspiracy before and after the murders took place. The articles were based on letters alleged to have been written by Parnell, one of which was reproduced in facsimile by the *Times*. Parnell stated that he had never written, never signed, never authorized any of the letters, and eventually a Government Commission was set up to examine the case. The commission established that spies and informers were paid to seek out evidence relating to the murders, and that the letters in question were procured by Richard Pigott. At the enquiry it began to emerge that Pigott himself had forged the letters. The denouement hinged on a phrase in one of the letters, "Let there be an end of this hesitency." Pigott was asked to write down several words by the Defence Barrister, and he misspelled "hesitancy," as he had done in the forged letter.[4] He later confessed to the forgeries and committed suicide, events that figure later in *Finnegans Wake* (97.25–98.4).

The fatal word that was Pigott's undoing, but that saved Parnell, echoes through *Finnegans Wake* whenever hidden crimes exist or where guilt creates imaginary ones. The reverberations are felt when HCE is challenged by the Cad: "Hesitency was clearly to be evitated" (35.20). The encounter with the Cad takes place "ages and ages after the alleged misde-

meanour" (35.5–6), just as the allegations against Parnell were made five
years after the Phoenix Park murders. HCE meets the Cad "one happygogusty Ides-of-April morning" (35.3), and the *Times* published the first of its
articles on 18 April 1887.

Joyce had written earlier that Ireland was "an aristocratic country without an aristocracy . . . poor fallen kings, recognizable even in their decline
as impractical Irishmen,"[5] just as Humphrey Chimpden Earwicker is an
impractical but average Irishman. The comings and goings of past armies,
systems of government, and colonizers have all contributed to "a vast
fabric, in which the most diverse elements are mingled. . . . In such a
fabric, it is useless to look for a thread that may have remained pure and
virgin without having undergone the influence of a neighbouring thread."[6]
Joyce's view of the composite nature of Irish civilization is echoed in the
structure and technique of *Finnegans Wake*.

The world that exists in *Finnegans Wake* is created of many things; it
encompasses many almost incompatible strands and attempts to hold them
in the momentary harmony of a kaleidoscope. The response to it needs to be
sensitive and complex, created from a consciousness of as many disparate
elements as the mind can hold at a given moment. In relation to the history
of Ireland this involves a consciousness of multiplicity rather than of
simplicity, a sense of the variety of past inhabitants incorporated into the
variety of those who exist at present, or who existed in the present of Joyce's
moment. The Cad passage polarizes the extremes of Englishness and
Irishness, placing HCE and a shade of Parnell in the middle. HCE in the
passage under consideration, and indeed in the entire chapter, is both
invader and invaded, conqueror and conquered, king and subject.

Notes

1. St. John Ervine, *Parnell* (London: Benn, 1925), pp. 198–200.
2. James Joyce, *The Critical Writings*, ed. Ellsworth Mason and Richard Ellmann
(New York: The Viking Press, 1968), p. 162.
3. Ervine, pp. 194–202.
4. Ibid. pp. 240–66.
5. Joyce, *The Critical Writings*, p. 168.
6. Ibid., p. 165.

PART VIII

Joyce and the Gnosis of Modern Science

Joyce and the Gnosis of Modern Science

Ihab Hassan

What can the cryptic title "Joyce and the Gnosis of Modern Science" possibly mean? I hasten to reassure you: gnosis here refers simply to knowledge or wisdom, not to any hieratic cult or licentious heresy. Our interest lies in Joyce and Science. But isn't this like saying "Joyce and Green Peas"? I admit it: yoking incongruous themes together appears as a conceit. But I am not in the least cynical and hope to prove this by placing the topic of our discussion in two large perspectives that may vindicate its bizarre conjunction. The first concerns that drive toward abstraction, or derealization, or discorporation, or ephemeralization, or etherealization that I have elsewhere called the New Gnosticism. The second concerns science itself as a metaphoric activity of mind. Placed in this double perspective, the work of James Joyce reveals an aspect of itself both historical and tropological.

The perspective of abstraction or derealization comes quickly into focus when we place *Dubliners* (1912 or 1914, as you wish) by *Finnegans Wake* (1939). Did ever an author change so much his verbal skin within a mere quarter century? *Dubliners*, though consummately shaped, renders a reality that even Dubliners, even Messrs. Maunsel, Ltd., would spitefully recognize. The *Wake* renders—is—another kind of reality: "a very fairworded instance of falsemeaning adamelegy" (77), "making a bolderdash for lubberty of speech . . . letting punplays pass to ernest" (233), "half a sylb, helf a solb, holf a salb onward" (292), "the sibspeeches of all mankind have foliated (earth seizing them!) from the root of some funner's stotter" (96), "Silence in thought! Spreach! Wear anartful of outer nocense!" (378). The *Wake* explodes reality, collapsing it into language, explodes language, collapsing it into reality. We are reminded of Foucault's dream of dispersal and the "disappearance" of man: "Is this not the sign," Foucault asks, "that this whole [humanist] configuration is now about to topple, and that man is in the process of perishing as the being of language continues to shine ever brighter on the horizon?"

This immanence of language, this derealization or dematerialization of existence into the play of the logos, constitutes my first gnostic perspective, one that Joyce's work supremely enacts. But the tendency, of course, is older than Joyce. Ortega traces it back to the painting and philosophy of the Renaissance:

> The guiding law of the great variations in painting is one of disturbing simplicity. First, things are painted; then sensations; finally, ideas. This means that in the beginning the artist's attention was fixed on external reality; then on the subjective; finally, on the intrasubjective. . . . Now, Occidental philosophy has followed an identical route. . . .
>
> The philosopher retracts his attention even more and, instead of directing it to the subjective as such, fixes on what up to now has been called "the content of consciousness," that is, the intrasubjective.

It may be that the theoretical physicist "retracts his attention" even more than the artist or philosopher wants—but let that for the moment pass. What we now need to recognize *about* the tendency toward abstraction, derealization, is its universalist implications—or rather, its implications of a *concrete universalism*, both idiosyncratic *and* immanent, idiolectic *and* ubiquitous.

> Man humanizes the world, injects it, impregnates it with his own ideal substance and is finally entitled to imagine that one day or another, in the far depths of time, this terrible outer world will become so saturated with man that our descendants will be able to travel through it as today we mentally travel through our own inmost selves—he finally imagines that the world, without ceasing to be the world, will one day be changed into something like a materialized soul, and, as in Shakespeare's *Tempest*, the winds will blow at the bidding of Ariel, the spirit of ideas.

Was this Teilhard de Chardin? Not at all: Ortega again. Nor does Erich Auerbach reach a different conclusion in his compendious work on Western realism, which ends with the emergence of "the technique of multiple consciousness" in modern works, including *Ulysses*, "in which the technique of a multiple reflection of consciousness and of multiple time strata would seem to be employed more radically than anywhere else." (What would he have said of *Finnegans Wake*?) The tendency leads Auerbach finally to presage "a common life of mankind on earth," perhaps a long way off still, yet already visible in the derealizations of literature, the extended immediacies of its consciousness.

Auerbach feared "the approaching unification and simplification" that this extension of mind seemed to portend. But Northrop Frye came closer to the mark when he recognized that whenever "we construct a system of thought to unite earth with heaven, the story of the Tower of Babel recurs: we discover that after all we can't quite make it, and that what we have in the meantime is a plurality of languages." Frye, we recall, ended the vast synoptic task of his *Anatomy* by taking *Finnegans Wake* as his exemplum: creation and knowledge, art and science, myth and concept, dream and language, are all therein diffused, diffracted, disseminated—and at the same time, wholly patterned, if not exactly unified. For the Logos, as Derrideans never cease to remind us, the Logos is "decentered," actually rather like an inverted God, whose circumference is everywhere and center nowhere.

Let me summarize this first perspective on Joyce. The startling development of his fiction, from *Dubliners* to the *Wake*, may be construed as a movement away from realism toward fantasy, abstraction, derealization. But that movement recapitulates within the author's lifetime a larger historical trend, accelerated by science and technology in the last half century, a trend toward dematerialization, the dispersal of languages, thus the (near) immanence of mind. This, to repeat, is the new gnosticism, which avers that nature is becoming culture, and culture is becoming less artifacts than symbols and signs. Ernst Cassirer put it thus in his *Essay on Man*, published in 1944, before McLuhan or Frye, Foucault or Auerbach:

> Physical reality seems to recede in proportion as man's symbolic activity advances. Instead of dealing with the things themselves, man is in a sense constantly conversing with himself. He has so enveloped himself in linguistic forms . . . that he cannot see or know anything except by the interposition of this artificial medium.

Conveniently, this statement brings me to the second perspective on Joyce. For Cassirer also believed that in the symbolic universe, science held a special place, and could be regarded as "the highest and most characteristic attainment of human culture," precisely because it was theoretical, metaphorical, because it possessed, together with language and art, that "spontaneity and productivity" which animate "the very center of all human activities."

I will comment presently on this metaphoric power of science, but before doing so, I want to reemphasize its historic role in the dematerialization of existence. Speculative, paradoxical, non-iconic, modern physics relies mainly on mathematical idealizations, abstract *Gedankenexperimente* and intuitive or aesthetic criteria—Paul Dirac thought it was "more important to have beauty in one's equations than to have them fit the experiment." Indeed, as Werner Heisenberg argues in *Physics and Philosophy*, atomic physics has rejected the materialism of Democritus in favor of a view far closer to Heraclitus, Pythagoras, and Plato. No less than Ortega on art and philosophy, Heisenberg argues, in *Across the Frontiers*, discorporation:

In art, as in science, we can discern a striving for universality. In the sciences we are endeavoring to interpret all physical phenomena in a unified way, to understand all organisms in terms of a single point of view, and we have already come a long way upon this road. In art we are seeking to present a basis for life common to all men on earth. This striving for unification and bringing together necessarily leads to abstraction, in art probably no less than in science. However, what we now see before us in modern art may well not yet belong to this stage of abstraction. Instead, it probably corresponds to that confused preliminary phase which also had to be undergone in science: a phase where we sense that the previous forms will not suffice to present the new and more embracing content; where this content can be seized but cannot yet be formed, since it is not yet clear or viable enough for that.

This statement may strike us as both condescending and naïve, for it deprecates the will to difference, diversity, indeterminacy—Heisenberg's own principle—that coexists with the universalizing drive in culture. Still, Heisenberg's point stands, and even applies to Joyce's later work, *Finnegans Wake* most particularly, which William Troy called "a kind of Logos of the Einsteinian vision of the universe," a text that despite all its decreations, invokes the gnostic totality of the Book: "light phantastic of his gnose's glow as it slid lucifericiously within an inch of its page" (182).

But I must now turn to the metaphoric capacity of science, which defines my second perspective on Joyce. That metaphoric capacity inheres in all thought, as Nietzsche knew, and in all languages as well, which in their "counterfactuality"—the term is George Steiner's—defy "that which is the case." That same capacity, however, inheres especially in certain assumptions of modern physics. I wish to make but seven points about the epistemology of science.

1. Science cannot be entirely free of faith or metaphysics. The immanence of the laws of science in the cosmos is *not* apodictic. As Einstein once remarked, the true mystery of the world is its comprehensibility. Nor can scientists dispense wholly with metaphysics: "When we think we can," Schrödinger tartly observed, "all that is apt to happen is that we replace the grand old metaphysical errors with infinitely more *naïve* and petty ones."

2. Advanced scientific work is an imaginative act; on this almost everyone now agrees. The axiomatic basis of scientific theories cannot be extracted from sensory data; it must be freely invented. Even so austere a geneticist as Jacques Monod admitted: "to be absorbed in thought is to be embarked upon an imagined experience." Dream, play, poesis are complicitous in the scientist's work as in the artist's, for neither really is satisfied merely to confirm.

3. Since scientific models are mainly heuristic fictions, they must be viewed as speculative instruments designed to order rather than describe

experience naïvely. In reaction to older positivist and empiricist views of science, as Ian G. Barbour shows in *Myths, Models, and Paradigms*, most scientists now believe that all facts are "theory-laden"; that general theories cannot be easily "verified" or "falsified"; and that no "objective" criteria exist for choice between such theories since such criteria would already be "theory-dependent."

4. Perhaps all this is implicit in Heisenberg's statement that "what we observe is not nature in itself but nature exposed to our method of questioning . . . in the drama of existence we are ourselves both players and spectators." In fact, the statement could serve as one formulation of Heisenberg's own Uncertainty Principle, which introduces the subject, if not subjectivism, in all experiments.

5. Heisenberg's Principle of Uncertainty as well as Bohr's of Complementarity also raise the radical issues of language, logic, and assertion in ways that artists may find congenial. Indeed, Bohr himself once said to Heisenberg: "When it comes to atoms, language can be used only as in poetry. The poet, too, is not nearly so concerned with describing facts as with creating images."

6. As new fields and new disciplines emerge—general systems theory, cybernetics, information, decision, and game theories, etc.—the epistemological boundaries of the sciences shift; their methods vary. Bertalanffy believed that these disciplines "differ in basic assumptions, models, mathematical techniques and intentions, and occasionally contradict each other." Paul Feyerabend went farther in *Against Method* to argue that science "is essentially an anarchistic enterprise," and this encourages progress far more than "its law-and-order alternatives."

7. Yet if no universal Logos of human knowledge is within sight, the paradigms of science, art, myth, religion, increasingly reveal their homologies. Beginning with such thinkers as William James and C. D. Broad, scientists as different as Einstein, Bohr, Heisenberg, Schrödinger, Bernal, Dobbs, Weizsächer, Oppenheimer, Sherrington, Le Noüy, Haldane, Waddington, Bertalanffy, Wiener, Bateson, Hoyle, Sagan, Delgado, Bohm, Lilly, and Capra have explored the reciprocities of knowledge, the limits of mind bordering sometimes on the supernatural. And Jung and Pauli, we recall—we are in Zurich, after all—once collaborated on a work entitled *Naturerklärung und Psyche*, which speculates on the influence of archetypes on scientific concepts.

But I must now return to the restive question: what in the name of Gnosis does all this have to do with Joyce? True, the physicist Murray Gell-Mann found a quark on page 383 of *Finnegans Wake*, and, more recently, Phillip Herring gave "solase" (p. 470) to the Department of Nuclear Engineering at the University of Wisconsin-Madison, by providing a Joycean name for an experimental laser fusion reactor: "their solase in dorckaness, and splattering together joyously the plaps of their tappyhands." Still, I repeat, what has all this to do with Joyce, who confessed in a letter to Harriet Shaw Weaver (25 February 1920) that he could never learn chemistry or "understand in the least what it is about," and who said to Tom Kristensen: "I don't believe in any science but my imagination grows when I read Vico as it doesn't when I read Freud or Jung"?

Imagination: that may be precisely the point. My introductory remarks concerned not science *in* Joyce but a historical and imaginative matrix that may clarify a little: a. the culture of dematerialization, or better still, of semiosis, in which Joyce's later work situates itself; and b. the figurative or imaginative structures that complex literary works share with scientific theories.

As to science *in* Joyce, I defer that question to the authorities, who may defer it as well to you and the gnostic spirit of Joyce himself.

The Newtonian Nightmare of *Ulysses*

Alan David Perlis

After reading *Ulysses*, one is tempted to engage wholesale in "Joyce and the gnosis of modern science." "Ithaca" 's miasma of pseudo-scientific jargon in particular and characters' multiple perceptions of the same event and their wildly various internal time clocks in general suggest that Joyce is an exemplar of relativity. One Joyce scholar, in fact, calls *Ulysses* "an epic of relativity" and alludes to Heisenberg's indeterminacy principle as a fit analogue to Stephen's and Bloom's wanderings through a city to which they do not wholly belong.[1] One likes to see in writers signs that they are truly of their age. To link Joyce with the Einsteinian revolution in physics would greatly satisfy such an impulse.

But if Joyce needed a predecessor or a contemporary to establish his credentials for demonstrating how different individuals perceive the same duration of clock time as different spans of internal time, he did not need to go to Einstein and the Special Theory of Relativity. Bergson's "durée" and Proust's "moment privilige" could have served Joyce's fictional purposes better, their notions of perception being far less restrictive than Einstein's, which depend on incredibly rapid motion through four-dimensional space. One might well argue, on the other hand, that a preoccupation with relativity developed in the first two decades of this century on a number of fronts, including at the very least physics, philosophy, psychology, and, as an attendant handmaiden, literature. It is entirely possible that this general surge of interest came to meet Joyce the expansive novelist and that a merger ensued. This is quite different, however, from arguing that Joyce comprehended certain theories of modern physics and responded to them in *Ulysses*.

Since my colleague Mr. Friedman will be considering various mis-appropriations of modern physics to Joyce, I shall now propose a way in which a scientific theory *has* found currency first in philosophy and in psychology, then in the novel, and finally, in a great, culminating moment, in *Ulysses*. This proposition involves modern physics' classical ancestor and, more particularly, certain observations in Isaac Newton's *Principia*.

A statement that rings throughout the *Principia* is that "in philosophical disquisitions we ought to abstract from our senses, and consider things themselves, distinct from what are only sensible measures of them."[2] When Newton argues that bodies in space create a field between them that establishes the maximum distance at which they continue to attract one another, and that the universe operates like a well-functioning machine that needs for its perpetuation only God's occasional repairs, he proposes that these elements of nature's behavior are absolute in themselves, and not the formulations of the physicist who observes them. Having adduced these absolutes, Newton speculates that "It seems probable to me that God in the beginning formed matter in solid, massy, hard, impenetrable, moveable particles, of such sizes and figures, and with such other properties, and in such proportion to space, as most conduced to the end for which he formed them."[3] Newton's universe, then, is the manifestation of intention and not the caprice of blind matter. And in this universe, the presence of objects, and not the perceiver who would observe them, is what confirms the absolute reality of existence. This is, in fact, Newton's most persistent statement in refutation of Descartes's notion that thought is the source of existence. Otherwise, Newton is more interested in refining and correcting his precursor than he is in disproving him.

It is Newton's argument for the supremacy of the object world, for its behavior as the embodiment of truth, that most appealed to his eighteenth-century sycophants and disciples. In *The Enlightenment* Peter Gay documents philosophers' and psychologists' tremendously enthusiastic response to Newtonian mechanics. Newton had accomplished for science what Francis Bacon had hoped someone would accomplish—the demythification of the universe through some mechanical explanation of its operation—and now his efforts began to prod thinkers in other fields to confirm the unchanging center of their own disciplines. Gay writes of the "Newtons of the Mind," of a movement to isolate and explain the absolute qualities of human behavior, and in particular the distorting role perception plays when it internalizes external truth.[4] In the works of Hartley, Hume, and Locke, for example, there is an implicit recognition of an unchanging, mechanically explicable presence called "Nature," which the act of perceiving inevitably fails to record with verisimilitude. What Newton contributed to philosophy and psychology, then, was a renewed and incredibly confident faith in the rightness and inevitablity of nature's behavior. The machine of universal operation worked perfectly; it was only imperfect man who failed to understand and respect it.

It might be argued that the emergence of the novel in the late seventeenth century required adaptation of the Newtonian world view in order to take the shape that it so quickly assumed. The universe, Newton proposes, is unified by a succession of gravitational forces and operates through the mutual attraction of bodies. The early novel likewise operates through the mutual attraction of bodies, which not only describes but also circum-scribes motion. Within a few years after the publication of the *Principia*, while philosophers were wrestling with the notion of a *Deus absentia* that the existence of a well-functioning machine suggests, separation and collision begin to dominate as literary motifs, and the lengthy narrative begins to seem like the ideal form for expressing these phenomena and hence embodying motion. In the works of, say, Cervantes, Defoe, and Fielding, characters move through their lives and across nations and separate from their friends, loved ones, and enemies. But invariably they meet once again, usually in some remote and unexpected place. While coincidence is the ostensible explanation for these surprise encounters, we might also consider the explanation that like bodies attract, or that in a world appear-ing to be vast, the shared needs and characteristics of certain individuals almost guarantee their continual meetings, even when the world seems to militate against them. In the earliest novels, the world has a strikingly Newtonian cast: motion and attraction, rather than the more nearly poetic phenomenon of contemplation, dictate meaning.

It might also be argued that the novel's tendency to draw heavily from fact is an extrapolation from the Newtonian world view. In describing what he calls the novel's "paradoxical relation to reality," A. Walton Litz dis-cusses its hybrid quality. The novel, Litz suggests, manifests a convergence of myth and fact (journals, diaries, and news) and provides the first literary instance in which raw data play a significant role. Litz makes this point in a treatment of the "Ithaca" section in *Ulysses*, but his general theme is that the novel as a whole corresponds to the quotidian aspects of its eighteenth-century predecessors.[5]

One need only consider the many catalogues, newspaper headlines, ledgers, and budget sheets that Joyce includes in *Ulysses* to appreciate the extent to which data occupy the novel. It is the *role* of these data, however, that reveals the extent to which Joyce evokes a Newtonian, mechanistic view of universal operation. The stuff of the eighteenth-century novel that Litz calls "facts"—mainly letters and diaries—has a writer who is also a character in the novel in which these "facts" appear. Though the typical eighteenth-century novelist attempted to be as compendious as he possibly could within whatever constraints a circuitous plot established, he had yet to confront Newton's most abiding concern: the existence of an absolute reality independent of human perception. In fact, we have to wait for the appearance of Joyce to find a novelist willing to address this concern.

It is because so much of Joyce's data is literally "raw"—data neither filtered through any systematic process of thought nor drawn into the arena of his characters' preoccupations—that its presentation seems to suggest the world as Newton would have it appear. In fact, Joyce includes far more information in *Ulysses* than the traditional standards of aesthetic decorum would allow, information that leads neither to a revelation of character nor to a richer sense of June 16, 1904. Things themselves often become the author's subject, and even the most assiduous reader of *Ulysses* must confess that some of these things lack the symbolic inferences that lead back to character or to the significance of events. One is hard-pressed, for example, to return a list of medieval church divines, another of Irish heroes and heroines of antiquity, another of trees with human surnames, and still another of modern clergymen, to their normal place in the traditional novel: thematic relevance. They simply do not fit such an aesthetic pattern. Rather, what strikes the reader who encounters these lists is the sense of an author who refuses to edit himself. A universal mind is set loose in the world of things, and what it records, Joyce allows to evolve into words. Because of its catalogues, the novel acquires an unrestrained quality, as if the world has exploded the boundaries placed on it by perception itself in wanting to declare its own independent truth.

Rather than enhance character and action, many of *Ulysses'* details threaten to obliterate them. An example of this phenomenon can be found in "Cyclops," where a catalogue serves to interrupt the energetic bigotry of the garrulous Dubliner in Barney Kiernan's tavern. Throughout the chapter, Bloom suffers the ignominious distinction of being ignored in a bar, a place for friendly and open conversation. First his observations are sidestepped:

> —But, says Bloom, isn't discipline the same everywhere? I mean wouldn't it be the same here if you put force against force?
> Didn't I tell you? As true as I'm drinking this porter if he was at his last gasp he'd try to downface you that dying was living. (*U* 329)

Then his observations are interrupted:

> —Perfectly true, says Bloom. But my point was . . .
> —We are a long time waiting for that day, citizen, says Ned. Since the poor old woman told us that the French were on the sea and landed at Killala. (*U* 330)

Finally, Bloom's observations are totally rejected with the convenient device of silence:

> —What is your nation if I may ask, says the citizen.
> —Ireland, says Bloom. I was born here. Ireland.
> The citizen said nothing only cleared the spit out of his gullet and, gob, he spat a Red bank oyster out of him right in the corner. (*U* 331)

The citizen takes out his handkerchief—presumably of the ordinary variety—and with this act, a noserag becomes a "muchtreasured and intricately embroidered ancient Irish facecloth" on which appear a variety of country scenes, all described in sterile travelogue tones which could be from the voice of virtually anyone ("all these moving scenes are still there for us today" [*U* 331–32]). Unfiltered fact once again impinges on action and sets the human drama against a panoply of details that threaten to smother the novel's own plot in the enormity of things the world contains. In fact, the significance of plot-directed events in the chapter fades in what seems to be the powerful threat of objects rumbling, glacierlike, across its pages.

Of all *Ulysses'* chapters, however, "Ithaca" contains by far the most catalogues. One might well argue that "Ithaca" is a single catalogue from beginning to end. The question-and-answer format reminds us of a catechism, or perhaps the four questions in the *Haggadah* from the celebration of Passover, or perhaps a scholastic inquisition between some unmoved teacher and his obsessively verbal pupil. As the critics have by and large resolved, "Ithaca" 's two poles are Stephen's artistic and Bloom's scientific casts of mind. But neither mind is represented in the act of thought. Rather, observations are summarized by an omniscient and detached voice that conveys not only the essence of the protagonists' conversations and thoughts but also a mass of data that is outside of either character's knowing. Again, fact threatens to overwhelm what one ordinarily expects to learn from human interaction in a novel.

But if we remember that *Ulysses* is, indeed, a novel, something extraordinary happens to the pseudoscientific voice that, for example, offers a lengthy discourse on the content of Dublin's water or describes in geometric detail the arcs of urine sent simultaneously out into the world by Stephen and Bloom. The voice draws things so expansively that they assume the role of characters. At the same time, characters seem to shrivel behind the arras of objects and events and assume the role of insignificant things. The effect achieved by these reversals is that of a world in such a state of flux and movement that human meaning is not only slighted but indistinguishable. *Ulysses* is the post-Newtonian mechanical world turned into a nightmare: one in which the mechanism plays itself out beyond the reach not only of the reader who would try to contain it but also of the author who would try to restrain it for the sake of aesthetic decorum.

It may be said that *Ulysses* demonstrates how the world looks to the person who can successfully abstract from his senses, or rather fully exercise all his senses without imposing any patterns on the received stimuli. In his *Essay Concerning Human Understanding*, Locke considers the "white paper" mind with which we are born and projects how it would continue to function were it to lack the memory that inscribes an associative network for perception. Joyce engages precisely such a mind, and he sees it operating in two different ways. The first is a disburdening of memory, in which, as most fully realized in Molly's soliloquy, the mind unknots and unwinds its tangled thread of associations back to sleep and forgetting. The second is the mind in a state of utter forgetfulness, where no preconceptions dictate perceptions. Here one experiences only *re*ceptions, and the world exceeds the limits that the mind itself might impose on it.

A passage from "Ithaca" demonstrates my point. Bloom reminisces with Stephen that he often took Mrs. Riordan to the corner of the North Circular road

> where she had remained for a certain time scanning through his onelensed binocular fieldglasses unrecognisable citizens on tramcars, roadster bicycles, equipped with inflated pneumatic tyres, hackney carriages, tandems, private and hired landaus, dogcarts, ponytraps and brakes passing from the city to the Phoenix Park and *vice versa*. (*U* 680–81)

In this short passage, the point of view changes markedly. Initially, we assume that we are seeing the world through Mrs. Riordan's eyes. Gradually, however, we come to realize that the description is simply too inclusive to involve only one person's brief observations. The fieldglasses seem to have their own eyes. Since they cannot discriminate, their vantage point takes in virtually everything in sight. And the hectic pace of Dublin life seems to maintain itself on its own momentum, almost as if it were eluding the author's efforts to contain it within the scope of his characters.

Implied in my application of the Newtonian world view is a caution against any facile argument for the novel as an "epic of relativity," or one in which an Einsteinian vision of a world bound by the limits of how we perceive it prevails. While it is impossible to attribute Joyce's adaptation of a Newtonian viewpoint to the author's study of his physicist precursor, however, it is at least possible to trace *Ulysses'* evolution from its eighteenth-century forebears, which did respond to Newton in a direct fashion, and to show that in refining out point of view from much of his narrative, Joyce was able to realize Newton's world in a way they could not. All readers of *Ulysses* are struck by its awesome materiality. At the same time that Joyce evokes our sympathies for his characters, he reduces their magnitude to fit the noisy and often impersonal world that they inhabit. Frequently, Joyce smothers them in a list of faceless names and swirling objects that swarm across the pages of *Ulysses*. Perhaps he is suggesting that in our high regard—in this, the most material of ages—for things, we have given life, even myth, to the material. Now, in the Newtonian nightmare I have described, things regard us and seem even to write novels in which we are the subject of their greatest interest.

Notes

1. Marilyn French, *The Book as World: James Joyce's "Ulysses"* (Cambridge, Mass.: Harvard University Press, 1976), p. 17.

2. Alexandre Koyre, *Newtonian Studies* (Chicago: University of Chicago Press, 1968), p. 106.

3. Isaac Newton, *Sir Isaac Newton's Mathematical Principles of Natural Philosophy*, trans. Andrew Motte (1729) and rev. by Florian Cajori (Berkeley: University of California Press, 1934), p. 76.

4. Peter Gay, *The Enlightenment*, II, *The Science of Freedom* (New York: Alfred A. Knopf, 1969), pp. 174–87.

5. Clive Hart and David Hayman, eds., *James Joyce's "Ulysses": Critical Essays* (Berkeley: University of California Press, 1974), p. 391. These observations are made in A. Walton Litz's essay, "Ithaca."

Ulysses and Modern Science

Alan J. Friedman

LOOKING FOR CONNECTIONS

At least two geniuses were in Zurich in the spring of 1919. James Joyce was living on the Universitätstrasse[1] and working on *Ulysses*, while Albert Einstein was staying on the Hochstrasse for a lecture series.[2] The revolutions these two men created were becoming manifest. An experimental confirmation of Einstein's General Theory of Relativity would soon make Einstein the most famous physicist alive. As the publication of *Ulysses* approached, Valery Larbaud could remark in 1921 that Joyce's notoriety had made him as familiar to the literary world as Freud and Einstein were to the scientific world.[3]

The literary innovations of Joyce and the scientific ones of Einstein had even more in common than their European cultural settings and their contemporary development. Both men were concerned with manipulations of time and space, with the relations between subject and observer, and with the role of language in our understanding of the universe.

As Professor Perlis remarked, we would like to find connections between these coexisting revolutions. We are pleased when our work illuminates links between diverse disciplines, and perhaps we can learn about the process of intellectual revolution itself by exploring the relations between such parallel events. There are also specific invitations to consider the relations between *Ulysses* and the scientific revolution of the early twentieth century. The "Ithaca" section, with its explicit science content, was written in 1921, and Einstein's work had been front page news since November 1919.[4] Not only had Joyce described "Ithaca" as "a mathematico-astronomico-physico-mechanico-geometrico-chemico sublimation of Bloom and Stephen,"[5] but he also noted that in revising and proofreading "Ithaca," "the question of printer's errors is not the chief point. The episode should be read by some person who is a physicist, mathematician and astronomer and a number of other things."[6]

We can also be encouraged in this study by the fruitful examinations of the relations between literature and science. Later novelists, like Lawrence Durrell, Vladimir Nabokov, and Thomas Pynchon, demonstrate fascination with and productive literary uses of the new science.[7]

198

My brief survey of possible connections between *Ulysses* and twentieth-century physics has three parts. First, I want to make a short comment on the two revolutions of modern physics, both involving Einstein, but with very separate potential meanings for authors and critics. Then I'll review some of the criticism from my own perspective as a physicist and a recently recruited student of Joyce. Finally, I'll offer my own observations on *Ulysses*, science, and style.

EINSTEIN'S REVOLUTIONS

Albert Einstein participated in two very different revolutions in twentieth-century physics. Many nonscientists blur these together or misunderstand both. These mistakes are primarily due to the physicists' inabilities to communicate with the public. Getting the physics wrong is not a fatal sin, however. If a novelist like Lawrence Durrell misunderstands one aspect of relativity, that does not prevent him from making new structures for literary purposes from whatever he imagines relativity to be.[8] And a critic who is trying to illuminate Durrell's work needs to know Durrell's version more than Einstein's. But misconceptions must be recognized if we are trying to understand cross-cultural transfer and its possible usefulness in understanding culture beyond simply literature or science.

The first revolution was Einstein's theory of relativity. That work was essentially completed by 1917, although the implications and applications of it are still very much blooming as new instruments probe black holes, neutron stars, and the curvature of the universe. Relativity announced new relations between previously independent features of our physical universe, such as mass, time, and space. Some features formerly absolute and independent become relative and dependent. But new absolutes were created. The speed of light and the new laws of physics no longer need to change according to the uniform motion of each observer. The marvelous structure that Einstein created is just as causal, just as deterministic, just as reliable as the structure of Newton's universe. Einstein did not say that "everything is relative," or that truth itself was now uncertain. Different observers may record different numbers to describe some phenomena, but those numbers can all be successfully predicted, and all are rigidly linked, by Einstein's new equations. Einstein's relativity gave a violent shake to the old order but left in its place a gleaming new order.

This essay is too short to elaborate on Einstein's theory, which many physicists regard as the most surprising and beautiful vision of science. My own expectation of the uses literature would make of Einstein's relativity would be as metaphor and image for finding new, more subtle relations between apparently unrelated phenomena; discovering new absolutes to replace unreliable old ones; and appreciating the power of the imagination to create unprecedented global visions.

Unfortunately, early popularizations and even many today present relativity as just breaking down knowledge and leading to uncertainty and confusion.[9] Physicists have learned much since the 1920s about the meaning of Einstein's work and about science education, so that in an appendix to this paper I can recommend recent, accurate, and readable popularizations of modern physics.

THE OTHER REVOLUTION IN PHYSICS

The second revolution in physics, known as quantum theory or wave mechanics and manifested in the "Heisenberg Uncertainty Principle," was longer in the making than Einstein's relativity. Einstein himself contributed to this second revolution, beginning in 1905 and continuing throughout the first quarter of the century. Quantum theory was vigorously debated in the 1920s, with Einstein championing those who thought the theory seriously incomplete. The "Copenhagen School" formed by Niels Bohr in the mid twenties declared that the incompleteness was that of the universe, not the theory. Bohr's interpretation has won, so far, although Einstein's challenges are still being tested.

In a word, the current interpretation of quantum theory is that the theory requires *uncertainty*. An observer of atomic particles disturbs the particles he or she is measuring in an irreducible manner. The more carefully you measure the position of an electron, the more you might be disturbing its motion, so that any knowledge of its motion becomes less precise. That is one direct outcome of the "Heisenberg Uncertainty Principle," formulated in 1927. In some cases, such as the breakdown of a radioactive nucleus or the reduction in energy of an excited atom, we have no ability to predict the time when the event will occur. We can give excellent odds and averages, but no precise moment can be forecast. A nucleus may break up immediately or wait a billion years.

This second revolution is a legitimate source for literature of images, metaphors, or structure dealing with uncertainty and inescapable observer-observed distortion. Those qualities are often attributed inaccurately to relativity. The confusion would surely have distressed Albert Einstein, who could not accept a quantum theory that required "God to play dice with the universe."[10]

Major popular expositions of quantum theory were not published until the late 1920s. While anyone living in European society in 1921 and reading the newspapers would have heard much about Einstein's relativity, quantum theory in 1921 was still a confused area of debate among a few scientists, with any consensus several years off. We might well find that an uncertainty principle and inescapable subject-observer interaction are apt descriptions for major themes in *Ulysses*. Nevertheless, we cannot claim these descriptions as physics-inspired metaphors, since *Ulysses* preceded the physics. It is not impossible that the inspiration even worked the other way around—perhaps physicists (consciously or not) found some of their imagery in works of art and literature, like *Ulysses*.

CONNECTIONS PROPOSED

Several literary critics have used the terms "relativity" and "uncertainty principle" in relation to science and *Ulysses*. The terms are often used inappropriately, or at least without attention to the special meanings they have been given in twentieth-century physics. As an example, Professor Alan Perlis has called my attention to Marilyn French's mention of these terms and of science. In a note, French claims: "Joyce clearly intended to show incertitude as operating in the cosmos as well as the world."[11] Her examples are all the subjects of classical nineteenth-century Newtonian astronomy. They would represent "incertitude" for a sixteenth-century Ptolemaic scholar, but not for a Newtonian.

Richard Kain discusses science occasionally throughout his very useful study, *Fabulous Voyager*: "The picture of modern science given in *Ulysses* is that it constitutes a new folklore of a 'believe-it-or-not' nature and that its principal appeal to modern man is as a materialistic aid to wealth or to the saving of effort."[12] The modern science Kain is discussing is not relativity, however, which has provided no material aid or wealth or saving of effort. Bloom fails to distinguish between technology (waterworks and tram cars) and science (Newtonian or Einsteinian world views), and Kain is following his lead. Kain's uses of the term "relativity" in his final chapter refer each time to single measurements of time or space, with no particular meaning for Einsteinian physics.[13]

Littmann and Schweighauser accurately and thoroughly examine the astronomical terms in *Ulysses*.[14] All the examples are comfortably nineteenth-century, and Littmann and Schweighauser suggest mostly direct symbolic uses of that science.

Wyndham Lewis, in 1927, directly claimed a relation between *Ulysses* and Einstein, but more a spiritual connection than a scientific one: "This torrent of matter is the Einsteinian flux. Or (equally well) it is the duration-flux of Bergson—that is its philosophic character, at all events."[15] This requisition of a common feature of two very different approaches to time is too broad to provide much analytic exercise for our purposes.

Avrom Fleishman gives a different direction for searching out connections between *Ulysses* and twentieth-century science: style.[16] Fleishman reasonably points out that the science content of *Ulysses*, set in 1904, should

not directly mention Einstein's relativity, which was first published in
1905. Joyce's fussiness about literal details applies here, too. Although
Fleishman gives one example from "Ithaca" that he claims is clearly intended to refer to Einstein's cosmology,[17] his main comments are on the
catechism of "Ithaca" and its implications for the value of the scientific
approach. Like a catechism, science normally treats the universe by breaking it up into minutely small elements, then limiting consideration even
further, to those few elements that readily lend themselves to treatment
with available tools. "Ithaca" 's catechism is also like science, says Fleishman, in that it exhibits "no criterion of esthetic taste or human relevance to
direct the response."[18]

The highly self-restrictive inquiry of science, like other methods of
knowing, has positive but limited value. The major encouragement Fleishman sees "Ithaca" offering us is that of the courage of Bloom and of
mankind, using these limited tools to probe a terrifying universe.

Science as style is also the most convincing aspect of Tindall's treatment.
He also sees the style as cold, to "project the inhumanity of science."[19]
Edward Watson too finds the science in "Ithaca" directed at demonstrating
the objective, impersonal style of science, to be contrasted with the romantic, humanistic approach of other chapters.[20]

None of this critical material makes a strong case, at least for me, that
Ulysses has a specific *content* connection with twentieth-century science.
Fleishman's arguments come closest, showing that, for example, "parallax," a classical science concept, fits in well with the spirit of relativity if
not in its literal cosmology. But I think we must wait, at least until *Finnegans
Wake*, and our next paper, to find direct evidence of links between the two
modern revolutions in science and James Joyce. The question of the style of
science in *Ulysses*, however, bears further thought here.

WHOSE QUESTIONS?

The loss of religious faith, along with the gains of scientific knowledge,
had left Leopold Bloom in a vast universe without teleological motive or
moral center. Newtonian as well as Einsteinian world views could serve to
illustrate that position. Perhaps hope lies not in the specific physical facts
seen by science but in the success of its style, so evident as Einstein's
theories were celebrated in 1919. I contend that *Ulysses* examines the
subjective human values in scientific style, rather than trying to apply any
of Einstein's new findings themselves.

The style of science, however, should not be taken on the assessment of
scientists alone. Scientists have often thought of their method of inquiry as

not only highly self-restricted in subject and method but also totally objective, cold, or even inhuman. Lewis, Tindall, Fleishman, and Watson shared this perception. That attitude may have is origin in the rigid style conventionally used in writing about science. That style is based on total reconstruction, a narration produced if and when the narrator has reached full intellectual and emotional accommodation to his conclusions. Accounts of the human process of reaching accommodation are deleted.

Ulysses, as well as recent histories of science,[21] illustrates that the style of written science is only a partial depiction of the human process that has occurred. We are led to laugh at the irrelevancy of answering a question about whether water flowed by a detailed account of the entire waterworks. The clumsy, pedantic jargon used to describe Bloom's thoughts on being a cuckold appears needless. But these questions and responses serve subjective, human ends far more than scientific ones. After a day of humiliation, a water tap that works, and works in a manner Bloom can fully comprehend, demonstrates mastery of at least that phase of life. The pain of returning to a marriage bed still marked by a rival's presence can be distanced by concentrating on learning the minute technical details. The fear of the coldness of the universe is balanced by the comfort and pride of succeeding in the stunning feat of measuring the universal temperature.

The selection of facts presented in *Ulysses*, and in its contemporary science, involve warm and personal choices: which of the innumerable aspects of the universe should be examined; what possible interpretations exist; which of those interpretations should be accepted; what should be done with the results. A cold intellect suffices to catalog answers, but a total human act was necessary to select the questions.

Who asks the questions in Ithaca? The selection of subjects for inquiry and the mode of response are entirely human choices. Leopold Bloom's accommodation to a universe of bitter facts is made through a dignity and calm he finds in the style of written science. His needs are met with limited but significant success. The science-minded questioner of Ithaca is no less a human than the impressionistic-, romantic-, or dramatic-minded humans who illustrate the limitation and successes of their styles in other parts of *Ulysses*.

Ulysses comments on our understanding of the relations between science and literature by illustrating that we can place no more, but perhaps no less, reliance on the particular style of science than we can on our other modes of inquiry. Success in viewing waterworks, atoms, and stars is only a hint, but a welcome one, that we might just succeed in understanding civilizations, scientists, and novelists.

Appendix: Physics Sources for Literary Critics

Our physical world-view has been reshaped since Newton by the discoveries and creations of nineteenth- and twentieth-century physics. Three concepts are of particular importance and happen to be very rich in new images: (1) Einstein's Theory of Relativity, (2) the Second Law of Thermodynamics, and (3) the Quantum Theory. These concepts have proven of some use to novelists like Joyce, Nabokov, Coover, Woolf, Pynchon, Durrell, and others. Here are some sources of nonmathematical introductions to these three fundamental notions about our universe.

(1) Einstein's Relativity is the most famous and most misunderstood of these concepts. Einstein rethought the relations between the basic measures with which we describe our universe: mass, space, and time. In common sense, these three are absolute, independent quantities that can uniquely describe an event or observation ("An ounce of gold was sitting on that corner of the table at noon"). It turns out that these quantities are not independent and may vary according to precise laws in relation to each other and to the observer. It is *not* correct to say that "everything is relative"—on the contrary, Einstein began with the postulate that the speed of light is absolute in circumstances that were thought to make it relative. New, more subtle absolutes replace the old commonsense ones.

Martin Gardner's *Relativity for the Millions* (New York: Macmillan, 1962) is a clear and colorful first introduction (in *Ada*, Nabokov quotes Gardner quoting Nabokov). George Gamow's *Mr. Tompkins in Paperback* (Cambridge: Cambridge University Press, 1965) is a highly imaginative presentation of the new possibilities suggested by all three of the basic concepts of physics, although some of the explanations of the physics are not too successful.

Once a reader finds the basic images and language manageable, more detailed and historical presentations are in order. Three excellent biographies of Einstein are available. Ronald Clark's (note 2 below) is exhaustive but not at all tedious reading. Jeremy Bernstein's *Einstein* (New York: Viking, 1973) is a compact scientific biography, but I found the explanations of the physics too brief. Banesh Hoffmann, with Helen Dukas, wrote my favorite treatment of both the biography and the physics, in *Albert Einstein: Creator and Rebel* (New York: Viking, 1972).

(2) Thermodynamics describes which way time flows and how the universe becomes disordered. It has been little popularized although it is much easier to grasp than relativity and has served as a source of metaphor from Henry Adams to Thomas Pynchon. Norbert Weiner's *The Human Use of Human Beings* (1954; rpt. New York: Avon Books, 1967) is the only popularization to treat the full range of modern implications of thermo-

dynamics, but it is brief in describing the basic concepts themselves. Substituting the word "programming" for Weiner's now-obsolete "taping" will make the connections to computers easier to follow. Clear descriptions of the fundamental concepts may also be found in Jacob Bronowski's *Insight* (New York: Harper and Row, 1964).

(3) Quantum Theory is the least known, and perhaps the most important, of these three topics for the impact it has had on the philosophy of physics. Only one aspect, the Heisenberg Uncertainty Principle mentioned in this essay, is popularly known. While Relativity and thermodynamics are accepted by almost all physicists, the basic interpretations of Quantum Theory remain controversial, and efforts to find an alternative theory or at least a more palatable interpretation of it continue. One fine full-length treatment is Banesh Hoffmann's *The Strange Story of the Quantum*, 2d ed. (New York: Dover, 1959). There are also valuable discussions in the three biographies of Einstein and in Gamow's *Mr. Tompkins*, cited above.

Finally, the most detailed nonmathematical treatment that I can recommend is Adolph Baker's *Modern Physics and Antiphysics* (Reading, Mass.: Addison-Wesley, 1970). It tries to be too cute but nevertheless presents a remarkably complete and accurate discussion of all the major concepts of modern physics.

Because the art of science popularization has never caught up to the level of competence of science research, all of these reference sources are likely to leave the reader puzzling over some small but crucial point. Access to a physicist or physics student is therefore recommended. Most of us are delighted to try to initiate others into the excitement of modern physics, and we are often flattered to find that literary folk are curious about our work.

Notes

1. Richard Ellmann, *James Joyce* (1959; rpt. Oxford: Oxford University Press, 1976), p. 462.
2. Ronald Clark, *Einstein: The Life and Times* (New York: World Publishers, 1971), p. 220.
3. Ellmann, p. 537.
4. Clark, p. 237.
5. *Letters of James Joyce*, ed. Stuart Gilbert (New York: Viking Press, 1957), p. 164.
6. Ibid., p. 178.
7. Alan Friedman, "The Novelist and Modern Physics: New Metaphors for Traditional Themes," *Journal of College Science Teaching* 4 (1975): 310–12.
8. For a critique of the accuracy of Durrell's physics, see Alfred Bork, "Durrell and Relativity," *Centennial Review* 7 (1963): 191–203.

9. For a critique of the popularizations, see L. Susan Stebbing, *Philosophy and the Physicists* (1937; rpt. New York: Dover, 1958).

10. A summary of Einstein's concern and the origins of this phrase appear in Clark, pp. 340–45.

11. Marilyn French, *The Book as World: James Joyce's "Ulysses"* (Cambridge, Mass.: Harvard University Press, 1976), p. 287. Herman Broch also claims uncertainty operating as relativity in *Ulysses*: see Theodore Ziolkowski, "Hermann Broch and Relativity in Fiction," *Wisconsin Studies in Contemporary Literature* 8 (1967): 365–76.

12. Richard Kain, *Fabulous Voyager* (1947; rpt. New York: Viking Press, 1959), p. 18. See also comments on science in *Ulysses* on pp. 9, 22, 227.

13. Kain, pp. 228, 233, 236.

14. Mark Littmann and Charles Schweighauser, "Astronomical Allusions, Their Meaning and Purpose, in *Ulysses*," *James Joyce Quarterly* 2 (1965): 238–46.

15. Wyndham Lewis, *Time and Western Man* (1927; rpt. Boston: Beacon Press, 1957), p. 103.

16. Avrom Fleishman, "Science in Ithaca," *Wisconsin Studies in Contemporary Literature* 7 (1967): 377–91.

17. Ibid., p. 390.

18. Ibid., p. 381.

19. W. Y. Tindall, *James Joyce: His Way of Interpreting the Modern World* (New York: Charles Scribner's Sons, 1950), p. 90.

20. Edward Watson, "STOOM-BLOOM: Scientific Objectivity versus Romantic Subjectivity in the Ithaca Episode of Joyce's *Ulysses*," *University of Windsor Review* 2 (1966): 11–25.

21. See, for example, Jacob Bronowski, *A Sense of the Future* (Cambridge, Mass.: MIT Press, 1977); Gerald Holton, *Thematic Origins of Scientific Thought: Kepler to Einstein* (Cambridge, Mass.: Harvard University Press, 1973); Thomas Kuhn, *The Structure of Scientific Revolutions*, 2d ed., rev. (Chicago: University of Chicago Press, 1970).

Let's Hear What Science Has to Say:
Finnegans Wake and the Gnosis of Science

S. B. Purdy

Does the revolutionary modernity of *Finnegans Wake* include science? Specifically, does the book's mention of such things as quantum theory, Hertzian waves, atomic structure, spacetime, complementarity, and the expanding universe represent an incorporation of twentieth-century physical theory into its fabric in some way resembling, or even surpassing, its incorporation of science ancient, medieval, and Viconian?

At the outset, the negative evidence that bears on both questions must be considered. There is, for instance, little evidence that Joyce knew more of the revolution going on in physics and cosmology during his lifetime than the newspapers would have told him, or that he read deeply in any other field of science. Over the last twenty years Joyce criticism has tended to a revision, sometimes harsh, of the earlier picture of Joyce as universal polymath.[1] Furthermore, Joyce's intellectual background was one anti-pathetic to science, and his rupture with it was less than complete. Ellmann's biography amply documents Joyce's superstitions—his fear of thunder, his taking chance events as portents, his belief in number and word magic—concluding generously, "For Joyce life *was* charmed; nature was both stolid and magical, its ordinary details suffused with wonder, its wonderful manifestations permeated by the ordinary."[2] Atherton notes Joyce's claims "that to be mentioned in his book [*Finnegans Wake*] had an effect on the people named that was often drastic and sometimes fatal," and suggests that the thousands of names listed in the *Wake* are meant to exert power over the referents.[3] In a parallel vein Ellmann reports that for Joyce, "his books were not to be taken as mere books, but as acts of prophecy."[4] Religion and the supernatural were never far from Joyce's thoughts, and at the time he was starting the *Wake*, according to one source, his "favorite subjects were astronomy and the Jesuits,"[5] a combination seen by Leo Knuth as illustrative of his "theophobia."[6] The space devoted to divinity and its works in the *Wake* amply justifies Margaret Solomon's finding "deep religious inclinations" therein,[7] or Adaline Glasheen's statement, "*Finnegans Wake* is supremely a work of the imagination which treats, from first to last, the supernatural."[8]

Science in the *Wake* can therefore only with difficulty be seen as a thing given pride of place, or even as a thing independent. As a conceptual framework it is rather yoked, by the usual *Wake* machinery of coincidence and the union of opposites, to religion; and as the religions Eastern and Western, orthodox and heterodox, past and present, are set side by side, so are forms and periods of science. And for every science there is a pseudoscience, for every astronomy an astrology, often jostling it in the same paragraph. Myth, archetype, song, folklore, and joke, in multiple variation and repetition, mockery piled on mockery, constitute the major character of *Finnegans Wake* considered as a whole: not what one would think of calling a "scientific" book!

Furthermore, a great deal of what looks scientific in the *Wake* has a very taxonomical, nineteenth-century air, springing from its Homeric lists—lists of rivers, gods, heresies, historical events and characters, words. These are arranged according to various principles, the most obvious of which being simple addition. What other principles of structuring there may be present, whether geometrical, numerological, psychoanalytic, linguistic, or chronological, as Joyce critics of differing persuasions have suggested, they remain difficult to enumerate with certainty. The connection of such structure to the nature and hypotheses of modern science seems almost of necessity to be as imagined by David Hayman: "*Finnegans Wake* is more nearly an invitation to play than to read, to play according to rules that are amazingly consistent but that appear to be infinitely variable, if not imponderable, like those behind the workings of the universe."[9] The critical dilemma is escaped as neatly by Margot Norris, who argues for the idea that "the nature of structure is itself the central issue of *Finnegans Wake*."[10] As a structure of structures, the book remains an *ignotum* elucidated *per ignotius*.

None of the foregoing can remove the often striking reflections of twentieth-century science the *Wake* seems to give. They appear with varying degrees of philosophical or psychological application, and I think all of those I mention here have been adequately documented, if not presented in the same organization. Most generally present to my mind is a boundarilessness, an absence of the dividing lines and qualitative differences that give us our normal guideposts in acting and thinking. The most striking thing about the *Wake* is its apparent removal of linguistic boundaries, so that languages from different ends of the earth meet in the same word. This effect is not only *langue-langue* (as in "passencore," 3.4) but *parole-parole* (as in "nathandjoe," 3.12) and, even, *langue-parole*, in the production of unpronounced "hyper"-words out of living morphemic stocks (the thunderwords; probably others). A sense of loss and dismay has probably been felt on this account by every reader of the book at one time or another; it is certainly the initially rebarbative aspect of such language that keeps all but the select few

from ever getting very far in reading it. That the names of characters and
their attributes are subjected to the same distortion results in the boundaries between them and their attributes intermittently disappearing.[11] They
trade identities and sexes, and drop in and out of a background continuum
in which individual seems indistinguishable from mass. With these boundaries necessarily vacillate the moral identifications normally imposed. So
Hosty represents *hoi polloi*, the many-headed, and also Shem, the most
secretively private character of the book, "on the verge of selfabyss" (40.25);
H. C. E., the father of Shem, as individual—the host at the inn—but
himself the mass as well (Here Comes Everybody). "As the Host (*hostie*) or
Eucharist, Hosty is God. As *hostis* or enemy, he is the devil."[12]

The influence of Vico's science of humanity,with its intimate relation
between mass and individual and its concept of language as indicator-by-
etymology, has been shown in this portrait of H.C. E.,[13] along with that of
Giordano Bruno's theory of the coincidence of opposites, "eternally pro-
voking alio opposite equally."[14] Equally present are the shifting landscape
and overlapping narratives of dream, doubtless affected as a choice of
literary vehicle in Joyce's mind by the spectacular growth of the
psychoanalytical movement in the first quarter of the twentieth-century.
Nor is the initial impetus of Joyce's previous linguistic experimentation,
accompanied in *Ulysses* by the disruption of literary boundaries, to be
discounted. Armed with hindsight, we can say that after *Ulysses* something
as extreme as *Finnegans Wake* had an almost sinister inevitability on *formal*
grounds. Nevertheless, the science of the 1920s plays a role here too, one
outlined by reference in the text if we may suppose the description of light
in the wisdom of saint and sage greeting the dawn in chapter 17 to be
phrased in terms of Bohr's Complementarity principle (1928): "beingtime
monkblinkers timeblinged completamentarily murkblankered in their
neutrolysis between the possible viriditude of the sager and the probable
eruberuption of the saint" (612.21–24), and the command, or blessing, "let
every crisscouple be so crosscomplimentary, litte eggons, youlk and meelk,
in a farbiger pancosmos" (613.10–12). As the duality of waves and particles,
incompatible on a large scale, must be seen as complementary on the atomic
scale, so the members of all the *Wake*'s dualities, here in part greeting the
dawn, defy unification, but must be taken together. And in that those
co-occurring waves and particles illustrate Heisenberg's Uncertainty Principle, they lead us, as ideal readers, into a larger-scale consideration of the
problem of boundaries.

Directly mentioned in the text is the notion of an expanding universe,
perhaps the final blow to the secure boundaries of Ptolemy and Copernicus.
It was, as a blow, delivered by Hubble in 1929 when he discovered the red
shift, which shows distant galaxies rushing away from us. Chapter 10 sets it

mockingly within just that which it undermines in cosmology and religious doctrine: "all's loth and pleasestir, are we told, on excellent inkbottle authority, solarsystemised, seriolcosmically, in a more and more almightily expanding universe under one, there is rhymeless reason to believe, original sun. Securely judges orb terrestrial" (263.22–27). Shaun as Jaun and a barrel, in chapter 14, undergoes a further metamorphosis that combines cosmic expansion with a nova, or exploding star: "He was there, you could planemetrically see, when I took a closer look at him, that was to say, (gracious helpings, at this rate of growing our cotted child of yestereve will soon fill space and burst in systems, so speeds the instant!) amply altered for the brighter . . ." (429.10–13).

Here, as in most all passages treating space, time is not far to seek, for Joyce made of space and time one of his most frequently occurring warring pairs. In that they resemble many of the others in being opposed yet united, Shem-and-Shaun-like, it is tempting to see in their relationship the influence of Einstein and Minkowski's spacetime. Time as a function of space, as relative to the velocity of the observer, and as a fourth dimension, was made the subject of intense public speculation in the teens and twenties, and indeed, Joyce was publicly drawn into it by Wyndham Lewis's attack in *Time and Western Man* (1927; typically reversed in the *Wake* to "Spice and Westend Woman").[15] Joyce was already familiar with time as contingent upon experience, as ideational flux in literature—at least from Lewis Carroll to Proust—and in Bergson's philosophy,[16] but the time dislocations in the *Wake* are not easily pinned down to such sources. Time in the *Wake* not only undergoes the eroticization common to all major themes of the book—I cite here only the magnificent "lace at night" of the Prankquean (21.33)—but a complete freeing from the linear chronology of fiction and the universal instant of Newtonian physics. The word "planemetrically" in the citation above from the cosmic expansion of Jaun serves to key it to an entry in the Scribbledehobble notebook, "planimetry (2 dim) sterometry (3 dim): man on tightrope a 1 dim being: write as if future exists."[17] Much in the *Wake* suggests that the future exists, that it is, from a specified point of view, past. It is as "If there is a future in.every past that is present" (496.35), a narrative "Time: the pressant. With futurist onehorse balletbattle pictures and the Pageant of Past History" (221.17–19). The observer goes into the future "looking forward to what will in no time be staring you larrikins on the postface" (582.18–20), or into the past, "yon beam of light we follow receding on your photophoric pilgrimage to your antipodes in the past" (472.16–18), or remains frozen at a null point, as when receiving from around the world the data of the atom splitting: "*Similar scenatas are projectilised from Hullulullu, Bawlawayo, empyreal Raum and mordern Atems. They were precisely the twelves of clocks, noon minutes, none seconds"* (353.27–30). The picture may be compared to one of time symmetry, a general principle of the modern physical view of the world, by which time runs as well either "way," clocks run up as well as down, and predictions of the past (retrodictions) may be made as well as those of the future. It fails to hold only in certain subatomic phenomena like K meson decay, and it is coherent with relativistic time, that other great unsettler of the boundary between past and future.

Those sections of the *Wake* where time runs backward[18] are justified by time symmetry, and by such literary precedent as *Through the Looking Glass*, but they are not coherent with our resolutely asymmetrical experience of the world. For us shuffling the cards never results in ordering them, the past can be recalled but not the future, and teams of archaeologists never dig up future cities. The *Wake* gives us no such guarantees. This seems to contradict the concept of the Viconian cycle, which determines a linear unidirectional chronology. The text restarts its end with its beginning, punctuates its internal structure and coincident ages of human history with thunderclaps, and periodically inserts statements of the type "The same renew" (226.17); "The Vico road goes round and round to meet where terms begin" (452.21–22); or "We move in the beast circuls" (480.24). This puts the future into the past, or the past into the future, so even "The man in the street can see the coming event" (583.15). But the cycles do not comprehend all that is going on with time in the book; they do not express the "freed of time" quality of so much of its narration. Nor is there any guarantee that their being is proof to the universal dissolving power of the mocking scepticism pervading that narration. The announcement of a cyclical operation is always slightly ridiculous: the divine thunder is an almighty fart, and if it be lacking (I take p. 613 as an example), there is sure to be some other form of flatulence—here the ridiculous posturings of Irish and German nationalists, the outpourings of sun worshippers, and the march through the heavens of the saints: "Good safe firelamp! hailed the heliots. Goldselforelump! Halled they. Awed. Where thereon the skyfold high, trampatrampatramp" (613.1–3). Their prayers call upon Shem, or illusion: "Shamwork, be in our scheining!" (613.10). The mathematics of the change itself works out to nothing, with a self-cancelling divine *fiat!* of creation-defecation: "Yet is no body present here which was not there before. Only is order othered. Nought is nulled. *Fuitfiat!*" (613.13–14). This is suitable, because they are undergoing a transformation into the marching dupes of Hitler, whose 1936 Olympics gave the world a glimpse of the "New" Order: "The folgor of the frightfools is olympically optimominous; there is bound to be a lovleg day for mirrages in the open. . ."

(613.28–30). A fine guarantee of a cycle that is! It'd take a Sinn Feiner to believe it. Or a devotee of Irish cuisine: "Change the plates for the next course of murphies . . . the still sama sitta. I've lapped so long."[19]

That the change brought about by the cycles is illusory seems clear; that the cycles themselves are illusory follows logically. The Liffey will still reach the sea, but we have freed ourselves to see it doing so in spacetime, a 4D continuum, or in a manifold rather than in a process. In a manifold, man's progress through time is an illusion. Everything looks normal, and men are free to evolve grandiose theories about time flow, but it's not there. "Future" is simply "later than" or "elsewhere" in regard to an act of writing or speaking, and it is as illusory to speak of changing the future as to speak of changing the past. What happens in the future is, when it happens, what the future was; it is *determinant*, because it has no other existence, but not *determined*, as by some process occurring in the past and "bringing events into being." This strikes me as a more accurate picture of the *Wake*, where a consciousness is free to consider events in any order it wishes, or spatially rather than temporally.

It is true that the position of this consciousness above a hypothetical time track is quite parallel to that proposed by J. W. Dunne, whose qualifications as a *Wake* source have been dealt with by Joseph Phillips and William Dohmen.[20] For Dunne, as a process philosopher, there is not a spacetime stasis, but a constant move ahead into the future. This future is visitable, and thus would seem to be determined. Not visitable by anyone anytime, but by certain receptive types in precognitive dreams. Dunne's dreamer thus bears a resemblance to the dreamer in *Finnegans Wake*; as Dohmen puts it:

> Joyce's representation of dreaming corresponds very closely to Dunne's theory of dreams: Dunne's dreamer is freed of conscious chronology, so that both past and future events have free access to his mind. Accustomed to a three-dimensional view of reality, the mind attempts to impose a vague chronology on this four-dimensional matter, with the result that time seems to move very erratically and spatial surroundings are unstable. Similarly, the *Wake* conveys material freed of all restrictions of time of [or?] place by means of superimposed verbal levels built up from an extremely flexible, nonsequential narrative. (P. 386)

These "superimposed verbal levels" embodying perceived spots of time, first noted by the *Our Exagmination* writers, fairly represent the continual co-occurrence or juxtaposition of events distant in time in the *Wake* text. If personages such as Tristram, Wellington, Tom Sawyer, and St. Patrick appear coterminously in the same sentence and are interpreted as points on a single time track, then that track cannot be passing by in review but must be arranged in folds, so as to bring these points into conjunction. That Dunne's dreamer sees confusedly, and has the future open to him, does make him like HCE-as-dreamer (the point also made by Phillips, p. 61), but there is also in Dunne a very clear, and necessary, "Time One" linear track, that of our daily experience. This the *Wake* lacks, and it also lacks the infinite regression of dimensions in hypertime that Dunne must posit in order to give a time flow to the existence of each of his successively superior observers. We need not question Dunne as a *Wake* source, but we may question the size of the role the source plays.

Dunne has another use, however; he leads us to Jung, and thereby to another of the slightly bizarre reflections of the twentieth-century view of the physical world. Joyce, of course, knew Jung, both personally and as the second Grand Panjandrum of Psychoanalysis. Jung is in the *Wake* by name, and the book's mythic symbolism resembles Jung's archetypes in more than one way.[21] Jung, like Bergson, Dunne, and so many other writers and thinkers of the teens and twenties, undertook to adjust his world view to the drastically altered nature of time advanced by Einstein's Special Theory of Relativity. It might be said that Jung undertook to kidnap the Special Theory, for he presents, on a basis of spacetime, time symmetry, and the statistical view of causality, a justification for his principle of "Synchronicity," which is "a psychically conditioned relativity of space and time,"[22] an intuitively perceived connection between spirit and matter. If causality can only be statistically valid and thus only relatively true, argues Jung, there is room for an *acausal* principle connecting events. Events so connected seem to fall together in time, with more than simple chronological linking (which is synchron*ism*), but without one causing the other. ESP demonstrates such linking, and so do dreams: Dunne dreams of the 1902 Martinique disaster, and the next day's papers bring him word of it; a patient of Jung's dreams of a golden scarab, and as she relates the dream in his office, there comes a tap at the window. Jung opens it, and in flies a rose-chafer, "the nearest analogy to a golden scarab that one finds in our latitudes."[23]

While the picture of the human mind that Jung advances here, divided between conscious receiver and unconscious transmitter of images of the future, is of interest as another twentieth-century analogue to *Wake* dream mechanics, there are several points of sharper similarity to the book's practice. First, in synchronicity chance dwindles away, since statistical laws do not apply; second, time fails to exert a "later than"–"earlier than" causal sequence but allows a future event (seeing the scarab at the window) to present a past image (the dream of the scarab); yet, third, there is meaning here, as there is in every unconscious image toward which intuition or even superstition guides us—number, or those numbers with a numinous aura (1–9, 10, 12, . . . 28, 32, 40), being an example. Fourth, and finally, the coexistence of a synchronous universe implies that we all are potentially implicated in the fate of all others. Schopenhauer's image of the lines of longitude (individual lives) and latitude (events) intersecting on a globe, which Jung cites as a source of synchronicity theory, symbolizes this point eloquently:

> the selfsame event, although a link in two totally different chains, neverthe-less falls into place in both, so that the fate of one individual invariably fits the fate of the other, in a drama foreign to him . . . something which surpasses our powers of comprehension and can only be conceived as possible by virtue of the most wonderful pre-established harmony.[24]

Could we have here what is expressed by the constant interconnection of the *Wake*'s character? Jung, who does not find Schopenhauer's First Cause attractive, leaves open the question of determinism and Divine Will—as did Einstein, and as did Joyce. Some mysteries are yet beyond us, but, he charmingly elucidates, "Synchronicity is no more baffling or mysterious than the discontinuities of physics."[25]

Of the CPT (Charge, Parity, Time) picture of its day, the *Wake* also employs the reversibility of Parity, or left-right in space. The mirror is the traditional literary source for left-right reversals; it enables all the *Wake* characters to have visible reversed twins, and it is not disorienting when it coincides with preexistent illusion: we know ourselves by mirror images, because we don't know ourselves by our true images. It's a long jump from there to "anything recognizes itself through some contrary,"[26] but many works of literature before the *Wake* have made it. The dog-god of *Ulysses* is multiplied many times in the *Wake*, and when a reversed name or word is counterposed by its normal form ("Tugbag is Baggut's," 491.6), it is true that an undoing is matched by a doing, and it is possible—if improbable—to receive the impression that "reversal means renewal."[27] More immediate is an impression of dislocation and confusion, especially when no key is given ("Elleb Inam, Titep Notep," 237.26–27). This returns me to the point I first cited, the power of disorientation in *Wake* language. Space tricks join with time frolics to puncture the boundaries of normal percep-tion and to increase our sense of the weakness of that perception as a guide to reality. Who has seen an atom? Yet, since we have no other means to perceive, we are thrown back on our poor resources with an increased sense of their fallibility. We can make sense of waves, and we can make sense of particles, but we cannot make sense of something that is both at once. Complementarity is a case of uncertainty that, in a manner of speaking, forces us to perceive our perception. Glasheen says of the *Wake* that it is "a model of our universe as we perceive it,"[28] and while there is nothing in that profound mirror reflection that can't be found in Plato, it was the new science of the twenties that gave it a new kind of physical proof.

Turning back to the first question posed, about possible correspondence between the structure of the *Wake* and the structure of nature, it is, of course, necessary to note answers already given. Joyce himself, Atherton feels, may have dictated the statement by Eugene Jolas that the Work in Progress involved a search for "a pansymbolic, panlinguistic synthesis in the conception of a 4D universe."[29] Clive Hart's assertion of "the new world of physics of which Joyce was trying [in the *Wake*] to build up a faithful verbal analogue"[30] follows this lead, if lead it be, and it is reinforced by Margaret Solomon's "It is a new universe Joyce is creating in *Finnegans Wake*," a "multi-dimensioned novel universe."[31] Other critics have made equivalent statements, but it is perhaps Margaret Solomon who has carried furthest the effort to work out of Joyce's insistence on a mathematical basis to the *Wake*,[32] and the geometrical forms he mentions in the book, an actual physical model. Her choice is the tesseract, a 4D hypercube[33] associated at one point in the text with HCE: the Coach With The Six Insides of 359.24 represents the book as a 3D cube, which is then rotated in 4D to become a tesseract, the fourth dimension adding the (narrational) point of view from which all six sides, the totality of our 3D existence, can be seen at once. This extradimensional observation is also like seeing inside and outside at once.

That the tesseract cannot be constructed in 3D makes it, in a way, worthy of the undefined structure of the *Wake*, but it also makes it difficult to visualize, as difficult to visualize as that to which it is offered as analogy. Of mathematical curiosities with philosophical potential, and potential application to the *Wake*, my own choice would be the Klein Bottle, named for Felix Klein (1849–1925). It suffers from the same disadvantage as does the tesseract: it is not constructable in 3-space; and an additional disadvantage, to those who think the *Wake* must contain its own interpretation: it is not mentioned in the book. The rest is an ideal fit: it is a closed space (a bottle) that is one-sided. For the tesseract's clearly demarcated boundaries, it substitutes boundarilessness. That is to say, its inside and its outside cannot be differentiated, like the two sides of a Möbius strip in 3-space. Thus it can serve—at least in my view—as a model for our universe, which the tesseract cannot, being finitely boundaried. The Klein Bottle's perfect union of inside and outside, form and content, is worthy of a revolutionary creator, and brings to mind the Gnostic view of early man expressed by Erich Neumann, Jung's disciple: "early man lived in the middle of . . . psychological space in which outside and inside, world and man, powers and things, are bound together in indissoluble unity."[34]

Further search for the shape in space of a "verbal analogue," the text of the *Wake*, should take greater consideration than I have of the language of the book. In other words, is it reasonable to expect sentences in the book (the *parole*), to make referential statements about the structure? And if such (pseudo) statements are found, to grant them special status? Our search for such reference seems doomed to do violence to the text. Would not that structure be in the *langue*? Until the study of *Wake* language passes its present lexicographical stage, it is perhaps wise to reserve judgment.

Our first question, then, about structural incorporation, finds itself somewhat come to grief over the matter of visualizable analogues, and the fact that we tend to see, looking at any literary structure at all derivative of the physics of the 1920s, our own eye looking back. To the second question, about themes, characters, and the debates in the book, we can advance a cautious affirmative. Cautious, because to call *Finnegans Wake* Einsteinian or Heisenbergian makes little sense, even less than it does to call it a scientific work. No twentieth-century science provides more than a superficial source for the book; if we took it as the sum of its sources and the profundity of its description of scientific matters, we should be forced to conclude that it had been written by Leopold Bloom. What remains between such a sum and what the *Wake* is, its revolutionary novelty, the power it has exerted over two generations of readers, constitutes the real challenge of interpretation. The combination of medievalism, psychoanalysis, and spacetime physics in Jung's Synchronicity may be our closest scientific analogue, or the closest thing to a scientific analogue, to events in the *Wake*. If we leave the humor out. With it in, the pseudoscience falls away, and *Finnegans Wake* remains our century's greatest artistic expression of the sense of a changed world science has given us.

Notes

1. Ellmann's *James Joyce* (New York: Oxford, 1959) gives much information on Joyce's way with sources, and points out his slight knowledge of the sources of exotic lore to which he repeatedly alludes in *Ulysses* and *Finnegans Wake*; James S. Atherton, *The Books at the Wake*, notes that "Joyce frequently uses Mark Twain's words without regard to their meaning in Twain's text" (Carbondale: Southern Illinois University Press, 1974, p. 15). William Y. Tindall, *Reader's Guide to "Finnegans Wake*," p. 185, states: "Despite his many references to Mark Twain, Joyce never read him," and "Joyce made excellent use of all he did not know—Thomas Aquinas, for example" (New York: Farrar, Straus, 1969). Bringhurst (*Wake Newslitter*, n.s. X, no. 6 [1973]: 92–93) questions Atherton's assumption, from a few common Arabic words appearing in the *Wake*, that Joyce read the Koran; Margaret Solomon, *Eternal Geomater* (Carbondale: Southern Illinois University Press, 1969) suggests Ous-

pensky (!) as a science source; Louis Mink in *Wake Newslitter* n.s. XII, no. 6, and Jacques Aubert, *Introduction à l'esthétique de James Joyce*, offer further sobering analyses.

2. Ellmann, *James Joyce*, p. 562.

3. Atherton, *Books at the Wake*, p. 45.

4. Ellmann, p. 562.

5. Ellmann, p. 567.

6. *James Joyce Quarterly* (Summer 1974): 313.

7. *Eternal Geomater*, p. ix.

8. Adaline Glasheen, *A Second Census of Finnegans Wake* (Evanston, Ill.: Northwestern University Press, 1963), p. lix.

9. Hayman, *JJQ* 11:338.

10. Norris, *JJQ* 11:353. The point is well argued in this article and may unjustly suffer from a certain suspension of belief thanks to its resemblance to the relentlessly similar conclusions of French structuralist critics writing on everything from *Das Kapital* to *Tintin*.

11. "There are in a way no characters." Joyce to Vinding (Ellmann, p. 709).

12. Tindall, *Reader's Guide*, p. 61. See also Glasheen, *Second Census*, p. 119.

13. Particularly as put by Atherton, *Books at the Wake*, pp. 33–34: "All history is to be deduced from any part of the created universe. Yet it is found most completely in the mind of any human being."

14. *FW* 488.9–10; Atherton, *Books at the Wake*, p. 36.

15. For the Lewis-Joyce quarrel, and its appearance in chapter 13 (The Ondt and the Gracehoper) and elsewhere, see Atherton, *Books at the Wake*, p. 266; Tindall, *Reader's Guide*, p. 226; Dohmen, *JJQ* 11:368–86.

16. Bergson had himself tried to incorporate "les thèses d'Einstein" into his *Durée et Simultanéité* (1922). Leo Knuth, among others, sees Joyce's experiments with time as essentially Bergsonian (*JJQ* 11:317).

17. *James Joyce's Scribbledehobble: The Ur-Workbook of Finnegans Wake*, ed. Thomas Connolly (Evanston Ill.: Northwestern University Press, 1961), p. 162.

18. Chapter 13, "Shaun The Post," was so identified by Joyce ("a description of a postman travelling backwards in the night through the events already narrated") in a letter to Harriet Weaver of 24 May 1924; as was Jaun's departure in chapter 14 ("He is seen as already a Yesterday . . . turning back his glance amid wails of 'Today' from Tomorrow," *Letters I*, 263). David Hayman, in *JJQ* 11:340, describes the opening of chapter 1 as running like a reversed movie film; so Glasheen, *Second Census*, p. xxxvii, ALP's childbearing 201–204.

19. *FW* 625.7–8, 27. As Tindall ultimately notes, *sama sitta* is Estonian for "same shit" (*Reader's Guide*, p. 331).

20. Joseph M. Phillips, "Locating J. W. Dunne in *Finnegans Wake*," *Wake Newslitter*, n.s. XI (1974): 4, 59–64; Dohmen, op. cit., n.15.

21. See Ian MacArthur, "Self Archetypes in *Finnegans Wake*," *Wake Newslitter*, n.s. XIV, no. 1 (1977): 3–5.

22. C. G. Jung, *Synchronicity: An Acausal Connecting Principle* (London, 1972), p. 28.

23. Ibid., p. 36.

24. Schopenhauer, "On the Apparent Design in the Fate of the Individual," *Pererga and Paralipomena* I, 1891, quoted in Jung, *Synchronicity*, p. 16.

25. Jung, *Synchronicity*, p. 141.

26. Tindall, *Reader's Guide*, p. 178.

218

S. B. Purdy

27. Ibid., p. 161.

28. Glasheen, *Second Census*, p. xvii.

29. "Frontierless Decade," in *transition* 27 (April–May, 1938): 8; Atherton, *Books at the Wake*, p. 60.

30. Hart, *Structure and Motif in Finnegans Wake* (Evanston Ill.: Northwestern University Press, 1962), p. 65.

31. *Eternal Geomater*, p. vii.

32. Ellmann, p. 627: "He wished also for Ogden to comment, as a mathematician, upon the structure of *Finnegans Wake*, which he insisted was mathematical."

33. *Eternal Geomater*, pp. 120 ff. Tesseract is mentioned at *FW* 100.35, in the paragraph on Einstein. See also Thomas A. Cowan, "St. Humphrey as Tesseract," *Wake Newslitter*, n.s. X, no. 2 (1973): 19–20.

34. *Encyclopedia Britannica*, 15th ed., 1975, 8.219, s.v. "Gnosticism."

PART IX

Joyce and Judaism

Joyce and Judaism

Edmund L. Epstein

There are two basic questions that must be asked about Joyce, the writer on Jews: Is Bloom a Jew? Was Joyce anti-Semitic? The answers to these questions are not easy to arrive at. What is a Jew? What is an anti-Semite? On the first question, the speakers on the "Joyce and Judaism" panel presented a great deal of evidence that Bloom was disqualified as a Jew on many counts—he was uncircumcised; his mother was not Jewish; he does not "keep kosher" (he buys pork twice during the day); he was baptized (as a Protestant *and* as a Catholic). On the second question, no one on the panel suggested that Joyce was an anti-Semite, but the suggestion has been made elsewhere, by Robert Martin Adams in *Surface and Symbol*,[1] on the basis of some journal entries that record anti-Semitic slander (but, then, the journals record everything). Therefore, both questions have not yet received their definitive answer.

IS BLOOM A JEW?

The eminent scholar Gerschom Sholem, in an intervention at the Symposium, reported a conversation with David Ben-Gurion on the subject, in which Ben-Gurion said, "Well, the rabbis might not say that Bloom was a Jew, but *I* do." Indeed, the question of Jewish identity is still a vexed one in Israel. Perhaps we had better ask, Did *Joyce* think Bloom was a Jew? Here the answer is unequivocally *yes*. He wrote to Carlo Linati that *Ulysses* was an "epic of two races—Irish-Israelite."[2] Joyce really believed in national races, not as a proto-Nazi pseudobiologist, but as a nineteenth-century liberal mystical nationalist in the mould of Herder and Mazzini. His statement on the Irish race shows clearly how he regards "race"—not as a biological *donnée* but as a mystical "tutelage," which turns native Firbolgs and invading Milesians and Normans and Danes and Englishmen (and Jews?) into Irishmen and Irishwomen, by some mysterious process.[3] The process remains mysterious in *Ulysses*, where the Citizen rejects the notion of Bloom as an Irishman with contempt and expectoration. In *Finnegans Wake* Joyce's Irishman is Finn McCool, and Finnegan, and the Norman Persse O'Reilly, and the Dane Earwicker (Eirikr = Eric), and the English-named Porter, and

221

myriad foreigners (including the American Indian "Hapapoosiesojibway"), all merging into his quintessential Irishman. So it is useless to look for a legal or biological definition of "Jew" in Joyce. We should, of course, look for a psychological definition, and, oddly enough, there is one.

In the Nighttown chapter, Bloom is treated to a display of Zoe's back-view by Lynch (U 511). Since behinds are for Bloom the supremest objects of desire (as Molly could testify!), the sight of Zoe causes an instant and total revolution in his psyche—he splits in half. All of his instinctual drives, his will, his essential inner creative madness, coalesce into the bizarre figure of Lipoti Virag, Bloom's grandfather, but here bearing no resemblance to any normal human being. The rest of Bloom—the parts divorced from will and drive—appear languidly in Bloom's disjointed and feebler responses to the daemonic Lipoti Virag, and later as the feebly romantic Henry Flower. It seems clear to me that in Lipoti Virag we have the essential Bloom. Joyce, who does not engage in depth-psychology elsewhere in *Ulysses*, here pro-duces a figure from the depths. Here if anywhere we may find the answer to our question, now phrased as, Is Bloom a Jew in his heart? The answer is a deafening *Yes*. Bloom as Virag refers to "our tribal elixir of gopherwood" (U 512) and to "Fleshhotpots of Egypt" (U 513). However, when he reaches his nadir of madness, it is anti-Gentile fury that impels him into a series of insane charges against the purity of the Virgin Mary. Beginning with a curse against Gentiles ("Verfluchte Goim!") Lipoti-Poldy takes up the discourse on the religion of Christ that had been broken off hastily in the "Cyclops" episode:

> And says he:
> —Mendelssohn was a jew and Karl Marx and Mercadante and Spinoza. And the Saviour was a jew and his father was a jew. Your God.
> —He had no father, says Martin. That'll do now. Drive ahead.
> —Whose God? says the citizen.
> —Well, his uncle was a jew, says he. Your God was a jew. Christ was a jew like me. (*U* 342)

Lipoti-Poldy picks up Bloom's profession of faith ("Christ was a jew like me") and turns it into an attack. The surface-Bloom reacts mildly to the memory of anti-Semitism in *U* 642–44, where he denies that he is a Jew, though defending Jews ably against historical calumnies. But in his heart, or in his Id, Bloom reacts furiously as a Jew attacked by anti-Semites. In his heart Bloom identifies himself as a Jew. This is enough for Joyce, and it should be enough for us.

WAS JOYCE AN ANTI-SEMITE?

Bloom may be a Jew, in Joyce's mystical-psychological nationalism, but Joyce may still be an anti-Semite. After all, Joyce was mildly amused at the notion of a Jewish navy—Jews in the stereotype are city-men, merchants, not jolly Jack-tars (see Ellmann, p. 408). And how about those journal entries noted by Adams? To answer this question, we should know what we mean by "anti-Semite." It seems to me that an anti-Semite is not someone who makes mild jokes about Jews, or even one who records (and perhaps believes) traditional calumnies about Jews. An anti-Semite in his purest form is not someone who says that *some* Jews do silly or wicked things. He is not even someone (though this comes closer) who says that *all* Jews do silly and wicked things. The true anti-Semite, in his full development, is someone who says that *only* Jews do silly and wicked things. An anti-Semite is a person who has invented a new virtue—not-being-Jewish—and this high virtue (taking the place of charity, of course) excuses all crimes. An anti-Semite does not so much lie about Jews as he lies about everybody else. To an anti-Semite, the human faults of Jews are regarded without charity; this always turns the object of analysis into a hideous, stinking, dangerous, pernicious sub/superhuman, a type of deadly virus or vermin (imagery much in the mouths of anti-Semites like Hitler), which must be ruthlessly exterminated so that the rest of humanity, ennobled by their virtue of not-being-Jewish, can exercise their humanity, unendangered by the nonhuman enemy.

This is anti-Semitism as a historical system, the anti-Semitism of the Anti-Semitic League, of Maurras and Drumont and the anti-Dreyfusards, of Belloc and (at times) Chesterton. However, the "anti-Semitism" of Hemingway, among others, does not qualify, nor does the "anti-Semitism" of Chaucer, Shakespeare, or Dickens. The Jews in the Prioress's Tale, Shylock, or Fagin are not the only villains in the works of Chaucer, Shakespeare, or Dickens, nor are they the worst people in the works of these writers. The Pardoner is more vividly pernicious; Iago, Edmund the bastard, Macbeth, are worse than Shylock; Bill Sykes, lawyer Tulkinghorn are both worse than Fagin. So long as Jews are not uniquely exempt from the otherwise universal charity of the writer, the writer is not anti-Semitic.

Anti-Semitism derives its name from the naïve historical theory promulgated in the nineteenth century and afterwards that the Jews were the fifth-column *avant-garde* for a general Semitic counter-crusade against European Christendom. T. S. Eliot and (perhaps) Ezra Pound seem to have subscribed to this notion during most of their careers. Eliot's Tiresias-figure in *The Waste Land* views his father, Europe, as a comatose, commercial, Semitic figure, a drowned Phoenician sailor. In Eliot's other poems, the Jews are underneath the lot, as red-eyed scavengers for Eliot, presiding over the over-chartered real estate of modern rootless cosmopolitan civilization, squatting on the windowsills of the houses they lease to the hapless inhabitants of Christendom.

No one sensitive to tone in Joyce can hold that he was anti-Semitic in any of these senses of the word. But the case against Joyce's anti-Semitism is even stronger than feeling. A true anti-Semite, as I said above, considers Jews as not human at all; they are "Judaeorhynchi," Jewish insects, as a splenetic anti-Semite in Huxley's *Antic Hay* calls them. Joyce not only was *not* this sort of anti-Semite, he was the reverse. As we have seen, his Everyman is a Jew—Leopold Bloom. An anti-Semite would make any Jew he writes about an Anti-Man. Here we see Joyce not simply not as an anti-Semite but as an anti-anti-Semite, in the fullest sense of the word.

However, we would know this from the balanced but sympathetic account of some unattractive French Jews in *Ulysses*:

> On the steps of the Paris Stock Exchange the goldskinned men quoting prices on their gemmed fingers. Gabbles of geese. They swarmed loud, uncouth about the temple, their heads thickplotting under maladroit silk hats. Not theirs: these clothes, this speech, these gestures. Their full slow eyes belied the words, the gestures eager and unoffending, but knew the rancours massed about them and knew their zeal was vain. Vain patience to heap and hoard. Time surely would scatter all. A hoard heaped by the roadside: plundered and passing on. Their eyes knew the years of wandering and, patient, knew the dishonours of their flesh. (*U,* 34)

Bloom is a Jew in his heart, and Joyce is an anti-anti-Semite. What else remains to be said?

Notes

1. (New York: Oxford University Press, 1962), pp. 99–106, 146. See also Adams's *James Joyce: Common Sense and Beyond* (New York: Random House, 1966), p. 122.

2. Richard Ellmann, *James Joyce* (New York: Oxford University Press, 1959), p. 535.

3. *The Critical Writings of James Joyce*, ed. E. Mason and R. Ellmann (New York: Oxford University Press, 1959), p. 166.

The Humanity of Bloom, The Jewishness of Joyce

Morton P. Levitt

My epigraph comes from Frank O'Connor's *A Short History of Irish Literature*. "Jewish literature," says O'Connor, "is the literature of townsmen, and the greatest Jew of all was James Joyce." As a sort of subepigraph, I might also cite David Ben-Gurion's perception that anyone is a Jew who says that he is—on the supposition, presumably, that no one would make such a claim unless he had to. The obverse of this, of course, is the definition provided by history: you're a Jew if someone else says you are.

In past essays and talks, I've dealt with the identity of Bloom as a Jew, with his Jewishness (especially his family connections) as a metaphor of his broader humanity, and with Joyce's use of the Passover ritual (amidst a larger context of fertility myth) as a central metaphoric pattern in *Ulysses*—a pattern more truly functional, I believe, than that of Homer. I propose now to deal with some larger, less specifically textual issues that are raised by this metaphor of Jewishness as it affects Joyce and other Modernist novelists. The legalistic question of whether Bloom is a Jew no longer activates me: had Joyce meant him to be demonstrably not Jewish, he could easily have continued to call him Hunter and omitted the more than two hundred Jewish references in the novel.

Coming this week to Zurich from Italy, I'm struck by the fact that of the three dozen or so synagogues still functioning in Italy, very few remain vital: testimony to the Holocaust, to emigration to Israel, to assimilation, and to the movement of people in all nations to a relatively few large urban centers. What is surprising is that the community endures and that so many of the important Italian novelists of this century—from Svevo to Carlo Levi and Natalia Ginzburg, from Moravia to Giorgio Bassani—are either Jewish or have strong Jewish ties. The phenomenon is not restricted to Italy, and it has another, metaphoric dimension: what made the ten-year-old Nikos Kazantzakis convince his father to take him from Iraklion in Crete to Khania (a trip that is difficult even today on a modern highway) to take Hebrew lessons from the rabbi there? (Lessons that family pressure soon

225

put an end to.) Why has Jorge Luis Borges, with no supporting evidence, claimed to be part-Jewish himself? (It cannot be simply, as his translator has told me, "to bug his mother.") Why did Mr. Joyce make his hero a Jew? It is not enough, I think, to answer merely that he was a Jew and to recount Joyce's ties to the Jews of Dublin and Trieste.

Jews have exerted a profound appeal, both positive and negative, on the Modernist literary imagination: the conventional critical wisdom claims that Jews, as sufferers and outsiders, have served as convenient symbols of modern alienated man. There is surely some truth in this, just as there is in the usual explanation for Christian anti-Semitism, i.e., that the Jews' refusal to recognize Jesus as the Messiah seemed to cast doubt on the legitimacy of Christianity itself. But just as the latter explanation omits economic motivations or imagined political needs, so too does the former simplify what is, in fact, a most complex issue. Joyce's use of Bloom—the first significant use of a Jew in Modernist fiction—is important not only for what it may tell us about *Ulysses* but for what it reveals as well about the larger Modernist usage and perhaps even about modern life itself.

Removed from insular Dublin, living in the international port city of Trieste, Joyce was well situated to observe a phenomenon still recent in European history: the movement of the long-inbred Jewish culture into a larger European context, a major cultural infusion comparable to the effects of the Crusades, but one more direct and easily traceable. It was, after all, only in the middle of the nineteenth century that Jews were emancipated politically by the Austro-Hungarian Empire and other nations of Europe. This did not mean, of course, that Jews were immediately and universally accepted as equals by their European countrymen (or that they are today). Witness the fictions and autobiographical writings of Jakov Lind or Peter Weiss or Elie Wiesel or Jerzy Kosinski; witness Bassani, Canetti, or Kafka; witness the Citizen's not-so-atypical question, "What is your nation if I may ask," and Bloom's trusting if ingenuous answer, "Ireland. . . . I was born here. Ireland" (*U*, 331). Yet the knowledge that they now enjoyed at least civil rights, if not widespread acceptance, did effect an outpouring of Jewish creative energies—energies directed outward, into Central and Western and Southern European cultures, and not, as they had been for centuries, inward, into the ghetto, into the study of Torah, Talmud, and Cabbala. I. B. Singer's comment a few generations later (that after six hundred years in Poland, he and his brother were the first in their family to learn Polish, for they were the first to feel that they might actually be welcome) points up the hope and disillusionment inherent in the new situation. (Within a decade, both Singers had been forced to emigrate to America.) The events of *In My Father's Court*, which so closely parallel those of *A Portrait* and which we can envision happening in the lifetime of

Rudolph Bloom, have some bearing here: new laws aside, Jewish optimism aside, the pattern of centuries did not change so easily. Witness history.

Before the late nineteenth century, those Jewish artists and thinkers who would make an impact on the larger, gentile world would have to do so, as did those in Bloom's infamous catalogue, as something other than Jews: by assimilating, like Mendelssohn; by becoming themselves anti-Semites, like Marx; by outraging their coreligionists and thus becoming outcasts, like Spinoza (a major influence on Singer, by the way). Only the Saviour, as Bloom sees him, is truly creative within a fully Jewish context. But fully Jewish contexts were no longer very common in Bloom's day (except in the Pale, where Malamud's Fixer could be forced to be a Jew, despite himself). Out in the gentile world, exposed in some ways more than they had been when they were forced to wear pointed hats and yellow stars and to live behind locked gates and walls (we tend to forget that ghettoes were invented for Jews), European Jews nonetheless retained the potential for alienation and suffering that would so attract the Modernists to them.

More significantly, I believe, they brought with them into the outer world certain pivotal aspects of their long tradition—this is true even of those Jews, such as Svevo and Joyce's other Triestine friends, who may have wanted to leave the past behind them. And it is these qualities which would function so centrally for Joyce, as for Proust, Kafka, Mann, Kazant-zakis, and others. They brought with them, to begin with, their respect for learning (despite his problems, Bloom seems the only intellectually curious person in all of Dublin, aside from Stephen) and their respect for family ties (the Blooms' home life, ironically, is the most stable that Joyce depicts). They brought with them a sense of their history—not necessarily profound knowledge of that history ("that brought us out of the land of Egypt and into the house of bondage," thinks Bloom [U, 122]) but a powerful sense of it and its significance (Bloom knows well the difference between bondage and freedom and what it means to be free—hence his Irish patriotism). They brought also a broader sense of continuity than their neighbors had known (with all his confusion of dates, Bloom understands that Jewish history is much older than Western [U, 658]).

The Jews of Rudolph Bloom's time also brought forth from the ghetto a deeply humanistic tradition, one that is distinct from and not dependent upon the neo-Aristotelian borrowings of the Renaissance: a tradition in which the individual is valued both as an individual and as part of a larger community. Centered on the worship of the one God, this humanistic spirit would survive even among those for whom God was a functionless concept. Finally, evolving from this humane spirit and from the emphasis in Judaism on this life, as opposed to some potential future life, they brought with them into the world a sense of individual responsibility—and thereby of individual worth—a perception that would predict existential belief, as it predated both Renaissance and Aristotelian humanism. (This is true even if Aristotle was not, as Poldy would have it, "a pupil of a rabbinical philosopher, name uncertain" [*U*, 687].) Matthew Arnold, you see, had it all wrong in "Hebraism and Hellenism."

Joyce, it seems to me, partly perceived and partly intuited this. At least, this is the prime thematic function of Bloom in *Ulysses*: in a European world from which traditional humanistic values seemingly have fled, he provides a new (yet old) form of continuity, of individual responsibility and worth, of humanism itself. As their forebear, he would provide a model for many of the Modernist heroes (not antiheroes after all, then) who would follow him. It is perhaps because of this insistence of his that he would be made to suffer and, despite his best efforts to belong, to remain alienated. It may not be coincidental that Joyce could identify so strongly with just those aspects of Bloom which made him, too—far more than did his stereotyping of himself as a Romantic artist—a suffering, affirming outsider. O'Connor's strange formulation seems not so strange after all.

The Jewish Connection, Cont'd

Marilyn Reizbaum

Joyce's connection with Judaism has been a source for much discussion since he made Leopold Bloom the hero of *Ulysses*. There are many aspects of this "connection" that are controversial and, in the debate over them, hard to elucidate. *Ulysses* has either been criticized or praised, and interpreted in various ways, on the basis of conclusions drawn in this matter: Erwin Steinberg disputes Bloom's Jewishness and thereby calls for another approach to the character of Bloom and to the book as a whole;[1] Harold Fisch, in *The Dual Image: The Figure of the Jew in English and American Literature*, praises *Ulysses* for being the first modern novel written in English to have a Jew as a hero.[2] Many have seen Joyce's treatment of the Jew as antipathetic. Maurice Samuel, noted Jewish author and translator, was very interested in the subject of Joyce's relation to Judaism. In an article that appeared in 1929, Samuel, citing passages from "Circe," asserted that Joyce treated Bloom in a loathsome and malevolent manner, and that he seemed to exhibit a "cosmic loathing for the little Jew, Bloom."[3] In his attempt to account for this he goes so far as to suggest that, while it may seem "stupid" in this connection, Joyce might have been an anti-Semite. This notion that Joyce harbored hatred for the Jew and the extension from that to a consideration of Joyce as an anti-Semite has been voiced by others:

> Sentimentalists who simplify Bloom the Jew into a pathetic and admirable little man who forgives his enemies and so is apotheosized into the perfect Christian hero would do well to face the sizeable element of anti-Semitism in Joyce himself. This element is not distinct from powerful feelings of self-loathing; it involves also a shrinking from excessive self-awareness and a scorn of prudent self-interest.[4]

To aid them in understanding the novel and for biographical reasons, many have attemped to bring Joyce's statements about Judaism to bear in their assessment of his attitude toward the people and the religion. The task is a difficult one, for, when compiled, the statements are often contradictory, making an assessment on the basis of them alone virtually impossible. Joyce has expressed anything from respect and admiration—"it was an heroic act on the part of the Jews when they refused to accept the Christian revelation. Look at them, they are better husbands than we are, better fathers and better sons"[5]—to what can be construed as disdain—"By the Lord Christ I must get rid of some of these Jewish bowels I have in me yet."[6] Others argue over the depth and accuracy of Joyce's knowledge about Jews. The credence that they give to Joyce's statements depends upon what view they hold. Again, the evidence is hard to assess. Many claim that Svevo as a prototype for Bloom and as a source for Joyce's knowledge about Jews is a poor choice, in that his knowledge of and connection with Judaism are dubious. And certainly Joyce was no master of the Hebrew language, having made mistakes throughout *Ulysses* in his transliterations: e.g., "Agendath Netaim" (60),[7] which should read "Agudath Netaim," and as in the quote from "The Song of Songs" (477)—"Schorach ani wenowach benoith Hierushaloim," which, regardless of how one tries, through Ashkenazi inflection or otherwise, cannot be justified. It should read: "Schrorah ani venavah, banoth Yerushalaim."

If we use the text to document Joyce's connection with Judaism, then we are faced with what might seem to be irresolvable ambiguities, or we might be able to interpret those ambiguities as artistically significant—Bloom as Jew and non-Jew, Bloom as loathsome and admirable. It seems to me that both Samuel and Adams are narrow and reductive in their assessments of what are inherent and complex ambiguities in the presentation of Bloom. A more profitable way of approaching these ambiguities and their significance is by examining a source that Ellmann mentions in the biography. Ellmann claims that this source, Otto Weininger's *Geschlecht und Charakter*, contains theories that Joyce generally believed, especially where they pertain to women.[8] Ellmann does not make clear how well Joyce knew the book, and he does not discuss in any depth the relevance of Weininger's theories to Joyce's concept of Jews. In fact, it is not clear from Ellmann's source that Joyce read the book. But even if Joyce did not use the book, the ideas put forward by Weininger about Jews and about women (or variations on those ideas) were prevalent in the late nineteenth and early twentieth centuries.[9] Assuming that Joyce might have used this source, I believe that it can be, at least, of heuristic value to examine his theories and how Joyce might have used them. Considering Weininger's book as a possible source could seem damning to any favorable reading of Bloom as Jew because of Weininger's flagrant anti-Semitism, but upon closer examination of the way in which Joyce used these theories or themes—and whether or not Joyce used Weininger, he did plainly use the themes—one can see that the development of those themes appears with a complexity of tone and attitude that transcends Weininger's concept of them. It is important to remember that regardless of where Joyce got the ideas, it would be uncharacteristic of him to use any source (e.g., Bérard, Homer) in a straightforward manner. We have come to expect a "Joycean" adaptation of some kind.

In his book Weininger expounds upon what he feels to be the inferiority of women and the inhumanity of Jews. A kind of metaphorical link is set up between the two, and it is this link which I believe Joyce gathered up to use in *Ulysses*. Weininger based his theory about the inferiority of women on what he saw as a fundamental relationship between sex and character. He saw every human being as a combination of both sexes, in which the male is the positive, productive, logical, conceptual side capable of genius, and in which the female is the negative side, incapable of any of these virtues. Woman has two functions according to Weininger—either prostitution or procreation. The ideal woman accepts her role as dependent upon the phallus, and her only emancipation comes in the ending of coitus.

Just as the woman is the negative force in every human being, so too, according to Weininger, is the Jew. The Jew has no redeeming qualities. He believes in nothing and therefore is useless. Because he is undirected he gravitates toward all "destructive" institutions and beliefs—communism, anarchism, materialism, and atheism. The Jew is detestable and the detestable part of every human being is the Jewish part—"Doch die eine bliebt darum nicht minder gewiss: wer immer das Jüdische Wesen hasst, der hasst es zunächst in sich."[10] To cement the link between woman and Jew, Weininger proclaimed that Jews were "weiblich"—the clue that they are the embodiment of the negative.

We can see that many of the connections that Weininger makes suited Joyce perfectly; they appear most prevalently and climactically in "Circe." It is important to keep in mind that the dream world of Nighttown is a kind of metaphor for or presentation of subconscious activity. Joyce depicts Bloom there as he exists in his own mind, a womanish man filled with self-loathing, among other things. As Bloom says in "Circe"—"Sleep reveals the worst" (546). With this in mind it seems reasonable to postulate that rather than taking and accepting Weininger's theories literally, Joyce perceived them as an expression of Weininger's own subconscious mind. In that mind feelings of self-loathing (as Adams either consciously or unconsciously implies) are linked with being Jewish. The Jew internalizes his plight of being an outcast and accepts for himself the sense of that self which others have foisted upon him.

If Joyce knew Weininger's book, then he might have known that Weininger was a Jew who converted to Christianity and then committed suicide at the age of twenty-eight, the very year the book was published. Joyce might have seen Weininger as a man who when confronted with his own philosophies could not reconcile them with his origins. He is a man like Bloom, as were many of the prototypes whom Joyce used in his creation of Bloom—a Jew and a non-Jew, struggling to accommodate both worlds. But Weininger was the exemplar of the "jew who hates the jew in the jew."[11] Ellmann and others may see Bloom's actions in "Circe" as exemplifying Weininger's theories, but if we examine those actions and perceive Joyce's use of Weininger's theories as an expression of the subconscious, then we may conclude that, in fact, Joyce does just the opposite—he does not exemplify the theories in his work, he exposes them. The difference between Weininger and Bloom is that Weininger exorcised his fears by theorizing and dying, whereas Bloom exorcises his through imaginative action and by emerging with a sense of who he is, an acceptance of that self, and with a son, symbol of the continuation of life.

In the section of "Circe" where Bloom embarks upon his series of transformations, we have Dr. Dixon reading Bloom's "bill of health": "Professor Bloom is a finished example of the new womanly man. His moral nature is simple and lovable. Many have found him a dear man, a dear person. He is a rather quaint fellow on the whole, coy though not feeble-minded in the medical sense" (493–94). Bloom is a "womanly man," "weiblich" in Weininger's terms, but it is important to note that he is a "new womanly man." (It is also important to note the double entendre in the word "finished"—just as Stephen is, according to his self-description later in the episode, a "most finished artist," meaning that he is at once polished and impotent, so too here Bloom is exemplary of qualities that make him a "dear man" while he is at the same time impotent. It may also be a clue to his redemption in the episode—he is "finished" with the "old" womanly man and is ushering in the new.) The "womanly" characteristics that are attributed to him in this description are not the negative ones of Weininger's theories, but the stereotypical ones of gentleness. (Joyce once said to Wyndham Lewis that he thought the Jews to be a very "gentle race," and in that way more like women than like the Irish, whose similarity to the Jews he insisted upon.[12])

Furthermore, this womanly man is about to give birth, which for Joyce, on both the literal and the symbolic levels, was a positive purpose. This fecundity was not a limitation in Joyce's eyes, but a celebration of man's ability to immortalize himself on earth—as was art. Bloom is not relegated to the status of an instrument of procreation; he is given the ultimate power. And he is not, as he would be in Weininger's terms, lacking in a logical, conceptual side. He is "coy though not feeble-minded in the medical sense." By allowing for what is considered characteristically feminine—coyness—and intellect, Joyce is departing from Weininger's notion that woman, or what is "womanly," is incapable of genius. Joyce also seems to indicate that Bloom is feeble-minded in the sense that he is not totally

governed by his intellect. The strength of his intellect could be said to be
enfeebled by his emotional capacity, and this is to his advantage. We see
this borne out later in "Circe," when Stephen and Bloom come together—
"extremes meet." Stephen is challenged intellectually by Lynch's cap, and
Stephen has to make an effort to continue with his sterile intellectual
analysis. It is with "woman's reason" that this happens, the "cap" says
(504). Man's logical powers do not enable him to make the connections that
transcend the reasonable, leading into the mystical, the cosmic, that which
allows Stephen and Bloom to come together.

These extensions, which are not immediately logical, lead us to Joyce's
notion of lineage. It might be useful to point out here that the word
"geschlecht" may mean "race" as well as "gender," allowing both concepts
to collapse together in Joyce's creation of character. (This is essentially
what Weininger does but with a negative purpose in mind.) Bloom gives
birth to a kind of mini-universe that is in accord with Joyce's concept of the
world. He produces eight white and yellow (exotic) children, who have
either Greek or Jewish names, and they run the economic world (495). But
then "A Voice" questions the origins of Bloom and his brood: "Bloom, are
you the Messiah ben Joseph or ben David?" "You have said it," Bloom
answers "darkly." In other words, Bloom's lineage, his religion, is being
questioned—does he stem from the Christian messiah or from the Jewish
one? And his is the answer: there is essentially no distinction between them
according to lineage. The distinction is in men's minds; they have created
that distinction, not according to parentage but according to dogma. With
the distinction gone Stephen and Bloom may come together. Jews and
Christians are from the same lot: "*Leopoldi autem generatio. Moses begat
Noah and Noah begat Eunuch and Eunuch begat O'Halloran and O'Halloran begat Guggenheim and Guggenheim begat Agendath. . ."* (495). This
is Joyce's line, where mankind descends from mankind. At the same time
an acknowledgment of the distinction made between races, religions, points
up the split within Bloom—Jew and non-Jew, the self and the alien self.

It is with these ideas of the "new womanly man" and the Joycean notion
of lineage (sex and character, race and character) that we may most profit-
ably look at the Bella/Bello in Bloom and at the final section of "Circe" in
which Bloom meets his son, Rudy/Stephen. In "Circe" the sexes take turns
being both dominant/sadistic and subservient/masochistic. These extremes
are separated out and embodied in the figments Bella and Bello. Their
interaction with Bloom is a working out of Bloom's relationship with
Molly. Weininger's theory states that each person is made up of both female
and male, and therefore both are always present. Joyce has, however,
altered Weininger's distribution. Not only does Bella have olive skin,
signalling the exotic element that Joyce so often evokes, but she has a

"sprouting moustache." In her fan's interaction with Bloom we see the
inversion of roles in Bloom's relationship with Molly:

THE FAN
(*Flirting quickly, then slowly.*) Married, I see.
BLOOM
Yes . . . Partly, I have mislaid . . .
THE FAN
(*Half opening, then closing.*) And the missus is master. Petticoat government.
BLOOM
(*Looks down with a sheepish grin.*) That is so. (527)

This is an internal condition as well as an external one ("the missus is
master"), for it is true in the relationship between Bella and Bloom, Bella
being a projection of Bloom's subconscious. Yet when the Bello side comes
out, the positions are reversed. Whereas Bella turns Bloom into an animal,
in the parallel with *The Odyssey*, Bello turns Bloom into a woman as well.
The Bello side of Bloom enables him to see his ineptitude rather than
simply to wallow in it, and symbolizes Bloom's feelings of impotence and
self-hatred. We see Bloom's debasement, but it is externalized and finally
exorcised:

BELLO
(*Sarcastically.*) I wouldn't hurt your feelings for the world but there's a man of
brawn in possession there. The tables are turned, my gay young fellow! He
is something like a fullgrown outdoor man. Well for you, you muff, if you
had that weapon with knobs and lumps and warts all over it. He shot his bolt,
I can tell you! Foot to foot, knee to knee, belly to belly, bubs to breast! He's
no eunuch. A shock of red hair he has sticking out of him behind like a
furzebush! Wait for nine months, my lad! Holy ginger, it's kicking and
coughing up and down in her guts already! That makes you wild, don't it!
Touches the spot? (*He spits in contempt.*) Spittoon! (541)

Bloom has been able to wallow in his debasement by having Boylan be a
sexual substitute, but he is now prepared to reject Boylan as a substitute for
the father/creator aspect of his relationship with Molly. He now sees that
they are inextricably connected (sex, race, character).

In both cases, Bella and Bello, the key to understanding is Molly, the
woman, as in the metaphorical link that Weininger makes between gender/
race and character. Bloom, the Jew, the cuckold, the debased, forces
himself to confront the fact of Blazes Boylan, and his reaction after this
direct confrontation is one of self-recognition. He realizes his own part in
the difficulties in his relationship with Molly, as she does later in "Penelope." There is acceptance here, rather than the avoidance that Bloom has
been practicing throughout the book until now:

BLOOM
To drive me mad! Moll! I forgot! Forgive! Moll! . . . We . . . Still . . . (541)

With the word "Still" we get an inkling of Joyce's intention; there is still hope for their relationship. The "still" corresponds to Molly's "yes" at the end of the book.

Furthermore, we can see another parallel to *The Odyssey*, which Joyce has manipulated for his purposes, and this parallel also marks a departure from as well as a manipulation of Weininger's theories. In *The Odyssey* Ulysses uses the drug "moly" to ward off Circe and to save himself and his men from destruction. Similarly, here, "Molly" is the key to Bloom's salvation. What happens to him in "Circe" is the process whereby he can come to terms with what he needs. He sees his life pass before him, like the man who proverbially sees all in the moment before his death. As I have suggested before, Weininger experienced this with the publication of his book—he was unable to exorcise the debasement, the "jew who hates the jew in the jew," the alien self. Bloom sees things for what they are instead of distorting them as a means of exorcism. He experiences a kind of death of the "old" Bloom, but his is a death into life. The parallel between Weininger and Bloom works out on a personal level as well as on a mythical one in Joyce's terms. Bloom's emergence brings him into a societal myth through his relationship with Molly. Both of them have mixed parentage, Jewish and non-Jewish, and this allows for the superimposition of Stephen onto Rudy. In effect it is Weininger's theories that allow for the denouement. Lineage and sexuality come together positively to complete Joyce's probable adaptation of Weininger's book.

As for Samuel's contention that Stephen emerges undefiled while Bloom remains loathsome,[13] I would argue that, while they are contrasted, in fact, the opposite is true. Their experiences in "Circe" are paralleled: both meet their parents—Bloom meets them head on while Stephen recoils in horror; both are confronted with their sexuality—Bloom faces his problems (and after all he is already a father) while Stephen wants to know "the word known to all men." At the end of the episode, it is Bloom who helps Stephen to rise.

And so all the associations that Joyce makes with Bloom are complete— he is Jew, Irishman, Greek, and Savior; Elijah ben Bloom, Lord Mayor of Dublin, and spiritual father of Stephen, Ulysses, and Christ. "There is a flower that bloometh" (517). The final association, I would suggest, is with Joyce himself, the father/creator, who possessed all the qualities and ambiguities of the characters he created. He was the Stephen who cried "non serviam" and the Bloom who perceived the tortured alien self. He could also probably see the potential for the Weininger in himself—the self that hates the self in the self—and through his art he was able to exorcise what is irreconcilable in Weininger's creation.

In all of this it is significant, it seems to me, that Joyce made Bloom a Jew. In this regard Adams writes: "Bloom is Jewish because Joyce as an artistic outcast and voluntary exile identified with the Jews; their status as special vessels of divine purpose and their long history of pariah treatment correspond with the conditions of the artist."[14] I agree with Adams here. Joyce's affinity with the Jew seems to have arisen out of this—that his vision of himself as an artist was most closely reflected in the image, his image of the Jew. Because of the Jew's condition and because of his nature, he had contained within him all the ambiguities which Joyce perceived in himself: exile, wanderer, assimilator, achiever, survivor, equally at home and a stranger in every country in the world. The Jew was for Joyce the perfect exemplar of the noman/everyman, "bearing the tables of the law graven in the language of the outlaw." If "Circe" has been Bloom's personal myth of degradation and exorcism, then perhaps *Ulysses* can be said to have done the same for Joyce.

Notes

1. Erwin Steinberg, "James Joyce and the Critics Not Withstanding, Leopold Bloom Is Not Jewish," *Journal of Modern Literature* (in press).
2. Harold Fisch, *The Dual Image* (London: World Jewish Library, 1971).
3. Maurice Samuel, "Bloom of Bloomusalem," *The Reflex*, Feb. 1929, no. 2, Vol. IV, p. 14:

> . . . somehow Stephen emerges from all this undefiled in the eyes of the reader. *His* madnesses are those of poets. Bloom's are those of a wretched, indecent little person, none the less so because there is something pathetic in the way he clings to the young Irishman. Joyce's malevolence can do no more. By the time the scene closes the worst that can be revealed concerning human beings, the most loathsome, has been unfolded about the figure of Bloom. One should not be personal, but one cannot help feeling that for the character of Bloom, the Jew, Joyce harbors a mad, insatiable hatred. As he sees into the soul of Stephen with the mercilessness of great love, he sees into the soul of Bloom with the mercilessness of hate. . . .

4. Robert M. Adams, *Surface and Symbol: The Consistency of James Joyce's "Ulysses"* (New York: Oxford University Press, 1972), p. 104n.
5. Frank Budgen, "James Joyce," *Horizon III*, Feb. 1941, p. 107.
6. *Selected Letters of James Joyce*, ed. Richard Ellmann (New York: Viking Press, 1975), p. 76: from James Joyce to Stanislaus Joyce.
7. All parenthetical citations to page numbers in *Ulysses* refer to the Vintage Books edition, New York, 1961.
8. Richard Ellmann, *James Joyce* (New York: Oxford University Press, 1972), p. 477.

9. An example of a source that verifies the prevalence of these ideas at the time Joyce was writing is Viola Klein's *The Feminine Character* (London: Routledge & Kegan Paul, 1971). Klein devotes an entire chapter to Weininger's theories. She also examines, to some degree, the similarity between, for instance, Weininger's ideas and Freud's.

10. Otto Weininger, *Geschlecht und Charakter: Eine Prinzipielle Untersuchung* (Wien & Leipzig: Wilhelm Braumüller, 1917), p. 413 (originally pub. 1903).

11. *Joyce's "Ulysses": Notesheets in the British Museum*, ed. Phillip Herring (Charlottesville: University Press of Virginia, 1972), p. 18.

12. Richard Ellmann, *James Joyce*, p. 529.

13. See n. 3 above.

14. Robert M. Adams, *James Joyce: Common Sense and Beyond* (New York: Random House, 1966), p. 122.

PART X

Re-Joycing in Sex (Or, Come Again?)

Prefatory Note

Morris Beja

The original panel on Joyce and sexuality at the Zurich Symposium had no formal papers; instead, there was a lively discussion. What we talked about included such things as sex, promiscuity, celibacy, virginity, adultery, cuckoldry, homosexuality, heterosexuality, onanism, masturbation, sado-masochism, fetishism, incest, impotence, contraception, sin, pornography . . . the same old stuff. Oh, and love.

And joy: how much, we asked, of the joys of sex are there in the Joyce of sex? We came up with varied answers, as suggested by the papers here, which develop a few of the points and positions briefly explored at the Symposium. By agreement among the panelists, our talk tended to concentrate on *Ulysses*, with a foray into *Finnegans Wake* as well.

By way of introduction, I want to begin with a comment on Judge Woolsey's decision about *Ulysses*. The practice by Random House of reprinting that decision in all American editions of the novel has always seemed to me reprehensible and misleading. For about half a century, it has assured newcomers to the book that *Ulysses* is a quite proper work, which ought not to be banned—presumably because it is safe and harmless. Obviously the United States owes a debt to Judge Woolsey, but I suspect that his decision has done more to remove the excitement that American readers should rightly feel on coming to *Ulysses* for the first time than almost anything else—except, maybe, courses in modern literature, or critical and scholarly studies. But there are some exceptions, and we hope the present essays are among them.

James Joyce and Those (K)nights of "Ruful Continence"

Jane Ford

Any attempt to assess the evidence for the joy of sex (or for the lack of it) in Joyce's work can only be based on an evaluation of the experiences of his fictional characters. This experience is, more often than not, one of "ruful continence." Just as it is true that the history of the development of the novel can be traced in the Joyce corpus, so is it also true that the evolvement of attitudes toward sexuality in our time can be discerned in its progressive delineation from *Stephen Hero* through *Finnegans Wake*. I believe that Joyce, in his concern with the problem of satisfactory sexual relationships, moved from a focus on the solipsistic quest in the one-to-one relationships of *Stephen Hero*, *Dubliners*, and *A Portrait of the Artist as a Young Man*, through the shift to the transitional experiences of the characters in *Ulysses*, and on to the blurring and merging of identities (which includes incest) that we find in *Finnegans Wake*. He thus foreshadowed the present-day acceptance on the part of an increasing number of people of more casual sexual encounters, devoid of commitment, which have culminated in the "cruising" phenomenon in many of our larger cities. As a response to the inherent difficulties in long-term sexual relationships, there has been a shift in some quarters to spontaneous, one-time encounters, and the Joyce corpus reflects this shift.

In general, Joyce's view of the possibilities of joy in sex was close to Freud's pessimism, which focused on a low statistical probability, considering the array of factors militating against it. One of the most obvious obstacles is the lack of spontaneous response on the part of the Other to the desire of the primary initiator. This immediately introduces the problem of the exertion of one person's will over that of the Other. Richardson's Lovelace was reduced to obliterating Clarissa's consciousness, and sexual desire is always a useful paradigm for the exploration of the desire to control, based on genuine need. Both Proust and Sartre (to name only two) explored this theme extensively. The failure to prevail in this battle of wills is frequently what leads to the "ruful continence" of Joyce's characters.

Beginning with *Stephen Hero*, we have Stephen's first attempt to persuade another to succumb to what he perceives as a mutually compelling sexual desire. In his refusal to assume hypocrisy, or to feign a sophisticated indifference calculated to seduce Emma, Stephen adopts an honestly open, frontal approach, which offends both the girl and his friend Lynch. He attributes her recalcitrance to the "fathers"—in this case the church fathers. His outrage at the refusal of the Other to take advantage with him of a fleeting moment in time when their mutual desires coincide leads, in a natural progression, to his encounters with the prostitutes in *A Portrait*: if compliance cannot be obtained by coercion, it can be bought.

But with *A Portrait*, we must pause briefly to note another aspect of Joyce's attitude toward sex—the relationship between sexual fulfillment and artistic achievement. Ibsen before him, in a series of plays that included *Hedda Gabler* and *When We Dead Awaken*, depicted the sublimated sexual impulse (with a concomitant frustration of the potential female partner) as necessary for successful artistic or intellectual production. Joyce seems to have been at least partially attracted by this concept, as expressed in the distanced encounter with the bird-girl in *A Portrait*, explored more thoroughly with Richard in *Exiles*, and suggested by Stephen's chosen isolation at the end of *Ulysses*. This was a view not shared by Freud, however.

Dubliners provides a series of incidents of "ruful continence." In these stories, sex is never the one consolation and pleasure for people leading otherwise drab and uneventful lives. In "An Encounter," we have the frustrated attempt of the older man to entice the two young boys, and although the reader shares their sense of escape, from the point of view of the man, it is a nonencounter. In "The Boarding House," we have a version of Joyce's outrage at possible lifelong entrapment based on succumbing to the passing desire of the moment. But Polly is as much the victim of her own sexual desire as is Bob Doran; both are being manipulated by Mother/ Society. "The pleasures of love lasts but a fleeting but the pledges of life outlusts a lieftime" (*FW* 444.24–25). In "A Painful Case," the "ruful continence" is not the knight's but the lady's, and Joyce again reiterates a failure to seize advantage of what life offers. Mrs. Sinico, defeated by Duffy's refusal (or perhaps inability) to accept a mutually satisfying sexual relationship, loses the will to survive and try to find it again. In "Eveline," the girl's inability to tear herself away from her father forces a "ruful continence" on her would-be husband, as he sails without her. And finally, in "The Dead," we have yet another version of consistent failure to achieve fulfilled desire simultaneously. Gretta, still fixated on a romanticized past, which Joyce would surely have seen as being no better than the present, had it materialized, is unable to take advantage of the only real possibility life has for her at that moment, and Gabriel becomes yet another of Joyce's knights of "ruful continence" in what promises to be a long night of same.

But Cervantes's Knight of the Rueful Countenance and Joyce's knights of "ruful continence" have more than a punning relationship. All these characters from *Dubliners* (with the exception of the man in "An Encounter"), being true Quixotes themselves, fail to grasp at possible joy in the present moment because they are so locked into an idealized other place, person, or time, summed up in Molly's "were never easy where we are." In *Ulysses*, the characters begin to break out of this bind, and we move toward the blurred and merged identities of *Finnegans Wake*, where "everybilly lived alove with everybiddy else" (*FW* 21.9).

As Joyce moved into *Ulysses*, he was still contending with the same basic barriers to mutually satisfying sexuality. In a country in which contraception was—and is—a grievous sin, Mrs. Purefoy epitomizes the result of unbridled, legalized sexuality, the production of costly-to-feed "hardy annuals" (*U* 161.11). The possibilities for joy in sex are explored by Leopold and Molly against the backdrop of Mrs. Purefoy's prolonged labor, in counterpoint to Mulligan's "no more marriages, glorified man, an androgynous angel, being a wife unto himself" (*U* 213.26–27). Faced with this dilemma, Bloom concludes, "Eunuch. One way out of it" (*U* 82.26–27).

Although something can be made of Stephen's "I will not sleep here tonight" (*U* 23.20), in terms of his relationship to Mulligan, sexual experience seems scarcely a real concern for him, especially in contrast to the importance it has for the two other main characters in the novel. And any good Freudian would quickly point out that his unresolved preoccupation with the loss of his mother precludes such activity on his part. But he also fits the Ibsen/Joyce concept of sexual activity and artistic achievement being mutually exclusive in his rejection of Bloom's offer of a haven and, for whatever reasons, functions as another knight of "ruful continence."

Joyce's preoccupation with the effects of intense involvement with another human being, and with the pain that it can entail, is worked out primarily in Bloom's consciousness throughout the day. Joyce had earlier confronted the ramifications of allowing the Other his or her freedom in *Exiles*, and Richard discovers that it is not as easy as he had hoped it would be in theory. Bloom not only attempts to come to terms with Molly's defection at 4:00 P.M.; he is also trying at the same time to accept Milly's projected involvement with a "young student." In the lives of both these women, he must face the fact that he is indeed only "always the last term of a preceding series even if the first term of a succeeding one, . . . neither first nor last nor only nor alone in a series originating in and repeated to infinity" (*U* 731.19–23). But this had been a problem for Joyce himself, and he seems to have oscillated between wanting to be the one-and-only love object and needing the goad of jealousy of others. Bloom shares this dilemma, and in his honest musings admits his need for fresh stimulation to whet his sexual appetite: "Returning not the same. . . . The new I want. Nothing new under the sun" (U 377.13–14).

Again, Joyce shared Freud's insight that total freedom does not necessarily lead to joy in sex or provide the necessary excitement. In spite of the fact that prior to Molly (with the exception of Mrs. Sinico) he depicts a series of uncooperative women, in real life Nora was compliant, even agreeing to abjure marriage for many years. But we know from the Letters that he needed the stimulation of uncertainty and jealousy to keep himself interested. He here corroborates Ibsen's emphasis on triangular desire, so well elucidated by René Girard, and termed by Freud the "need for an injured third party." Freud also contended that human beings would always have a need to set limits and obstacles for their sexual behavior in order to keep themselves sufficiently stimulated.

But Bloom moves from his nagging absorption with missing wife and daughter ("All is lost now") to the depersonalized encounter with Gerty on the beach, a peculiarly modern solution to the barriers to sexual satisfaction in Joyce's world and a foreshadowing of the blurring of identities in *Finnegans Wake*. Gerty and Bloom remain nameless to each other; she cannot become pregnant; there can be no demands for an unwanted marriage and no nagging jealousy or haunting sense of loss as there has been in Bloom's personal life.

Molly, on the other hand, has moved more readily toward the acceptance of depersonalized sexual experience. In spite of the controversy over her function in the novel, no one would argue that she would feel much pain—or feel much of anything. But this is not new for Molly; when first involved with Leopold Bloom she had accepted him on the basis of "as well him as another" (U 783.9). We get the sense from her comments on Boylan that, were he to drop out of her life, she would coolly begin looking for his replacement—indeed she is already contemplating an affair with a "young poet" (U 776.9–10). In spite of both the Blooms' preoccupation with the past, neither accepts "ruful continence." Their separate solutions partake, however, of the same absence of emotional involvement, which, when present, can only result in pain and eventual loss—one way or another. Has this become for Joyce the alternative to the sort of commitment that had ended in the suicides of Ophelia, Mrs. Sinico, and his father?

In *Finnegans Wake*, Joyce seems to move close to Nietzsche, who conceived of individuation as the root of mankind's problems, and who linked its removal to the obliteration of incest-boundaries. In fact, *Finnegans Wake* itself seems to have fulfilled Nietzsche's prescription:

In these notions we already find all the components of a profound and mystic philosophy and, by the same token, of the mystery doctrine of tragedy; a recognition that whatever exists is of a piece, and that individuation is the root of all evil; a conception of art as the sanguine hope that the spell of individuation may yet be broken, as an augury of eventual reintegration.

Sexuality and Survival in *Finnegans Wake*

Shari Benstock

In handing down a decision on the possible obscenity of *Ulysses*, Judge John Woolsey remarked that "whilst in many places the effect of 'Ulysses' on the reader undoubtedly is somewhat emetic, nowhere does it tend to be an aphrodisiac."[1] Indeed, Judge Woolsey held that the book was not "pornographic" because he did "not detect anywhere the leer of the sensualist." The common reader in search of a sensual thrill probably lacks the patience, if not erudition, to make *Ulysses* the instrument of his pleasure. And if this be true of *Ulysses*, what of *Finnegans Wake*? By most accounts it appears to be a dirty book, where even a Judge Woolsey might find an occasional "leer of the sensualist" (belonging to a Dante Alighieri, a Jonathan Swift, a Charles Dodgson, or a Daddy Browning), and there certainly seem to be a number of nubile young women available as the objects of affection, disporting themselves for their own and others' pleasure. But is there sex in *Finnegans Wake*? And, if so, is it pleasurable?

Perhaps the prejudices of my own reading of this text should be revealed at the outset. From what I can tell, all the sex there is in *Finnegans Wake* (and there's not much, really) happened in the past and is rather foggily remembered in the present, making assessments of pleasure or pain a bit difficult to support; what sex there is in the present is unsuccessful, presuming a less than ecstatic estimate of its joyfulness. Indeed, more seems to rest in the sensual leer or the provocative come-on than ever gets itself actualized, and what's "dirty" about the book exists in dream, revery, fantasy, and memory. Depending on what limits of the narrative one subscribes to, all events may be displaced into the past, even those which seem to be happening in the present. And perhaps this displacement was important to Joyce, who certainly chose to keep the crucial events at 7 Eccles street on June 16 offstage of *Ulysses*, and whose linguistic encrustations in the *Wake* give the sense that all events hold sexual potential without the necessity of committing them to fact. The *Wake* seems premised on the notion that sex is the downfall of man ("First we feel. Then we fall"),[2] and all action conspires to sexual implication: brothers' battles, children's lessons, sister's make-believe, mother's worries, father's drinking. And history serves as well as the family: from Wellington's monument to Nelson's pillar, the landscape

247

of Ireland offers the potential for a sexual mapping, from the humptyhill-head of Finnegan himself down to his tumptytumtoes.

There is at least one scene in the *Wake*, however, where most readers agree that copulation progresses, and perhaps a look at this most unusual of Wakean events could shed some light on the joyousness of its sex. The scene opens foggily in a voice heavy with sleep, questioning both surroundings and events as though they belonged to a past time: "So, nat by night by naught by naket, in those good old lousy days gone by, the days, shall we say? of Whom shall we say?" (555.5–6). Slowly we move from room to room in this scene of "whenabouts," discovering members of the cast: the four old men, the young twins, the baby Isobel, a manservant, a maidservant, twelve good men and true, twenty-nine flowergirls, and, finally, "in their bed of trial, on the bolster of hardship, by the glimmer of memory, under coverlets of cowardice," a man and a woman: "he, Mr of our fathers, she, our moddereen rue arue rue." Evidence for the actual events taking place in the bed of trial must be deduced from linguistic artifice. Hardship is bolstered, finally, into a "mace of might mortified," an oblique suggestion that the male is erect; meanwhile, the woman is described as a "beautifell" waterfall, whose "dinny drops into the dyke." But the scene is interrupted by "A cry off," and the storyteller must begin again: "Where are we at all? and whenabouts in the name of space?" The awaited answer is a description of the bedroom itself, where there is a "Bed for two . . . Chair for one. Woman's garments on chair. Man's trousers with crossbelt braces, collar on bedknob" (558.26–559.9). The narrative shifts so that its appearance is of drama rather than a "once upon a time" story, and the dramatis personae must be enumerated again.

A time.
Act: dumbshow.
Closeup. Leads. (559.17–19)

This story/play seems to be having a very difficult time getting itself told. Perhaps there is something in its subject that makes its teller uneager to advance the plot. Again, the scene is set: "Man with nightcap, in bed, fore. Woman, with curlpins, hind. Discovered. Side point of view. First position of harmony." At long last, there is little doubt what the "dumbshow" constitutes, but there seems to be little joy in the act. "Man looking round, beastly expression. . . . exhibits rage. Business . . . Woman, sitting, looks at ceiling. . . . exhibits fear" (559.20–28).

At the second "Cry off," the woman leaps out of bed followed by the lumbering male, "Promiscuous Omebound to Fiammelle la Diva" (560.1). This unproductive scene is brought to a quick close by a "blackout." This most frustrating of narrative methods is typical of the *Wake*, where no scene is allowed to play out its drama without constant interruptions and digressions, which may eventually bring us back to Howth Castle and Environs, but not without venturing to farther lands. While sex seems to be at the center of what the *Wake* is all about, it is a subject that is constantly eluded and elided with multiple linguistic and semantic delay tactics.[3]

This particular scene is singularly unattractive. The opening glimpse of the bedroom strewn with garments suggests a homey enough atmosphere (and may well remind us of a similar scene at 7 Eccles street), but marital intimacy bears the stamp here of the all-too-familiar. Its effect is not unlike the "rumpled, shiny sole" of Molly's stocking looped over the bedrail (*U* 63): there is a hint of the sordid in these details of everyday life. And, indeed, the ensuing description confirms the worst—the man with his "beastly expression" and "fishy eyes," the woman with her "haggish expression" and "peaky nose." This scene of possible seduction is not romanticized by dewy-eyed anticipation, or dramatized by an insistent lechery, or even sentimentalized through revery. Rather, it brings "reality" into sharp focus: it offers the single opportunity in the *Wake* to pierce the surface of its structure, to meet Earwicker and Anna Livia as their human counterparts, the Porters. But one is relieved that the "Play!" is interrupted by the "cry off," since the characters as described are so disagreeably unaesthetic. The call of motherhood (to a son who has wet his bed) delays perhaps our only chance to observe "the act" that by its very mystery rests at the center of the Wakean universe.

To say that sex in Joyce's fiction is either remembered from the past or anticipated in the future denies us access to the facts we are led to expect. Do Molly and Leopold make love? How often? To what degree of mutual enjoyment? Under what circumstances? *How?* Well, we have Molly's word that she and Boylan made love on June 16, but her account is reconstructed several times over in the space of her one-hour monologue. And as her loyalties shift, so do her facts, so that she inflates the number of times they made love and exaggerates (perhaps) her satisfaction with her partner's performance. But then this is a performance that Molly had long anticipated (with a "someone," if not specifically Boylan); she arranged its details and set the stage for herself as a joyous cuckolder of her husband. Her afternoon matinee with Boylan, and its early evening reprise, are *not* standard fare for Molly. And it may be that the anticipation of it, the unusualness of its occurrence, the retrospective sense of its daring are of greater significance to Molly than the act(s) as such. If Joyce's fiction seems to argue that sex constitutes no moral fall, it does not go so far as to suggest that sex represents redemptive powers. James Joyce is neither John Milton nor D. H. Lawrence.

What the *Wake* suggests is that sex is a family affair, whether or not it always takes place within the confines of the family. The multiple displacements of the Wakean dream offer a cast of thousands, each somehow involved in the "sin" that serves as the dark center of the narrative. But when all the double-distancing of guilty dreams collapses into the "present" we discover a family of five, each linked to the other by sexual (as well as familial) design. And when we are introduced to Mr. and Mrs. Porter (560.23–26), we learn "They care for nothing except everything that is allporterous." They are subsumed by themselves, each appearing under the auspices of the other. When the present scene opens, the father is in bed with the mother but dreams of the daughter—who sees her father's "blade drawn to the full" in erection when he appears at her doorway (566.22)—while the sons war for the sister's affections. The mother is all the while more mother than mistress, attentive to her children's needs and speedily answering Jerry's nighttime cry. She is both the source of sexual interest for her husband (by her reincarnation in the daughter) and the agent of its frustration (by her responsibilities to her children).

At the level of the family, *Finnegans Wake* presents the inversion of sexual tension *chez* Bloom. Molly is less mother than mate. Her husband still commands the focus of her attentions and psychological energies, in large part because of her sexual frustration with him. Rudy has been displaced by time, existing in the "now" only in odd moments of regret; Milly has been removed in space, but existing even in her letters as an implied threat to her mother's sexuality. Molly thinks of herself as a mistress and eventually lives out her own fantasy. (Bloom, of course, lives out another fantasy with a lover who is present only in her letters.) Although Molly's intended adultery forms the backdrop to Bloom's day—determining his activities, his movements about Dublin—his thoughts return often enough to his children. His concern for his adolescent daughter is fatherly (almost motherly), but certainly is not predicated on sexual interest—except as it acknowledges her developing sexuality ("Sex breaking out even then"—*U* 63).

In the night world of the *Wake*, these roles reverse themselves. Bloom/Earwicker confronts in his dreams the possibility of incestuous longing, and Milly/Issy is present as a knowledgeable young temptress: "Undershift, by all I hold secret from my world and in my underworld of nighties and naughties and all the other wonderwearlds" (147.26–28). The dream provides multiple revisions of the scene in the park where the old man and young girl(s) play out a scene of seduction/masturbation/micturition, at the center of which seems to be the mutual desire of the old man for the young girl. A similar vision occurs to Bloom in "Circe" (*U* 542), when under Bello's spell Bloom plays a lustful Rip Van Winkle, dreaming of a young woman who turns out to be Milly Bloom (*U* 542). The youthful sexuality of the mother, meanwhile, is revealed through the daughters, recalled by Molly and Anna Livia in their reveries that close *Ulysses* and *Finnegans Wake*. Female sexuality exists here in its youth—in stolen kisses and remembered embraces—and is essentially absent from the present, adult marriage. Molly's sexual interest is in men other than Bloom (although her affections remain with him, and the defense of him against other men in Dublin— *U* 742—is a testament to the solidity of their relationship apart from the purely sexual). Anna Livia seems to have lost interest in sex. She leaves this aspect of womanhood to her younger generation, to the "daughterwife" who is even now "Swimming in my hindmoist" (627.2–3). Anna Livia looks forward to her death, an embrace with her "cold mad father" who "makes me seasilt saltsick and I rush, my only, into your arms" (a vision of sexual seduction involving father and daughter), while Molly looks back, to the moment by the Moorish wall when she was fifteen and with Mulvey, and to Bloom's long kiss on the Hill of Howth when she was eighteen.

This repositioning of the sexual act occurs on various levels in Joyce's fiction, not the least important of which is constituted by memory, revery, fantasy, and dream, all of which alter the sexual perspective. The subject of sexual interest (Molly, Milly, Anna Livia, Issy, Gerty, etc.) is always at some remove from the would-be seducer. The twilight encounter between Bloom and Gerty offers a striking example of this displacement. By their positioning on the beach, these two are able to see each other—but only dimly. The narrative facade of flowery nineteenth-century women's fiction filters the scene for the reader as the two participants gradually lose sight of each other in the evening darkness. What Gerty and Bloom know of each other they know by inflection, by supposition: "Nausicaa" offers one of the most difficult exercises in establishing fact in *Ulysses*, precisely because its linguistic forms are so opaque. (We assume, for instance, that Gerty MacDowell is lame, but by what evidence do we know? By Bloom's supposition: "Tight boots? No. She's lame! O!" Bloom's observation is corroborated only by Gerty's thoughts, which are formed so self-consciously and obliquely as to further the mystery about her "deformity.") But the narrative perspective of *Ulysses* at its most obscure is nonetheless consistent within the boundaries of its various styles; the *Wake*, in contrast, is a kaleidoscope, constantly shifting the perspective.

The scene that begins in the Porter bedroom at page 555 suffers the major interruption of Jerry's awakening and the opportunity to retell the story of Humphrey Chimpden Earwicker before returning the parents to the conjugal bed on page 582. We have progressed from the "First position of harmony" (559.21) to the "Third position of concord" (582.29–30) and through the narrations of Matthew and Mark to Luke, as the bedposts recount the night's events. The scene is described in terms of male games:

wars and naval battles, horse races (with Anna Livia as the "bucky brown nightmare"), and cricket. The description of coition is thus viewed through male eyes and told from the perspective of the male environ; Anna Livia, whom we have assumed to be a somewhat unenthusiastic sexual partner, shows herself rather full of life: "Kickakick. She had to kick a laugh. At her old stick-in-the-block" (583.26–27). Earwicker has his "waxened capapee . . . wick-in-her," and his game is strenuous enough to cause some concern that "he'd tyre and burst his dunlops and waken her bornybarnies making his boobybabies" (584.13–14). In the midst of this free-for-all, Anna Livia's voice may be heard as she chooses sides in the cricket match, rooting for Earwicker's opponent and the champion cricketer: "Magrath he's my pegger, he is, for bricking up all my old kent road. He'll win your toss, flog your old tom's bowling and I darr ye, barrackbuller, to break his duck! He's posh. I lob him" (584.5–8). The signals seem clear enough that Anna Livia, like Molly Bloom before her, is desirous of sexual activity that is athletic, uninhibited, and joyous, and that HCE (like Bloom) may not be up to her expectations any longer, "as he studd and stoddard and trutted and trumpered" (583.36–584.1). The game motif suggests that Anna Livia's hero, Magrath (the neighbor and cad, Earwicker's trickster enemy) wins the match: "(how's that? Noball, he carries his bat!) nine hundred and dirty too not out, at all times long past conquering cock of the morgans" (584.23–25). Sexual fulfillment is at the brink of satisfaction, spurred by Anna Livia's mental lovemaking with the neighbor in fulfillment of her physical duties to her husband. Her methods are psychologically sound and well known to both sexes when the interest and excitement of youthful sex has turned perfunctory and sour after years of practice with one's partner. Ironically, Anna Livia's moment of climax (signalled by the "Cocorico!" of the cock crowing) ends Earwicker's efforts. While she basks in the relief of orgasm ("her contractations tugowards her personeel"), Earwicker is still trying for "exclusive pigtorial rights of herehear fond tiplady his weekreations" (584.33–585.1). As "dawn drags nearing nigh," the marriage bond "repeals an act of union"; Earwicker withdraws his member (585.26); and Anna Livia discovers that he "never wet the tea."

The long-awaited lovemaking is unsuccessful except that Anna Livia has managed through mental disguise to achieve her pleasure. The narrative condemnation of Earwicker's poor showing ("You never wet the tea!") may suggest impotency, a fear that Earwicker has harbored in a secret that is safe with his wife: "Never divorce in the bedding the glove that will give you away" (586.5–6). Anna Livia knows too much (as does Molly Bloom), and if she were to play the role of sexual accuser, her evidence could be even be more damaging than the circumstantial supposition that surrounds the scene in the park. But the point is that Anna Livia is not and will never be

Earwicker's accuser, just as Molly Bloom will never say publicly what she thinks privately about Bloom's peculiar sexual habits. Indeed, both wives are the defenders of their husbands' honor in the face of a public that little understands or appreciates these men. While sexual tensions abound in the two works, and while sexual mystery lies at the center of "events" in *Ulysses* and *Finnegans Wake*, marital relationships survive by bonds of loyalty rather than sexual fulfillment. The sexual interests of these characters have changed over the years, altered by the responsibilities of parenthood and middle age: the moment by the rhododendrons on Howth Head will never occur again; Earwicker will never return the conquering hero to sail up Anna's river Liffey. Sexual capacity (if not desire) has been displaced.

If the process of sexual anticipation or remembrance—the vision that avoids the present by looking either backwards or forwards in time—makes Joyce's characters voyeurs of their own sexual lives, then the reader becomes a voyeur at second remove. We peep through the blinds and peer through the mists, our curiosity piqued by the sexual tensions appearing in the text by way of family relationships. And we suffer the worst frustrations of the voyeur, disappointed at the critical moment when the curtain is drawn and the sexual act itself is hidden from view. But the voyeur with the slightest bit of imagination can draw for himself, for his own sexual needs, the vision on the bed. And imagination is frequently more satisfying than the cold, factual thing itself. Having been denied the facts of Molly's tryst with Boylan, of Earwicker's first seduction of Anna Livia, of Milly's encounter with Bannon, of Bloom's misadventure with Bridie Kelly, the actual events between Stephen Dedalus and the prostitute, or of anything approaching sexual consummation in Bella Cohen's brothel, the reader surmises the real state of events shadowed by these various possibilities. Our minds play over the scarce remnants of the liaison between Molly and Boylan, plotting the progression of that relationship from first introduction, to the night of the bazaar dance when they walked along the Tolka, to the planned tour in Belfast in the "future." We speculate on the causes and consequences of Rudy's death, on the reasons for Milly's absence from 7 Eccles street, on Bloom's sexual potency and competency, on the frustration and gratification of Molly's sexual existence. But our fondest desires (like those of the characters we watch) are constantly frustrated. Even when we think we are viewing the "scene" itself, even when it appears that the cricket game that is being played out in *Finnegans Wake* is in fact the Porters making love, the scene is dimly lit and "we had only our hazelight to see with" (587.3): all rests in speculation.

In assessing these events seen dimly, I suspect that sexuality as such is only one aspect of the human survival in *Ulysses* and *Finnegans Wake*, and that the capacity for sexual experience that in and of itself is purely joyful exists only in youth, perhaps only in the first sexual encounter, and that it lives in the present through memory.

Notes

1. Reprinted in James Joyce, *Ulysses* (New York: Random House, 1961), pp. vii–xii. All parenthetical references to *Ulysses* are to this edition.

2. *Finnegans Wake* (New York: The Viking Press, 1947), 627.11. All further references are included parenthetically.

3. For a rather complete listing of all the various versions of the Phoenix Park incident, see Bernard Benstock, "Every Telling Has a Taling: A Reading of the Narrative of *Finnegans Wake*," *Modern Fiction Studies* 14 (Spring 1969): 3–26.

The Joyce of Sex:
Sexual Relationships in *Ulysses*

Morris Beja

In this essay, my aims will be to describe the sexual relationships the three chief figures in *Ulysses* have (or sometimes perhaps only seem to have) and to discuss why those relationships are the way they are, and where things stand at the end of the book. Obviously of primary concern is the sexual relationship between Leopold and Molly Bloom, and immediately we come upon an area where an effort to be as precise as possible goes against many of the assumptions that are usually made about this married couple. Of course everyone knows that Bloom and Molly have not had sex together for over ten years—since 27 November 1893, to be exact: that is, just before the birth and early death of their only son, Rudy. But what everyone knows is not always true, and Joyce is both meticulously precise and maddeningly vague, as he indicates that their abstinence has not been total. What they have not had is what the Ithaca chapter calls "complete carnal intercourse, with ejaculation of semen within the natural female organ"; instead, "carnal intercourse had been incomplete, without ejaculation of semen within the natural female organ."

For some reason, the term "incomplete," if noticed by critics at all, is apparently taken to mean "nonexistent," rather than "partial." But Bloom and Molly do have *some* forms of sexual activity with each other. Within just the last few weeks, for example, Bloom has—as Molly puts it—come on her bottom, and in the past he has performed cunnilingus. Indeed, when she thinks about her upcoming concert tour to Belfast and expresses doubts about the idea that Bloom and Boylan might both come with her—or, I suppose I should say, accompany her—her concern is not so much that she is afraid that Bloom would get sexually jealous as that he would get sexually active; and Boylan might be in the next room and hear, and *he* might get annoyed: "its all very well a husband but you cant fool a lover after me telling him we never did anything."

I am not trying to minimize the problems in Bloom and Molly's sexual relationship by pointing to the fact that their inactivity with each other is not absolute; rather, I wish to make sure that we realize what is *not* involved. And another thing that is clearly not involved is physical "impotence": despite the Citizen's question about Bloom, "Do you call that a man?" and Joe Hynes's answering reflection, "I wonder did he ever put it out of sight," Bloom can clearly achieve erection and ejaculate, as he does by masturbating over Gerty MacDowell; and, as we have seen, he has performed coitus interruptus with Molly, who is in fact of the opinion that he has "more spunk in him"—that is, more semen—than Boylan, who, she says, "hasn't such a tremendous amount . . . considering how big it is." If that is true, then it is no doubt especially wise that Bloom carries, as he does, a condom (or French letter). It is possible, as has been argued, that Bloom is a victim not of primary or physical impotence, but of secondary impotence, which entails the inability to perform actual sexual *intercourse*— or "complete carnal intercourse, with ejaculation of semen within the natural female organ"—or to perform it with some particular woman, from psychological rather than physiological causes. But I know of no specific evidence that that is so in Bloom's case; though who knows?—it would be one way out of it.[1]

Of course, for her part Molly does engage in complete carnal intercourse on June 16, although the degree to which that is so can be exaggerated. For the first few of Boylan's ejaculations—just how many times he came is unclear, since the number increases each time Molly thinks about it (from "3 or 4 times" early in her monologue to "4 or 5" around the middle of it, to "5 or 6 times handrunning" toward the end)—Molly recalls, "I made him pull it out and do it on me." In other words, carnal intercourse with Boylan too was incomplete— until the last time, when, she says, "I let him finish it in me." It seems quite possible, even probable, that this is the first nonmarital act of complete carnal intercourse in which Molly has ever engaged. In any case it does seem to be the first day on which the affair with Boylan has been consummated. And I hope it is too late in the day to have to prove that the list of twenty-five lovers in the Ithaca chapter does not represent reality, but at the most Bloom's vague suspicions. Very vague, I would guess, for surely even he cannot really believe that she has slept with all twenty-five of those men; actually, even the likeliest candidate—Lieutenant Gardner, who incidentally is not on that list—almost certainly never went to bed with her. No doubt debating how much of an adulteress Molly Bloom is sounds rather like asking how much of a virgin someone else is, but facing the facts may help to put in perspective some long-held assumptions about Molly's sex life—and her character, which, for example, has been described by no less acute an observer than Robert M. Adams as that of "a slut, a sloven, and a voracious sexual animal." To Adams, Molly is "a frightening venture into the unconsciousness of evil"[2]—a declaration that strikes me as a frightening venture into the unconsciousness of moral criticism.

Still, however limited, Molly's infidelity is there for us to face, and it reflects important problems in her relationship with her husband and in their attitudes toward each other. It may be argued, indeed, that a home without complete carnal intercourse, with ejaculation of semen within the natural female organ, is like a home without Plumtree's Potted Meat: incomplete (even if one is less certain that, with it, the Bloom home would be an abode of bliss).

Critics have long been concerned over whose doing Bloom and Molly's lack of full sex with each other is (whose "fault" it is): is it Molly's? Bloom's? Something for which they are *mutually* responsible? (As the *Wake* has it, "so long as there is a joint deposit account in the two names a mutual obligation is posited.") In the Nighttown chapter of *Ulysses*, copulation and the question of "fault" are brought together when, instead of thinking of "felix culpa"—the "happy fault" or happy sin that caused the Fall—Bloom thinks of "copula felix"; but his "copula" isn't very "felix," so that leads to a feeling of "culpa." The question of responsibility no doubt matters to us as well, but ultimately laying blame is less enlightening than finding causes. I have suggested, however briefly, the role of some of the key men in Molly's life, and I shall get back to that. But first let us consider Bloom's attitude toward her—and, indeed, toward just about all the women we see enter his life and thoughts on June 16.

Without at all asserting that the best way to examine Bloom is from a Jungian perspective, I would like to suggest that it is helpful to consider his attitudes toward women in terms of Jung's concept of the Anima, and three of the most common manifestations of that archetype: the Mother, the Virgin, and the Temptress, or what Jung calls the Seductress. Molly is seen by Bloom in all three of those roles.

Certainly we need not dwell on the degree to which she fills a maternal role in his life, even in his erotic thoughts—as when, in the first chapter, in which we meet both of them, he looks down "on her bulk and between her large soft bubs." Other significant mother figures for Bloom include Mrs. Purefoy, of course, and Bella Cohen—who becomes Jung's loving and terrible mother, the devouring mother. Folklore is filled with figures corresponding to the devouring or terrible mother—as in *Snow White*, *Cinderella*, and *Hansel and Gretel*. In such a figure as the Indian goddess Kali, the terrible mother is loving as well, and the child's reaction may be similarly ambivalent. For the child may *wish* to be devoured, at least in the sense of longing for a return to the womb, a desire that itself may have sexual overtones—as in Joyce's letters of 1909 to his wife Nora, while he was in Dublin and she was back in Trieste. He wrote of his desire to return and make love to her: "My body soon will penetrate into yours, O that my soul could too! O that I could nestle in your womb like a child born of your flesh and blood, be fed by your blood, sleep in the warm secret gloom of your body!" In other letters that same month, he stressed the terrible aspect of the devouring mother, itself no less sexually exciting for him, by, for example, telling Nora, "I feel I would like to be flogged by you. I would like to see your eyes blazing with anger."

As far as I can tell, the figure of the Virgin is to Bloom a good deal less important than the other two, the Mother and the Temptress, and certainly much less central than the Virgin figure is to Stephen Dedalus, as we shall see. And especially in Bloom's world, "virgin" seems a relative term. Almost certainly, Molly entered his life a virgin, after a fashion. But she remembers her actions one day in Gibraltar with Lieutenant Mulvey: "I pulled him off into my handkerchief pretending not to be excited but I opened my legs I wouldnt let him touch me inside my petticoat." Because Mulvey was not permitted inside her petticoat, Molly remained, technically, a virgin—just as Gerty MacDowell's virginity may strike one as more technical than spiritual. Yet even while Gerty is obviously aware of what the dark stranger is doing with his hands while she displays her hidden charms, she cannot quite admit it fully to herself, and so retains a certain naïve—indeed virginal—quality. But she is also, as Bloom perceives, a "hot little devil." In other words, she is (like Molly) both the Virgin *and* the Temptress, or Seductress, or indeed Whore.

As Fritz Senn has observed, the Nausicaa chapter is the first of three in a row in which we get "three archetypal manifestations of the Feminine": the Virgin here, the Mother in Mrs. Purefoy during the Oxen of the Sun chapter, and the Whore in Bella Cohen and the prostitutes during the Circe chapter.[3] Of course, other women also play the role of Temptress for Bloom—Molly, obviously, and Martha Clifford, as well as women whom he fleetingly glimpses or thinks of. But it is when Bella's role as Whore becomes blended with that of the loving, terrible, devouring Mother that we get a sense of Bloom's childish yet erotic submission, and our fullest sense of the masochistic elements in his personality and sexual being.

Nevertheless, they have earlier been brought out in, for example, his thoughts in the butcher shop about "the nextdoor girl," and her "strong pair of arms. Whacking a carpet on the clothesline. She does whack it, by George. The way her crooked skirt swings at each whack." And when she walks away from him, "the sting of disregard" glows "to weak pleasure within his breast." To some readers, these traits suggest an element of femininity in Bloom: Theodore Holmes speaks for a larger number of critics when he writes that the overtones of Bloom's "effeminacy are unmistakable"—and that they are seen in the way he is "dominated," "vain," and "pathetic," and even in his "affinity for scents."[4] To other readers, and sometimes the same ones too, those and similar traits indicate that Bloom is actually "perverse." Even Vladimir Nabokov has lamented that "in the sexual department Bloom is, if not on the verge of insanity, at least a good clinical example of extreme sexual preoccupation and perversity," indulging "in acts and dreams that are definitely subnormal in the zoological, evolutionary sense."[5] I shall return to such attitudes toward Bloom (and toward what it is to be feminine); but first, we ought to consider the third major figure in the novel, Stephen Dedalus, whose attitudes toward women also group them into similar patterns of Mother, Virgin, and Temptress.

Obviously, the chief archetypal Mother in Stephen's life is his actual mother, who is both loving and terrible—as well as devouring: in the first chapter, he calls her a "ghoul," and a "chewer of corpses." She is, then, symbolically like the Ireland he regards as—in a phrase that appears in both the *Portrait* and *Ulysses*—"the old sow that eats her farrow." But if Mrs. Dedalus represents in part Stephen's nation, she is even more emphatically connected with its church, and through and beyond that with the Holy Virgin, a figure much more important to Stephen than to Bloom. A number of the girls and women in the *Portrait* take on that role: Eileen, who in his childhood seems to him to reveal the meaning of "Tower of Ivory," and Emma (or "E.C."), and, of course, the girl wading in the water at the Bull Wall. But that girl on the beach—like Boylan's seaside girls and like Bloom's seaside Gerty MacDowell—also serves another role: that of the Seductress or Temptress. For while she is an "angel," she is a "*wild* angel," of "*mortal* youth and beauty," opening the "gates of all the ways of error and glory." Other such figures include, in the *Portrait*, Stephen's first prostitute, and Emma again (the "temptress," indeed, of his "villanelle")—and, in *Ulysses*, perhaps Florry and Zoe.

Perhaps. But so little is the Stephen of *Ulysses* tempted by those temptresses that we realize that sex in general now seems much less central to his existence than it had in the last half of the *Portrait*. He is twenty-two years old, but he thinks a good deal less frequently about sex than does the thirty-eight-year-old Bloom. Given the nature of Stephen's obsessions with sex in the *Portrait*, actually, we may be just as glad that he does not think all that much about it in *Ulysses*, for his desire in the earlier novel seems less to have sex with girls than to commit sin with them: "He moaned to himself like some baffled prowling beast. He wanted to sin with another of his kind, to force another being to sin with him and to exult with her in sin." Later, after the retreat sermons, Stephen thinks of his phallus as "a horrible thing," and he wonders: "Who made it be like that, a bestial part of the body able to understand bestially and desire bestially? . . . His soul sickened at the thought of a torpid snaky life feeding itself out of the tender marrow of his life and fattening upon the slime of lust."

One may be tempted to explain this horror of sex as disgusting and sinful by noticing that the same woman who has served as the chief exemplar for Stephen of both the Virgin and the Mother is in some respects the archetypal Temptress as well—Mrs. Dedalus. I do not wish to exaggerate the importance in Stephen's life of what the *Wake* will call the "eatupus complex," but it would be wrong to ignore its role altogether.

The first Temptress with whom Stephen has sexual intercourse is, of course, the actual whore—the prostitute in the *Portrait*—and when she says, "Give me a kiss," we are told: "His lips would not bend to kiss her. He wanted to be held firmly in her arms, to be caressed slowly, slowly, slowly. . . . But his lips would not bend to kiss her." That reluctance recalls the teasing he had endured while a little boy early in the novel:

> Wells turned to the other fellows and said:
> —O, I say, here's a fellow says he kisses his mother every night before he goes to bed.
> The other fellows stopped their game and turned round, laughing. Stephen blushed under their eyes and said:
> —I do not.
> Wells said:
> —O, I say, here's a fellow says he doesn't kiss his mother before he goes to bed.
> They all laughed again. (*AP* 14)

The question continues to bother Stephen: "He still tried to think what was the right answer. Was it right to kiss his mother or wrong to kiss his mother? What did that mean, to kiss?"

What it means to kiss—especially, to kiss one's mother—remains important to him. Years later, during his conversation with Cranly about his first major act of rebellion against his mother (his refusal to perform his Easter duty), Cranly claims that "whatever else is unsure in this stinking dunghill of a world a mother's love is not." Stephen's reply to that is interestingly oblique: "Pascal, if I remember rightly, would not suffer his mother to kiss him as he feared the contact of her sex." Cranly's response—"Pascal was a pig"—concentrates on Pascal; ours may concentrate on Stephen. We may think as well of his intense reaction to Davin's story about the peasant woman who had invited him to stay the night in her cottage—a woman who, Davin believes, was pregnant ("carrying a child"): another maternal Temptress.

In *Ulysses*, these themes remain subdued, although they may help explain why this young man's thoughts are so seldom about sex, despite his tendencies toward freedom of thought in so many other realms. The first time the theme of the mother appears at all in *Ulysses*, it is in the context of a relevant allusion, to Swinburne, when Mulligan asks, "Isn't the sea what Algy calls it: a grey sweet mother?" Swinburne's actual phrase is "great sweet mother," in his poem "The Triumph of Time":

> I will go back to the great sweet mother,
> Mother and lover of men, the sea.
> I will go down to her, I and none other,
> Close with her, kiss her and mix her with me;
> Cling to her, strive with her, hold her fast. . . .

In *Ulysses*, immediately after that allusion we get the first reference to the dream in which Stephen's mother has come to him in "her wasted body," "mute" and "reproachful." Clearly, Stephen's relationship with his mother is not without his resentment over what it is doing to him. In the Oxen of the Sun chapter, when everyone is talking about whether the doctor during a difficult birth ought to try to save the mother or the baby, Stephen is the only one to opt for the baby.

In *Ulysses*, then, we have two men and a woman who seem to have varied but pronounced problems in the sexual realms of their being. Probably the most important problem that they all share is that their sexual lives are cut off from their emotional lives: from love. None of them has completely satisfactory sex with a person whom he or she truly loves. In one of the "Notesheets" for *Ulysses*, Joyce writes: "Love? excuses all: Coition without love in & out of wedlock not desired." Yet without romanticizing, sentimentalizing, or minimizing all these problems, I hope to show that it is conceivable that they are either resolved by the end of the novel or, more certainly, shown as less catastrophic and problematic than they at first seem to be.

In regard to Molly's infidelity again, and Bloom's reaction to it, we have seen that one critic sees in Bloom's marriage evidence that he is "dominated," and that consequently his behavior reveals "effeminacy." Less extremely, Stanley Sultan laments that by serving Molly "ignominiously," Bloom fails to be the "master in the household." And according to Darcy O'Brien, Bloom's "unmanly weakness epitomizes the slavishness Joyce so lamented in his countrymen."[6] But I wonder: what ought Bloom to do in order to prove himself "manly" or "masculine"? Should he slap Molly around a bit? Or, avoiding such violence, should he leave in a huff? Do we really fault Leopold Bloom because he does not display the sort of machismo that would gain the admiration of someone like the narrator of the Cyclops chapter?

These are, of course, rhetorical questions, and I hope that the answers to them seem as obvious as answers to rhetorical questions usually are. For my point is that Bloom's attitude toward Molly's infidelity may in part—not entirely, to be sure: I am trying not to exaggerate but to set up what I perceive as a proper perspective—be correct, arguably heroic, even wise. He is not the possessive, dominant male that husbands are "supposed" to be, and for that he is the subject of ridicule within the novel and sometimes of ridicule, or sad sympathy or condescension, in criticism about the novel; but his mode of behavior seems to me not quite so clearly wrong-headed as those responses to him would suggest. In the Ithaca chapter, Bloom's "equanimity" in the face of Molly's affair is explained by his realization that her infidelity is "not as calamitous as a cataclysmic annihilation of the planet in consequence of collision with a dark sun," and is "less reprehensible than theft, highway robbery, cruelty to children and animals," and other transgressions that are meticulously listed—and finally is "not more abnormal than all other altered processes of adaptation to altered conditions of existence, resulting in a reciprocal equilibrium between the bodily organism and its attendant circumstances."

Few men in Bloom's "attendant circumstances" would or could display such "equanimity," to be sure. Certainly not James Joyce: when he was misled into believing in 1909 that Nora had once been unfaithful to him, his reaction seems to have been crazed. Personally, I doubt if that indicates that he was thereby stronger than Bloom. Rather, instead of showing that Bloom is weaker, it seems to me to indicate that Bloom is a *better* man—a better *man*—than his creator. But I do not mean to be condescending toward James Joyce either: the fact that he could not share his creation's attitude does not lessen his insight and discovery. Or if it does, then we may say of him what Stephen says of Shakespeare: that his "loss is his gain," as "he passes on towards eternity in undiminished personality, untaught by the wisdom he has written or by the laws he has revealed."

Even Bloom's resorting to masturbation may not be so contemptible as many critics—all of them, no doubt, themselves people with admirably active sexual lives—have assumed it to be, but instead may be a recourse to an outlet less destructive than others that (for various reasons we have not yet pursued) he avoids. It is probably an exaggeration to say, as Richard Ellmann does, that "Joyce has found an aspect of masturbation which every writer on the subject, from Rousseau to Philip Roth, has missed. For the first time in literature masturbation becomes heroic." But it is an exaggeration that serves as a healthy corrective to the snickering or clucking of the tongue that usually goes along with discussions of Bloom's sex life.

Nor do I have much patience with those who regard Bloom's general sexual bents as "perverse." Bloom may have—he does have—masochistic traits, for example; but that in itself does not make him "a masochist." And the equation between Bloom's so-called weakness and submissiveness and his so-called effeminacy and unmanliness strikes me as abominable. Bloom

is "the new womanly man": there are worse things to be. I recognize that
Bloom's androgyny, like every other serious theme in the novel, is undercut
and treated ironically: consequently, Bloom also has latent ambidexterity;
and he so wants to be a mother; and he sometimes seems less an adrogynous
being than a hermaphrodite or transvestite. Yet his androgyny is no less real
for all that, and no less to his credit. As Oliver St. John Gogarty long ago
observed about Joyce, he "was gifted with a seriousness that was unremit-
ting and could resist even his own jokes."[8]

In recent Joyce criticism, there has been an increasing willingness to
become aware that Bloom transcends the usual male stereotypes; unfortunately, there has not been a corresponding willingness to recognize that
Molly transcends the usual female ones. Yet to dismiss Molly Bloom as
Joyce's male projection of a woman is, while accurate, beside the point—as
it would be to speak that way of Emma Bovary and Flaubert, or Anna
Karenina and Tolstoy, or as it would be both accurate and beside the point
to dismiss Bloom as a gentile's Jew, or Joe Christmas as a white man's Black,
or Heathcliff, Lydgate, and Septimus Warren Smith as women's men.

After all, to whom does Molly seem to be an archetypal Mother or earth
goddess—this woman who has had one surviving child in an Irish Catholic
world where families as large as the Dedaluses' (Mrs. Dedalus had fifteen
children) are quite common? Not to us, I submit, and not to herself, surely,
and not so much to Joyce the artist either. It is primarily for and to Bloom
that she takes on that role. Thus Bloom's sexual problems may not be
entirely different from some of Stephen's. But in any case a key question is
what in Bloom's psyche more than in hers makes Molly seem to him an
archetypal Mother. A facile Jungian critic might explain everything away,
once again, in terms of "projection," but the forces behind Bloom's attitude
are neither easily dismissed nor easily understood. One such force seems to
be his *need* to deify her, for if she is a goddess, then she is unattainable: who
could fault him for avoiding sex with, and being submissive to, a goddess?
Yet even that, although I think it is an operative element in his attitude, is
perhaps more a mode of rationalization than it is a source.

Surely a key fact in his attitude toward Molly as an archetypal Mother is
Bloom's sense of guilt and loss over the death of their son, Rudy. But while
the relationship between sex and Bloom's agonizing over Rudy's early death
is often recognized, it is also often seen in overly simplistic terms. Bloom
and Molly's lack of sex does, to be sure, date from, and arise out of, that
event, but it is nevertheless a gross oversimplification of their lives, problems, and attitudes, and of the issues involved, to explain their abstinence
entirely or merely as a primitive form of birth control. Otherwise, why do
we explicitly learn from Molly's monologue that, in their last sexual act that
afternoon, she let Boylan finish it in her?

Much more importantly, Bloom seems to have taken upon himself the role of the child Rudy, who was lost to him and Molly, and of the child they shall now never have, because of his or her or their fears as a result of Rudy's early death in infancy.[9]

One is tempted to get a bit exasperated at this point and observe that actually the Blooms are not childless: there is, after all, Milly. And of course one's exasperation would be justified. Still, if we wish to understand and not simply to judge with self-righteous superiority, we must acknowledge the significance of the fact that Bloom's only *son* has died in infancy; and for a Jew, maybe even more than for most men with other heritages, even Irishmen, a son can be immensely important.

(There is a nice little story that illustrates my point, so I hope it is not too much of a digression. A man went to see his rabbi quite distraught, seeking advice, because his son was going to marry a Roman Catholic woman—and not only that, he planned to convert: "My own son!" the man said, "My own son with a new religion!" The rabbi sorrowfully replied, "*You* have a son?" *I* have a son! My son is going to shave his head and become a Buddhist monk. My own son with a new religion!" The man was shocked that such a fate should befall a rabbi, and he asked him what he had done, and the rabbi replied, "What should I do? I went to God with my problem." "And what did God say?" "He said, '*You* have a son? *I* have a son!'")

With such a context, for good or bad, it comes to Bloom to seem as if *he* is all they have left, so it is as if he becomes Molly's son, with Molly—from his perspective—"in the attitude of Gea-Tellus," and himself in that of "the childman weary, the manchild in the womb." My point is not that he has always been fixated in infantile sexuality, for which I see little or no evidence; his motivation is psychologically much more complicated than that, though the results may not be all that different.

Nowadays, of course, we are less reluctant to acknowledge the erotic elements in maternal relations than we used to be, and to that extent, if you will, we have learned to be Joyce's contemporaries. But we also inevitably recognize the forces working against that aspect of human sexuality. However symbolic and unconscious the relevance of the incest taboo will seem here, it may nevertheless be in large part what makes it seem impossible to Bloom to have complete carnal intercourse with Molly, given the fact that he is, however vicariously, her child. Consequently, Bloom recognizes the need for other men to take on the role in the mother's life that the child cannot fulfill. But if someone else can take on the role of husband-lover, then presumably it is also possible for someone else to fulfill the role of the child—of Rudy, or of the unborn child—as well. Enter Stephen Dedalus.

Now if Stephen becomes, as it were, Rudy—as, for example, in the climactic vision at the end of the Nighttown chapter, but in many more

subtle passages and ways as well—we have already seen that Bloom too is
associated with Rudy, or "is" Rudy. And if all A are B, and all B are C, then
all A are C as well; and, indeed, Stephen and Bloom *are* identified with one
another: they have been baptized into the church by the same priest; they
share an uncanny number of thoughts or allusions or images all day; and at
one point in Nighttown they even look into a mirror and see reflected back a
single image (that of Shakespeare). They well may be called Blephen and
Stoom. Moreover, this identification entails (more or less unconsciously in
Bloom's mind, a bit less so in Molly's) the possibility that Stephen may take
on the symbolic role of Molly's lover, or dream lover.

But if, from the perspective of Bloom's needs, the Stephen/Bloom identification stresses Stephen as a son, from the perspective of Stephen's needs
it stresses his going beyond dependence on the father. In *Ulysses*, despite
critical tradition, Stephen does not so much "find" a father as identify with
him. He must leave behind childish things; the trouble is, that is just as
difficult to do in sexual realms as in others, or more so. But one way for this
to happen—a mode that is psychologically beneficial for Stephen and
artistically feasible for Joyce—is to have Stephen cast aside his childish
stance by identifying with the father.

One may wonder, assuming that all this is not simply wrong, if a
corollary might be that Bloom will assume or resume his full roles as
husband and adult, enabling us to agree, at least in this instance, with the
Joyce who once told Frank Budgen that Jews "are better husbands . . .
better fathers, and better sons." But we cannot really know, since we do not
follow the lives of our protagonists beyond the early morning hours of June
17, and Joyce never produced a *Ulysses II*, or a *Ulysses Sails Again*. In any
case, I do not mean to suggest that Bloom will—or that wouldn't it be nice if
only Bloom would—take over and become head of his household. Joyce,
after all, shows that we can be heartened rather than disappointed that
Bloom is not built that way.

On the other hand, no doubt it would be pleasant or agreeable to think
that he and Molly could resume complete carnal intercourse. But things
have probably gone on too long now for that to be at all likely. As the Ithaca
chapter puts it, "the parties concerned, uniting, had increased and multiplied, which being done, offspring produced and educed to maturity, the
parties, if now disunited were obliged to reunite for increase and multi-
plication, which was absurd, to form by reunion the original couple of
uniting parties, which was impossible." Anyway, Joyce has shown that
maybe things are not so awful the way they are, or at least that they could be
worse.

Oddly, Bloom for all his deficiencies in respect to sexuality, becomes the
ironic yet serious exemplar in this novel of love—I mean the opposite of

hatred. And we may sense that for Stephen, the identification with Bloom entails an identification not only with fatherhood—important as that is—but also with all that Bloom represents or exemplifies in other ways, including his values. If so, then at the end of his day Bloom has a right to his satisfaction and to his feeling that he has "sustained no positive loss" and has "brought a positive gain to others. Light to the gentiles."

Notes

1. For cogent presentations of contrasting views, see Marilyn French, *The Book as World: James Joyce's "Ulysses"* (Cambridge: Harvard University Press, 1976), pp. 147–48, and Suzette A. Henke, *Joyce's Moraculous Sindbook: A Study of Ulysses* (Columbus: Ohio State University Press, 1978), p. 93n. In his lectures on *Ulysses*, Vladimir Nabokov also refers at least twice to Bloom as "impotent": *Lectures on Literature*, ed. Fredson Bowers (New York: Harcourt Brace Jovanovich, 1980), pp. 350, 352.

2. *James Joyce: Common Sense and Beyond* (New York: Random House, 1966), p. 166.

3. "Nausicaa," in *James Joyce's "Ulysses": Critical Essays*, ed. Clive Hart and David Hayman (Berkeley: University of California Press, 1974), p. 282.

4. "Bloom, the Father," *Sewanee Review* 79 (Spring 1971): 249.

5. *Lectures on Literature*, p. 287.

6. Stanley Sultan, *The Argument of Ulysses* (Columbus: Ohio State University Press, 1964), p. 132; Darcy O'Brien, *The Conscience of James Joyce* (Princeton: Princeton University Press, 1968), p. 183.

7. *Ulysses on the Liffey* (London: Faber and Faber, 1972), p. 133.

8. *As I Was Going down Sackville Street* (London: Reynal and Hitchcock, 1937), p. 299.

9. I wish to express my gratitude to Ellen Carol Jones for the discussions and arguments that first led me to examine this possibility closely and with full seriousness.

Contributors

CHESTER G. ANDERSON, University of Minnesota
MORRIS BEJA, The Ohio State University
BERNARD BENSTOCK, University of Tulsa
SHARI BENSTOCK, University of Tulsa
ANDRÉ BLEIKASTEN, Université de Strasbourg
ZACK BOWEN, University of Delaware
SHELDON BRIVIC, Temple University
JAMES F. CARENS, Bucknell University
ROBERT ADAMS DAY, Queens College and Graduate Center, City University of New York
EDMUND L. EPSTEIN, Queens College, City University of New York
JANE FORD, La Mesa, California
ALAN J. FRIEDMAN, University of California, Berkeley
MELVIN J. FRIEDMAN, University of Wisconsin, Milwaukee
SEÁN GOLDEN, Tianjin Foreign Languages Institute, Tianjin, People's Republic of China
S. E. GONTARSKI, The Ohio State University, Lima
NATHAN HALPER, New York City
IHAB HASSAN, University of Wisconsin, Milwaukee
DAVID HAYMAN, University of Wisconsin, Madison
PHILLIP HERRING, University of Wisconsin, Madison
JEAN KIMBALL, University of Northern Iowa
MORTON P. LEVITT, Temple University
J. HILLIS MILLER, Yale University
RIANA O'DWYER, University College, Galway
RICHARD PEARCE, Wheaton College
ALAN DAVID PERLIS, The University of Alabama in Birmingham
FRANÇOIS L. PITAVY, Université de Dijon
S. B. PURDY, Marquette University
MARILYN REIZBAUM, University of Wisconsin, Madison
MARY T. REYNOLDS, Yale University
J. P. RIQUELME, Southern Methodist University
GABRIELE SCHWAB, Universität Konstanz
BROOK THOMAS, University of Massachusetts
NANCY WALKER, Stephens College
FLORENCE L. WALZL, University of Wisconsin, Milwaukee